All Acts of Love and Pleasure: Inclusive Wicca

All Acts of Love and Pleasure: Inclusive Wicca

YVONNE ABURROW

Published by Avalonia
www.avaloniabooks.co.uk

Published by Avalonia
BM Avalonia
London
WC1N 3XX
England, UK
www.avaloniabooks.co.uk

All Acts of Love and Pleasure: Inclusive Wicca

First Edition, November 2014
ISBN 978-1-905297-73-3

Design by Satori, for Avalonia.

British Library Cataloguing in Publication Data. A catalogue record for this book is available from the British Library.

About the Cover Art

The Androgyne represents a union of opposites within a single, perfected being. S/he manifests balance and beauty on all planes, here evoked by a rainbow background. Curves and bolts of feminine and masculine force tattoo hir body, and the male and female symbols of torch and chalice strike another note of balance on each side of hir crossed arms. Overhead, the Mystic Rose at the Crown evokes the splendour of the Universe itself.

About the Artist: Paul Rucker

For me, making art is how I "think in Pagan." I have been making art from personal encounters with the spirit world from a very early age, and have attained a BA in Humanities, with an emphasis in Art and Spirituality, from the New College of California. The intersection of myth, theatre, ritual and the ennobled body compels me; I seek a visual language to render metaphors, and ecstasies.

Some of my work is out-rightly iconic; other work is intended to convey an impression or atmosphere of a heightened or magical reality. My thematic approach is always grounded in the figure-- usually but not always, that of the human being.

My work has been exhibited in Minneapolis/St. Paul, Tuscaloosa, Alabama, New Orleans, San Francisco, and Chicago; and has been seen online, in print, and in other venues in the USA, Canada, Australia, and Europe.

More of my work can be seen and purchased at paulruckerart.com.

About the Author

Yvonne Aburrow is a Gardnerian Wiccan author and poet who lives in Oxford in a small cottage with her partner Bob and two cats, Morrissey and Ziggy. She has a MA in Contemporary Religions and Spiritualities from Bath Spa University.

Yvonne Aburrow. Photo by Bob Houghton.

Previous works by Yvonne ..

The Endless Knot, poetry collection, Birdberry Books, 2012

Many Names, poetry collection, Birdberry Books, 2012

The Magical Lore of Animals, Capall Bann Publishing, 2000.

A little book of serpents, Birdberry Books, 2012.

Auguries and Omens: the magical lore of birds, Capall Bann Publishing, 1994.

The Sacred Grove: mysteries of the forest, Capall Bann Publishing, 1994.

The Enchanted Forest: the magical lore of trees, Capall Bann Publishing, 1993.

Table of Contents

For my beloved Bob

Dark glass that spills a variegated half-light
Onto the floor of a theatre of night,
Faces from old mythologies glimmer
In the twilight as the day grows dimmer.
I step into your theatre of dreams
To act my part where the limelight greenly gleams
And shows the tracing boards of mysteries
Half-glimpsed among the shadowed traceries
Of lodge or circle, where the heart's compass
Points true north, to the vast green wilderness
Where the green god springs from the deep places
Leaving his scent, his tracks and traces,
For those who will to join the merry dance,
In the wood's dark heart, the place of trance.

Introduction

The aim of this book

The aim of this book is to act as a guide to existing initiatory covens who want to make their practice more inclusive. It is not a how-to guide for people to do eclectic Wicca. People who are not Wiccan may find it interesting as it deals with group dynamics, ritual, ethics, and Wiccan theology and practice along the way.

Inclusive Wicca is about including all participants regardless of sexual orientation, disability, or other differences, not by erasing or ignoring the distinctions, but by working with them. Different people have different experiences, expectations, and perspectives, and including and working with different ideas and experiences can only enrich our Craft, not detract from it.

The book examines different ideas in relation to Wicca, such as eco-spirituality, science, truth, the sacred, sexuality, consent culture, tradition, and magic, and how these concepts can be explored as part of a liberal religious tradition and training as a priestess or priest in Wicca. Each chapter offers further reading, a meditation or visualisation, and practical ideas for rituals and discussions. These can be incorporated into your Wiccan practice or adapted as needed. The book is not a course in Wicca, but can be used as the basis for one if desired, or as a supplement to your usual training methods.

My style of writing sometimes comes across as dogmatic or prescriptive, but that is not the intention of this book. Like Douglas Adams' fictional philosophers, Majikthise and Vroomfondel, I think there should be rigidly defined areas of doubt and uncertainty. If my ideas resonate with you, then feel free to adopt and adapt; if you don't agree, then I hope that reading this book will enable a dialogue on the subjects discussed, and deepen your understanding of the Craft by presenting an alternative view.

Introduction to Wicca

Wicca (contemporary Pagan witchcraft) is primarily a Nature religion, honouring the deities and spirits of Nature, and seeking to commune with the divine through the contemplation and celebration of Nature and its mysteries.

Wicca was officially started in 1951 by Gerald Gardner, a retired civil servant. It seems that he joined a magical group which had been in existence since the 1920s, and which was modelled on concepts of witchcraft, which was then widely believed to have been a survival of ancient Pagan traditions. This was largely due to Margaret Murray's influential (but now discredited) book, *The Witch Cult in Western Europe*, published in 1921. Wicca was originally an initiatory tradition, and most groups still hold to this, although there are many popular books on the subject that suggest that this is not required, and many people identify as Wiccan who are not initiated. Given the taboo status of the word "witch", this is hardly surprising. Ironically, however, it is probably the glamour of the concept of the witch that attracts so many adherents to Wicca.

One of Gardner's initiates was Doreen Valiente, who wrote a lot of the core Wiccan liturgy (known as the *Book of Shadows*, meaning that written texts are mere shadows of actual performed rituals), including *The Charge of the Goddess*, which contains much that Wiccans interpret as theological statements. The most important of these from a LGBTQ perspective is "All acts of love and pleasure are My rituals", and most Wiccans take this to mean that the Goddess approves of sexuality in all its glorious diversity.

In the 1970s and 1980s, Wicca and other forms of witchcraft attracted many second-wave feminists, interested in reclaiming the negative stereotype of the witch (an embodiment of female and "deviant" sexuality) and celebrating women's power, and the nurturing qualities of darkness and Nature. The most celebrated of these was Starhawk, who has written many inspirational books on feminist witchcraft. It was around this time that Dianic witchcraft (which is mostly women-only and honours a single Goddess) started, and included a mixture of lesbian, bisexual and heterosexual women. A similar group was started in New York in 1975 by and for gay men, called the Minoan Brotherhood. It was started in response to the heterocentric culture of Wicca at the time and includes a strong current of queer spirituality.

Many lesbian Pagans find the idea of a single Goddess attractive, sometimes because they have been molested by men, [1] sometimes because they do not feel the need for 'balance'. Other lesbian Pagans try to work within existing models, but often find that they perceive them differently from the way heterosexuals do.[2]

Wicca became much more eclectic and open to innovation in the 1990s, and people began to experiment with different and more inclusive forms, including same-sex initiations and more polytheistic rituals. This trend has continued into the 21st century.

Wicca is a religion where the practitioners interact with the world on many levels – physical, spiritual, magical and emotional. Witchcraft is the craft of magic. Wicca and Witchcraft overlap – all Wiccans are also witches, but not all witches are Wiccans. But the practice of witchcraft (in the sense of doing spells and so on) is

---

[1] Foltz, TG (2000). 'Sober Witches and Goddess Practitioners: Women's Spirituality and Sobriety.' *Diskus*, 6: 1. [online] Available from: http://web.uni-marburg.de/religionswissenschaft/journal/diskus/foltz.html

[2] Lynna Landstreet (1999 [1993]), "Alternate Currents: Revisioning Polarity - Or, what's a nice dyke like you doing in a polarity-based tradition like this?" Originally appeared in *The Blade & Chalice*, Spring 1993. Slightly revised in 1999. http://www.wildideas.net/temple/library/altcurrents.html

only part of the practice of Wicca.

Initiatory Wicca is essentially an esoteric mystery religion in which every practitioner is a priestess or priest. This may also apply to other systems, but we are mainly discussing the initiatory Craft here. A mystery religion is one in which the dramas of the psyche are enacted by and for the benefit of its initiates, but because these mysteries often involve non-verbal concepts, they cannot be communicated. Also, some material is oathbound (initiates are forbidden to disclose it).

After the first degree initiation, the initiate is responsible for their own spiritual development; in some groups, the period between first and second is where the new initiate is helped to develop their spirituality by their Coven and High Priestess and High Priest; after the second, they may take on responsibility for assisting others' development; after the third, their psyche is fully integrated with itself. (The third degree is generally regarded as a personal step in British Gardnerian Wicca, not something that is required in order to be able to run a coven.)

Modern initiatory Wicca has many variants (Gardnerian, Alexandrian, offshoots of these, and independently-developed lineages such as Georgian Wicca) but all share an adherence to a similar ritual structure and the practice of initiation.

The term Wicca has come to be applied to many different non-initiatory variants of the original form, such as solitary Wicca. There is nothing wrong with this – it can be argued that this is a natural outgrowth of any religious impulse.

Everyone's experience of Wicca is different

Many people experience a feeling of spiritually coming home. The words, the energies, and the space are beautiful and resonant. Entering into the circle is like crossing the threshold into a new realm, a realm that feels closer to the gods and goddesses. This is the place between the worlds, where we walk on the edge of time and space, with one foot in the otherworld. The circle is a space where you can commune with the universe, develop the self, engage in sacred play, and honour the divine within each other. There is freedom from unnecessary social constraint. We celebrate the beauty of the night and the human body, and the firelight flickering on the naked flesh; the ecstatic leaping across the fire, wild and free. The flames are symbolic of life and passion. We revel in the feeling of journeying together to other worlds, communing with the ancestors, the land, and the spirits of the land; walking with gods and goddesses.

The above is just an example of how Wicca feels – it's not the same for everyone.

Sources of the Wiccan tradition

Early modern Wicca was inspired by the general interest in the early 20th century in ancient paganisms, esoteric orders of the 19th century, and a passionate interest in nature and magical realms. It appears that the basic structure of modern Wicca was devised by two women in the Bournemouth area in the mid-1920s. They passed this on to Gerald Gardner via Dafo. Gardner genuinely believed that he had found an ancient practice which could be traced back centuries, possibly even millennia. There were, however, other covens practising in other parts of Britain, but little is known about these other than that they existed, and most claims that traditional and hereditary Craft existed before Gardner have not been proven – but nor have they been disproved. As archaeologists will tell you, "Absence of evidence is not evidence of absence".

Gardner proceeded eventually to publish *High Magic's Aid* (a fictional account of medieval witchcraft) and *Witchcraft Today*, an account of the Wica (as it was spelt in those days, referring to the people and not the practice) that he had encountered. He augmented the rather sketchy rituals with material from Co-Masonry and Aleister Crowley.

Many people joined Gardner's early covens, including Doreen Valiente, who added quite a lot of new material into Gardner's *Book of Shadows*, and took out some of the more obviously Crowley-derived phrases (though she left quite a lot in).

There was and is a strong strain of folklore-inspired material in the Craft. Gardner was a member of the Folklore Society and had extensively researched the local folklore during his time in Malaya. Many of the themes found in the celebration of festivals are inspired by folklore.

There were also many literary influences on the Craft, in particular Rudyard Kipling, James Branch Cabell, and many other writers with a strong sense of landscape.

During the 1980s, the Craft became more left-wing, radical, feminist and ecology-oriented. Gardner's political stance was conservative, in spite of some of his more radical ideas. However, Gardner was by no means a typical conservative, as while in Malaya he actually talked to Malayans, unlike most of his contemporaries. He was also strongly committed to naturism, a very unusual interest in the 1940s and 50s.

The modern Craft both draws upon its roots in the Western Mystery Tradition, and looks to traditional forms of folk magic, folklore, and the pagan traditions of the British Isles for inspiration. The structure of rituals remains reasonably constant, but the content varies quite a lot according to the inclinations and tastes of individual covens. Only initiations remain fairly standard, in order to ensure that they will be recognised across the whole Craft, should a covener wish to transfer to another coven.

Deities and other beings

Wicca encompasses a variety of beliefs:

- A belief in many gods and goddesses, spirits of place, nature and elemental spirits (polytheism)
- A belief that "all the gods are one God and all the Goddesses are one Goddess" (duotheism)
- A belief that there is no duality of good versus evil (monism)
- Devotion to a specific deity (henotheism)
- Belief that there is only one deity, usually, the Goddess or the Great

Spirit (monotheism)

- A belief that everything has a soul, including trees, rocks, animals, birds, places (animism)
- A belief that the divine is immanent or manifest in the physical world (pantheism)
- A combination of one or more of the above

There is a strong emphasis in some early *Books of Shadows* on the union of masculine and feminine, but some covens have dropped this on the grounds that the universe is more complicated than that. Polytheist Wiccans honour the Horned God and the Moon Goddess as patron deities of the Craft, and do not regard them as "The God" and "The Goddess". This two-deity approach seems to be a feature of popular exoteric Wicca, though some initiated Wiccans adhere to the dictum that "All the Gods are one God, and all the Goddesses are one Goddess", regarding various deities as aspects or archetypes of the masculine principle or the feminine principle. Most people feel that polytheism and duotheism are incompatible, though some see this as a matter of perspective. Some Wiccans (mainly of the Dianic persuasion) are Goddess-monotheists. Most Wiccans believe that their deities are immanent in the universe, not external to it. Many are also animists, believing in nature-spirits and spirits of place. Polytheist Wiccans believe that each deity is distinct, and not an aspect of some other deity. They may take the view that some deity-names are a different culture's name for the same being, but they do not conflate all deities into one. Fortunately, it is possible to accommodate all these different views within Wicca because of the autonomy of covens and the diversity in unity of Wiccan practice.

Good and evil

There are no personifications of good and evil in Wicca, but there are personifications of destruction, disorder, etc. (Loki, Kali, Eris, etc.), but these are regarded as part of the natural cycle: agents of chaos or destruction, bringing change so that renewal may take place. There are also personifications of growth, life, and light to balance the agents of chaos and destruction.

There are obviously evil entities, people or beings who have given themselves mostly or wholly over to evil (defined as the unbridled pursuit of destruction, domination and control); but there is no ultimate personification of evil in the Pagan worldview.

According to some of the more extreme Christian doctrines, the old Pagan gods were actually demons (because they were regarded as false gods luring people away from the true God). When Christianity arrived in Europe, many of the gods and goddesses were assimilated as saints. Those that could not be assimilated were turned into demons; usually, these were the ones associated with unbridled sexuality. The Horned God is an obvious example here, and it is probably this that gives some Christians the impression that Wiccans are devil worshippers. This is impossible, as the existence of the devil is a Christian doctrine, and Wiccans do not believe in an ultimate personification of evil, and would certainly not worship one if we did.

In folk tradition, people have often dealt with manifestations of the evil or the uncanny by making fun of them, referring to the devil as "Old Nick" and other light-hearted epithets.

Dion Fortune says that we "cannot deal with evil by destroying it, but only by absorbing and harmonizing it."

> "Each Qliphah arose primarily as an emanation of unbalanced force in the course of the evolution of the corresponding Sephirah. The solution of the problem of evil and its eradication from the world is not achieved through suppression, or destruction, but through its compensation and consequent absorption back into the Sephirah from which it came."[3]

If the evil becomes separate, it may become an autonomous thought-form. If a person has committed an evil deed, you would try to deal with the outcome of that but then try to link with the good in person – appeal to their conscience, for example. Wiccans generally see evil as a result of imbalance. If evil is referred to as a process, it is in the social context (which we are also in) so we are connected with it, and can do something about it. It is all too easy to project evil onto others and fail to recognise that our own society has the potential to commit the same atrocities (e.g. blaming "the German character" for the Nazis, and failing to notice that there were and are fascist tendencies in British society too).

People and entities who are damaged and imbalanced want attention (e.g. terrorists, serial killers, sex offenders, and demonic entities) – if you feed them, they grow, like gremlins, or the carnivorous plant in *Little Shop of Horrors*. If the evil is not named, there is a possible danger of it becoming the unspeakable horror (or, in the case of Cthulhu, the unpronounceable horror). The power of malevolent entities can be reduced by giving them a silly name, like "oogly-booglies". Unfortunately, this does not work with physical manifestations of evil like serial killers, etc.

In *Religion without beliefs* (1997), Fred Lamond puts forward the idea that repressing and denying sexuality and the feminine principle is the cause of most of the evil in the world.

> "Let us be quite clear that 99% of all the evil in the world is caused not by deviant individuals but by state power, especially in wars....
>
> The Pagan solution to the problem of evil is to re-establish the worship of the Earth Mother Goddess and her daughter/aspect: the Goddess of Love and Sensuality. The more that people feel free to love and be loved without guilt, the fewer will be driven to acquire more goods than they need to live comfortably, which will lead to a fairer distribution of the Earth's resources. The fairer resource distribution is, the fewer will be tempted to redress the balance by criminal activities.

---

[3] Dion Fortune (1935), *The Mystical Qabalah*, page 302. Wellingborough: The Aquarian Press.

The greater the proportion of people who have been loved and love themselves, the fewer the number of psychopaths driven to seek more power over others, to climb to the top in politics, and, having got there, to use state power to unleash predatory and destructive wars."

The structure of Wicca

Many Wiccans gather in covens. All covens have a High Priestess and High Priest, but the extent to which these are leaders in the generally-accepted sense of the word varies from one coven to another. Their role is more like that of a facilitator or mentor; their aim is to empower their coveners to develop as priestesses and priests in their own right, passing on their experience and knowledge to their coveners, and usually learning from them in the process. Covens are autonomous, but as their founders will have been trained in another coven, they usually maintain contact with their previous High Priestess and sometimes seek guidance from her. The maximum size of a coven is usually limited by the size of the room where they meet.

Most coven members will also practice on their own (either a full ritual or meditation and visualisation), and sometimes will become solitary for a time if they move to another part of the country and cannot find a compatible coven or simply because that is what they wish to do at the time.

Solitary Wicca is also practised by non-initiates, either because they do not want to join a coven or cannot find a compatible one. Solitaries sometimes perform a self-dedication or self-initiation ritual.

Fraudulent groups

Sadly, as with many modern phenomena, there are fraudulent Wiccan and witchcraft groups. Some of these are actually dangerous; others are just a waste of time.

There are people who charge a lot of money for training in what they claim to be Wicca, but which you could get out of any popular beginners' guide. Usually, they are people whom no-one in the Gardnerian or Alexandrian communities has actually heard of. Real Wicca does not cost money. You will be asked to contribute food to share to the feast at the end of the evening; you may be asked to contribute to the cost of candles or incense; you will never be charged for training to be a priest or priestess. You might be asked to pay for services over and above training, such as Tarot readings, astrology, Rune readings, or being a celebrant at a handfasting (Pagan wedding); but these are optional extras.

There are people who claim that you need to have sex with them in order to be initiated. This is not the case; certainly not for first and second degree initiations. The third degree initiation can involve sacred sex, but it is optional and may be done symbolically.

One fraudulent group that I have heard of does not allow its coveners to socialise with each other outside of coven meetings. This is clearly very controlling behaviour, and a warning sign of dysfunctional groups.

Another fraudulent group claimed that LGBT people could not become Wiccan. This is completely false. I know many fine witches who are lesbian, gay, bisexual, and transgender, and they are initiates of Gardnerian and Alexandrian covens.

Phil Hine[4] has described a key set of danger signals to watch for:

1.	Do most of the members strike you as weak, passive individuals who let one or two forceful people dominate the proceedings?
2.	Does the group work entirely from one particular set of teachings or manual and not allow deviation from those principles or allow people to question them?
3.	Does the group demand that you observe a number of strict rules, or attempt to interfere in your life outside the group (i.e. telling you to avoid certain people or not to read particular books)?
4.	Do they insist that they are the best group to be in and that all others are second-rate?
5.	Do they make it difficult for people to leave the group and, if people do leave, are they then demonized, i.e., made into enemies of the group?
6.	Do they make all kinds of wild claims about how your life will be made better by being a member?
7.	Is there a complex and rigid hierarchy, where high-ranking members have impressive titles and seem to be beyond criticism or censure by others?
8.	Do they encourage members to demonstrate loyalty either by donating large amounts of cash to the group's coffers or devoting a good deal of their spare time to unpaid work for the group?
9.	Do they continually draw a distinction between themselves and the outside world, regarding themselves as superior initiates and depicting everyone else as ignorant?
10.	Do they strongly discourage the voicing of dissident opinions in meetings, and label anyone who does speak out as immature, unbalanced or weak?

If you meet a group who have more than one or two of the above characteristics, you would be well-advised to look for a different group.

---

[4] Phil Hine (1998), *Approaching groups*. Online, available from:
http://www.philhine.org.uk/writings/gp_appgrps.html

Countercultural aspects of Wicca

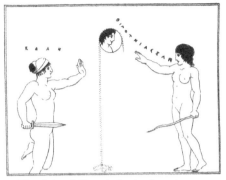

The witches of Thessaly drawing down the moon

There may be some genuine aspects of Wicca that make people uncomfortable, such as ritual nudity, scourging, and the erotic symbolism of the rituals. Not every group places emphasis on these aspects, but they are powerful means of transformation.

Witches have been depicted naked since ancient times, and there are several engravings by Albrecht Dürer, who also produced an engraving of four naked women who are frequently interpreted as being witches (left). The witches of

Thessaly in ancient Greece were also depicted naked.

Scourging or whipping was used as a means of producing altered states of consciousness by many cultures; one famous example appears in a fresco at Pompeii, which is interpreted as an initiation scene. The rites of Lupercalia included men running through the streets of Rome with rawhide whips; Roman women would get in the way of these whips, believing the rite to promote fertility.

Sexuality has been seen as a gateway to spirituality in many cultures, too. Hindu temples have a great deal of sensual and erotic art depicting the union of Shiva and Shakti. Medieval Christian mystics regarded the *Song of Solomon* as an allegory of the love between the soul and Christ. Many of them expressed their spiritual longings in highly-charged erotic sacred poetry. Wicca is steeped in erotic symbolism, and very positive about sex and sexuality. As it says in The *Charge of the Goddess*: all acts of love and pleasure are Her rituals.

Circle of Adam Elsheime (ca. 1578–1610), The Lupercalian Festival in Rome

If there were no challenging aspects of religion, that make people feel uncomfortable, there would be no opportunity to grow and develop by dealing with the internal conflicts; but one must be careful to distinguish between genuinely transformative practices, common to the whole of Wicca, and tried and tested means of transformation, and things that are merely manipulative behaviour.

Rites and celebrations

Wiccans celebrate eight festivals and the thirteen Full Moons of the year. We will sometimes meet on other festivals and other phases of the Moon. There are eight festivals in the Wiccan year: Samhain or Hallowe'en (31st October); Yule (21st December); Imbolc (2nd February); Spring Equinox (21st March); Beltane (1st May); Midsummer or Litha (21st June); Lammas or Lughnasadh (1st August); and Autumn Equinox (21st September). The dates, practice and meaning of these vary according to where the coven is located, when particular plants actually come out, and the local traditions where the coven members live. Some covens celebrate on the nearest weekend to the actual festival. Some writers have tried to fit the festivals to the story of the interaction between "The God" and "The Goddess", but few covens of my acquaintance actually celebrate the festivals in this way.

It is now generally recognised that the eight festivals were not all celebrated by the same culture (in spite of wild claims made on some web sites), and some of them are retro-engineered Christian festivals, but this is in keeping with the eclectic nature of Wiccan practice. Whatever the doubtful origins of the festivals, they have now taken on a life of their own, and could be considered a valid development of pagan tradition, provided that spurious claims for their antiquity are dropped.

While the Solstices and Equinoxes are fixed points governed by the movements of specific movements of the Sun and Moon, the other four, Imbolc, Beltane, Lammas and Samhain are moveable and relate to the passing of the seasons as they display themselves wherever the practitioner happens to be geographically. They do not have to be conducted on specific dates such as 1st May or 31st October. The allocation of specific dates to these festivals is an entirely modern feature.

In the Southern Hemisphere, the equinoxes and solstices are reversed, so the winter solstice is in June, and so on.

The structure of a ritual

The basic structure of a ritual is similar to that of a story. It has a beginning (the opening of the circle), a middle (the purpose for which the ritual is being conducted be it celebratory or magical) and an end (the closing of the circle).

Wicca is practised in a sacred circle, and most rituals have a structure broadly based upon the Western Mystery Tradition. This involves consecrating the space, orienting it to sacred geometry, raising some power, performing the ritual, sharing consecrated food and drink, and then closing the circle and bidding farewell to the beings and powers that have been called upon. Coveners usually bring a contribution to the feast.

Magic

Most Wiccans practice magic for healing and other ethical results. The intention behind the working of magic is not to impose one's will on the universe, but to bend the currents of possibility somewhat to bring about a desired outcome. Magic is generally practised at Full Moons rather than major festivals.

Ethics

The Wiccan attitude to ethics is mainly based on the Wiccan Rede, "An it harm none, do what thou wilt". However, it is significant that this injunction occurs as part of the first degree initiation, and was probably originally meant to show the new initiate that it is impossible to do anything without causing some harm, so it is necessary to consider carefully the consequences of one's actions (Dee Weardale, pers. comm.) The other famous (and often misquoted) injunction occurs at the second degree, and is generally known as the Law of Threefold Return. The actual text enjoins the initiate to return good threefold whenever s/he receives it. To my mind, the most important aspect of Wiccan ethics is the list of the eight virtues which occurs in the *Charge of the Goddess*. These are beauty and strength, power and compassion, mirth and reverence, honour and humility. Each of these pairs of virtues points to the need for balance. Virtue ethics seems to have originated in ancient Greek philosophy, though whether Doreen Valiente was aware of this when writing *The Charge of the Goddess* is not known.

After death

Most Wiccans believe in reincarnation, with the possibility of rest between lives in a region generally referred to as the Summerlands. Some believe that the spirit joins the Ancestors, whilst the soul is reincarnated. The degree to which the personality survives death is a matter of personal belief. Early Wiccan liturgy refers to the possibility of meeting one's loved ones again in future lives. Philip Heselton suggests convincingly that this is because the coven that Gerald joined believed that they had been in a coven together in a previous life.[5]

Wicca and other contemporary Pagan spiritualities

Wicca and Druidry are closely linked, both by their origins (Gerald Gardner and Ross Nichols were close friends) and by the fact that many Wiccans are also members of Druid groves. Owing to the large number of books available on Wicca, there are many people practising some form of Wicca outside the initiatory Craft, and much eclectic Pagan practice bears a close resemblance to the structure of Wiccan rituals and festivals. As more information becomes available on other paths and traditions, however, this may change. The rise of Heathenry and other reconstructionist paths should be welcomed as a valuable contribution to the diversity of Paganisms being practised in Britain today.

Queer Wicca

Wicca (and other contemporary Pagan traditions) are about celebrating our existence in this world, and gaining spiritual insight from Nature and the world around us. Wicca is also about honouring the qualities of darkness and the powers of the Moon. All of these themes are prominent in queer spirituality.

Witches in history

The main witch persecutions that resulted in actual deaths started in the 16th century, mainly due to economic and social pressures resulting from the Reformation. (See *Religion and the Decline of Magic* by Keith Thomas.) People had previously relied on the charity provided by the monasteries; once these were dissolved in England, there were a lot more poor old people around asking for handouts. People felt guilty for not helping them, so when the old women went away mumbling, they assumed that they had been bewitched when they got psychosomatic symptoms resulting from their feelings of guilt. Also, the Catholic Church had provided a lot of protection against sorcery, in the form of holy water, amulets etc., whereas the Protestants just told people to pray.

The Inquisition was more interested in persecuting heretics, especially *conversos* (Jews and Muslims forcibly converted to Catholicism) in Spain. The majority of people judicially killed for witchcraft were in Protestant areas.

---

[5] Heselton, Philip (2004). *Gerald Gardner and the Cauldron of Inspiration: An Investigation Into the Sources of Gardnerian Witchcraft*. Milverton, Somerset: Capall Bann.

The witch persecutions in England differed in character from those in the rest of Europe. The things people were accused of were different. In Europe, witches were accused of flying to Sabbats and having intercourse with the devil; frequently, midwives were accused of performing abortions and stealing children (source: numerous broadsheets in German). In England, they were accused of having witches' teats to give suck to their familiars; bewitching cattle, etc. In Europe and Scotland, witchcraft was a heresy, and therefore subject to ecclesiastical law, with the penalty of being burnt. In England, witchcraft was a felony, subject to criminal law, and the penalty was hanging.

There is no unbroken line of witch religion stretching back into the mists of time. The foundation date of modern Wicca appears to have been sometime in the 1920s, according to the latest research by Philip Heselton in *Gerald Gardner and the Cauldron of Inspiration* (an excellent book, as was its predecessor, *Wiccan Roots*). During the nineteenth century (and possibly the eighteenth century), there were various people who either self-identified as cunning folk or witches, or were labelled as such by their neighbours. However there was no organised movement of witchcraft, only isolated groups 'reinventing the wheel' - and they weren't necessarily pagan either - much of their magic was based on Christian symbolism (compare the story *Marklake Witches* by Rudyard Kipling). Note that the cunning folk were not witches - during the period of persecution they had often accused women of being witches and handed them over to the authorities.

In England, small snippets of Pagan belief and practice had survived and been incorporated into folk belief and practice - but again there was no large-scale survival of ancient Paganism. In some of the more remote corners of Europe (e.g. Scandinavia and Lithuania), ancient Paganisms survived much longer, and so when they were revived, the revivals were much closer to the original forms. There were also traditional practitioners of magic in Finland, particularly among the Sami people.

Chapter 1

What is the sacred?

Pagans don't have a holy book with commandments from a deity. We tend to derive our ethics from reasoning about the world around us. We cultivate virtues rather than following commandments. But we also have a specifically and recognisably Pagan response to the world.

I think the foundation of Pagan ethics is the idea that everything is sacred, because the deities are immanent in everything.

Pagan stories and mythologies illustrate the idea of deities and spirits being involved in the world, and of people taking care of each other and of animals and plants. These are the illustrations of the basic insight that the world itself is sacred and beautiful. The starting point for my realisation that I am a Pagan was the idea that physical reality and the body are sacred.

If you believe that the physical universe is an embodiment of the Divine, and life is something to be celebrated, then your mythology and your ethics will flow from that.

Each Pagan story, myth, and legend will reinforce the view that everything is sacred, but the stories are not necessarily the source of that insight. Rather, the insight rests in our emotional response to the world around us, a sense of being in right relationship with it when we treat it as a Thou and not an It. Regarding the world and Nature as divine is common to the vast majority of Pagans.

The Wiccan text *The Charge of the Goddess* includes the saying "All acts of love and pleasure are My rituals" (the speaker is the Goddess), and Wiccans take this seriously, regarding love and pleasure in all its glorious diversity as sacred.

Most Pagans regard consensual sexual activity as sacred, a form of worship (by which I mean celebrating that which is of great worth, not self-abasement). It is a way of celebrating being alive, connecting with the body, connecting with another person and honouring the divine in them.

The body is also sacred to most Pagans. Paganism mostly seeks to be an embodied spirituality – to connect more fully with the land, the Earth, and/or Nature. Eating and pleasure are sacred.

Some Pagans talk about the sacredness of the land. I feel connected to the land on which I live – its holy wells, stone circles, hills, rocks, trees, valleys, and rivers. I want to connect with specific places, and get to know my local spirits, the *genii loci* of the land around me. I want to know the geology, the history, the ecology, and the flora and fauna of my local landscape.

Other Pagans talk about the sacredness of the Earth. This is a concern for the whole planet, Gaia, and her interconnected eco-systems. Talking about the sacredness of the Earth is less about a concern for specific places, and more of an ecological focus. This is just as important as connecting with the land. Think global, act local, as they say.

Still other Pagans talk about feeling reverence for Nature. This seems different again from talking about the land or the Earth; perhaps it includes the sky and the stars as well as the Earth. Being aware of the whole cosmos is important too.

Most Pagans see the spiritual realms as being intertwined with the physical realms. Deities and spirits are immanent in the physical universe, not separate from it.

sacred versus holy

The word *"sacrifice"* is derived from the Latin "to make holy"; it was Shakespeare who first used it in the sense of giving something in exchange for something else, in *Romeo and Juliet* (which was written in 1592). In its original sense, it just meant to perform sacred rituals – so to make something holy was to include it in a ritual. When we include something in a ritual, we are really paying attention to it, treating it with love and affection, honouring it. So is a sacred thing something that has been set aside for religious use? Can it be used in other contexts without profaning it? To ancient pagans, all activities (planting crops, making love, preparing food, leaving the house) had a sacred dimension, and required ritual to make sure they were done correctly. Ritual was perhaps not really a separate activity from other aspects of life. If you look at Jewish traditions, there is a prayer for every occasion (even going to the toilet), which weaves the sacred into every activity in life. Modern usages of 'sacred' often imply something taboo or set apart; ancient peoples regarded it as an integral part of life.

Is there a difference between holiness and sacredness? Holiness is an Anglo-Saxon word and is possibly related to the concepts of wholeness and healing. Holiness has come to be associated almost exclusively with Christianity, with unfortunate overtones of "holier-than-thou" and the kind of piety associated with denying life and the joys of the body.

Interestingly, many Pagans (including myself) seem to prefer the word "sacred" to the word "holy". To me, 'sacred' implies something that celebrates the sanctity of being alive, and it can include the erotic and the wild.

'Holy', on the other hand, implies abstinence from the erotic and embracing 'civilisation'.

Interestingly, the first sense of 'sacred' offered by the *Merriam-Webster Dictionary* uses a Pagan-sounding example:

Definition of SACRED

1. a: dedicated or set apart for the service or worship of a deity <a tree sacred to the gods>
   b: devoted exclusively to one service or use (as of a person or purpose) <a fund sacred to charity>
2. a: worthy of religious veneration: holy
   b: entitled to reverence and respect
3. : of or relating to religion: not secular or profane <sacred music>
4. archaic: accursed
5. a: unassailable, inviolable
   b: highly valued and important <a sacred responsibility>

Contrast this with Merriam-Webster's definition of holy, which uses Christian and monotheistic examples:

Definition of *HOLY*

: exalted or worthy of complete devotion as one perfect in goodness and righteousness

: divine <for the Lord our God is holy — *Psalms* 99:9 (Authorized Version)>

: devoted entirely to the deity or the work of the deity <a holy temple> <holy prophets>

a: having a divine quality <holy ove>
b: venerated as or as if sacred <holy scripture> <a holy relic>

—used as an intensive <this is a holy mess> <he was a holy terror when he drank — Thomas Wolfe>; often used in combination as a mild oath <holy smoke>

The word 'sacred' is much more frequently used in contemporary Pagan discourse. (Try searching the internet for Pagan + sacred versus Pagan + holy if you don't believe me!)

Wiktionary unpacks the etymology of 'holy':

From Middle English *holi*, *hali*, from Old English *hāliġ*, *hāleġ* ("holy, consecrated, sacred, venerated, godly, saintly, ecclesiastical, pacific, tame"), from Proto-Germanic **hailagaz* ("holy, bringing health"), from Proto-Germanic **hailaz* ("healthy, whole"), from Proto-Indo-European **koil-* ("healthy, whole"). Cognate with Scots *haly* ("holy"), Dutch *heilig* ("holy"), German *heilig* ("holy"), Swedish *helig* ("holy").

The Old English connotation of 'tame' bears out my idea that the term 'sacred' can include wildness, but 'holy' cannot, and is associated with civilisation.

Interestingly, when an Anglo-Saxon Heathen set out to create sacred space, it was space set apart from the surrounding land, which was inhabited by spirits regarded as malevolent.

The etymology of sacred comes from Middle English, but ultimately from Latin.

> From Middle English *sacred, isacred*, past participle of Middle English *sacren, sakeren* ("to make holy, hallow"), equivalent to *sacre + -ed*.

Wikipedia defines 'holy' as associated with the Divine, whereas 'sacred' is associated with something more generally consecrated for ritual use:

> **Holy** (perceived by religious individuals as associated with the divine) or sacred (considered worthy of spiritual respect or devotion, or inspiring awe or reverence among believers in a given set of spiritual ideas).

So 'sacred' seems to be used here as a more general term without reference to the Divine.

Pagans use the term 'sacred' to refer to **sacred space** (usually a place consecrated for ritual), **sacred sites** (usually places that feel special and numinous, often because they were used for ritual in the past, such as stone circles, burial mounds, and holy wells), and **sacred sexuality** (consensual sexual activity for a spiritual purpose).

The word 'holy' is generally used only when it would be more easily understood by a general audience, in phrases which are already in general usage like 'holy book', 'holy well', 'holy water'.

Initially, I thought that the Pagan aversion to the term 'holy' was just an adverse reaction to its usage in Christian discourse, but I think the avoidance of it may be due to something deeper — the widespread Pagan view that everything is sacred in its own right, and does not depend on divinity to sanctify it. In addition to this, the connotations of 'holy' include abstinence from sex, whereas 'sacred' can include sexuality. In Christian discourse, 'holy' appears to mean something directly affected by God, whereas 'sacred' appears to mean something consecrated by humans. In Pagan usage, the sacredness of a thing or place can be either an inherent quality or something conferred on it by using it in a ritual or consecrating it. If we wanted to say that something was directly affected by, or associated with, a deity, perhaps we might use the term 'holy'. The phrase 'Holy Names' appears in a Gardnerian *Book of Shadows* dating from 1957.

Consecration

Who or what makes something sacred? Is it the Divine or deities that make it sacred, or us? Perhaps to the deities, everything is sacred, but we have to work at perceiving the sacred, and creating relationships with other beings – animals, places, people, and so on. When we enter into a relationship with something or someone, it is the relationship that makes it sacred. Most Pagans prefer to use natural materials such as wood, metal, clay, and stone for ritual implements, rather than plastic or other synthetic materials. Perhaps this is purely from aesthetic concerns, but the hand-made quality of most things made from natural materials, and their simplicity, means that the craftsman or craftswoman who made them has already entered into a relationship with them.

Is something more sacred if it is hedged about with taboos? In ancient times, the Roman priest-kings were surrounded by seemingly arbitrary taboos – not eating beans, for instance, or wearing a special hat, or not being permitted to touch certain types of people. I suppose the taboos kept them mindful of their sacred duty to be in touch with the gods at all times. On posing the question, "Why do we do such and such a practice?" I have never accepted the answer "Because it's traditional". It is alright as one of several answers, but for me to be satisfied, the other answers must include "because it works".

Does a sacred thing or place have power in it? Possibly, but it is the response that it evokes in us that is important. A place could be stuffed to the gunwales with Earth energies, but if the person visiting it was oblivious to the beauty and power of the place, then nothing would happen.

So, how do you make something sacred? You honour it – perhaps by performing a ritual to consecrate it, which could be something very simple or quite elaborate, depending on your tastes. If it is a quality you wish to cultivate, you could make and/or dedicate an object to remind you of that quality. If you have a personal shrine or altar, you could place it there.

I have often thought that sacred places, where there seems to be a spirit of place, are such because people have socially interacted with the place, and it has acquired extra numen (power) because of this social interaction; just as human consciousness is shaped by our social interactions.

What is sacred to you? A quality, such as love, forgiveness, peace? A place, like Stonehenge or Avebury or the Serpent Mounds in Ohio, or a place where something wonderful happened to you? Someone you love – a parent, a friend, a lover, a spouse? A thing – a keepsake from a special person, perhaps? Books? If you visit a Pagan household, you are very likely to see a lot of books. We do not have one holy book. because all books are sacred.

In most Pagan traditions, especially in Wicca, eros is sacred. Spirituality and sexuality are intertwined – both lead to feelings of oceanic bliss, which puts us in touch with the Divine in the depths of the soul.

Another very important concept in Pagan spirituality is that of liminality: the experience of being on the edge. Liminal means "of the threshold", so it is the quality of in-betweenness, which is often associated in folklore with the uncanny. Twilight, which is between night and day, is especially liminal; boundary paths and marginal land between civilisation and wildness are very liminal; likewise the state between sleep and wakefulness, when lucid dreams may occur. The boundary between the world of humans and the spirit world is also liminal, and often hedged about with taboos – both to preserve the sacred space, and to protect humans from the raw power of the deities. Dion Fortune, in *The Sea Priestess*, talks about how it is death to look upon Isis Unveiled – but it is an inner death that causes an inner transformation, or initiation. There is a good deal of folklore about dealings with the world of Faerie, and how to protect yourself from its uncanny powers; and how to harness those powers safely for magical uses such as healing, mediumship, second sight, and so on.

Deconsecration

What makes something not sacred? Perhaps when it is no longer dedicated to ritual use, it is less sacred, or deconsecrated. If everything is sacred, then consecration can only make things more sacred. I think that something is deconsecrated when the image of the divine in it is effaced, or defaced. Ugly buildings, rubbish tips, and polluted land come to mind as things that have lost their sacrality. A person who habitually thinks ugly thoughts, lies, cheats, and steals, seems to have lost their connection with the divine, or effaced the image of the divine in which they were formed. A thing that has caused pollution or suffering in its making seems less sacred than a thing that was made with love and reverence for all beings. Of course, sacrality can be restored in all these instances by re-consecration or rededication.

Discussion questions

- What kind of quality is sacredness? Is it the opposite of profanity, or something else?
- Is there a difference between holiness and sacredness?
- Is a sacred thing something that is set aside for religious use? Can it be profaned? Who or what makes it sacred? Is it more sacred if it is hedged about with taboos?
- Does a sacred thing or place have power in it?
- How do you make something sacred?
- What is sacred to you?

Meditation

Close your eyes, and choose something – a place, a concept, an object, a person – that you regard as sacred. What is the quality in it that evokes the sacred for you? What values or virtues does it represent? Are they values or virtues that find an echo within you? Is the sacredness an inherent quality of it? Or does it shine through it, as if its source is elsewhere? Just focus for a while on your sacred place, concept, thing or person. Allow its virtue to shine for you; hear its inner music, smell its perfume. Now let the place, concept, thing or person fade from your mind and just focus on the virtue itself, and recognise its reflection in your own heart.

Preparing for ritual: grounding and centring

Grounding: Visualise yourself as a tree, your roots extending deep into the earth, your branches waving in the sky. Feel water coming into your roots and coursing through you. Feel your connection to the earth; feel your involvement with the sky. Now extend your tap root deep into the earth until you find fire, and draw up energy from the earth. Feel its light filling you. Now draw fire from the heavens, and feel the two fires ascending and descending, meeting in the middle in an interlocking spiral. Now you have a column of energy running along your spine – this is the *sushumna*.

Centring: Visualise yourself lying with your head in the North. Extend your awareness to the horizon, and become aware of the place where the sun rises: the East. Now notice where it sets: the West. Your feet are in the South and your head is in the North. The Sun is in your left hand and the Moon is in your right.

Practical: Make an altar

- What does an altar consist of?
- Different altars for different purposes
- Seasonal altars – add objects which represent the festival or season
- Ancestor shrines – photos and objects of family or people who inspire you
- Wiccan altar – has the 8 tools of the Craft plus the chalice, seasonal fruit/flowers, Goddess and God statues
- Three candles on the altar: one for the Goddess, one for the God, and one for the coven or witch whose altar it is (traditional East Anglian custom)

Chapter 2

The Wiccan circle

Circle of power, elegant paradox;
Raised and yet grounded, floating yet anchored:
A sacred space set aside from the world,
but intimately connected with it.

Deep, dense, dark: a gravity-well.
Strange attractor, spinning bubble
in the space between - filmy rainbow colours
swirling on the surface of the sphere.

Alluring, fascinating, seductive - calling
to the elemental spirits, "Come and play,
dance with us in this anomalous place,
this silver jewel forged from thought and feeling."

A serpent's egg hatched by a woman;
A vessel both hermetic and porous,
wherein we may sail to the furthest reaches
of the archipelago of dreams.

The crossroads of the universe, unknown
to those who do not dare to step across
the abyss, over the sword-bridge
and into the castle of the grail.

Here all are gathered: earth, air, fire, water;
ancestors and the unborn, between the worlds,
suspended outside time and space,
at the marriage of darkness and light.

The chymical wedding, the resolution
of harmony and dissonance, beauty and the beast;
A celebration of the androgyne,
the source and origin of life

~ Yvonne Aburrow, 6 June 2006

The Wiccan circle is the space in which all Wiccan rituals take place. It is a container for the energies raised within it and a microcosm of the sacred cosmos. It also keeps out negative energy, as it acts as a filter. Many people think that a circle is meant to be impermeable, but it is a permeable boundary, and is actually a sphere rather than a circle.

Casting the circle in Wicca, usually, involves using a sword, and standardised words. The reason for these is that by using the same words frequently, it creates a groove or furrow for the mind to follow, in order to reach the liminal state of consciousness where one can encounter the deities. All preparation of sacred space creates a threshold between the world of humans and the world of spirit. Most words for opening a circle mention that it is a boundary, declare that only good may enter or leave, and mention its use as a container for energy. Most Pagans regard the realms of spirit as intertwined with the material world; as the Muslims say about Allah, "closer to me than my jugular vein".

The circle anchors us in a particular locality and orients us to the sacred. It is a spinning bubble in the place between the worlds, a means of voyaging to other realms and states of mind.

The circle space is first swept with a broom. I do this as one would sweep up physical dirt – starting at the edge, working into the centre, and then sweeping the heap out of the room. The sweeping gets rid of the accumulation of mundane energy – thoughts about the mortgage, or the car, or putting the rubbish out, or that argument you had last week.

The circle is then cast (usually with a sword) which delineates the boundary of the circle. I usually do this in three dimensions to indicate that it is a sphere.

The water and salt are then consecrated for use in blessing the circle. The ancient Greek philosopher Empedocles regarded these elements as "feminine", whereas air and fire were held to be "masculine". This seems to be why the water and salt are consecrated, and not the incense. This view was perpetuated through the Western Tradition of magic. I decided this was rather sexist, and started consecrating the incense as well.

Next, the circle is consecrated with water and salt. These represent the elements of Water and Earth respectively. The participants are also blessed with water and salt.

The circle is then censed with incense, which represents the elements of Air and Fire. The participants are also blessed with incense.

When blessing the participants with water, salt, and incense, in many covens, a priestess blesses all the men, and a priest blesses all the women. However, you don't have to rely upon the polarity of masculine and feminine to do this; you could use a different polarity, such as asking someone whose astrological birth sign is ruled by Fire to bless all those people whose sign is ruled by Water (and vice versa), and someone whose sign is ruled by Earth to bless all the people whose sign is ruled by Air (and vice versa). Obviously this requires knowing the astrological correspondences and which of the participants was born under which sign, but then that is the sort of thing that witches should know anyway. The reason for not having a woman bless all the men, and a man bless all the women, is that it reinforces the idea that heterosexual interaction is primary, and that the male-female gender binary is the highest form of polarity. However, polarity is much more complex than that, and should not be reduced to a simple gender binary.

Circular ritual space is inherently egalitarian and participatory. People can step into and out of the centre of the circle, and be the focus of the ritual while they are in the centre, but they can also speak from the edge. The ritual space is dynamic and not static – people move about.

If you are interested in the development of Wiccan liturgy, I would highly recommend reading *Wicca: Magickal Beginnings* by Sorita d'Este and David Rankine.

Calling the quarters

The quarters align us to the sacred cosmos. They also act as guardians of the circle. Most Wiccans use the Western Tradition correspondences of the elements. I use a different set of correspondences, and add the idea of above and below as well.

The Western Tradition correspondences are derived from ancient Greece, via medieval grimoires, magic, and medicine. The occultist Eliphas Levi switched the attributions of air and fire in the 19th century to give the ones that are now commonly used and described here. Prior to this Fire was attributed to East and Air to South, going back to the original ancient Greek attributions. Carl Gustav Jung associated them with four modes of thought and feeling.

They are as follows:

Element	Direction	Humour	Common quality	Jungian trait
Earth	North	Melancholy	Cold and Dry	Sensation
Air	East	Blood	Hot and Moist	Thinking
Fire	South	Choler	Hot and Dry	Intuition
Water	West	Phlegm	Cold and Moist	Emotion

The four elements and the directions also correspond to the seasons and the phases of human life.

Element	Direction	Season	Phase of life
Earth	North	Winter	Death
Air	East	Spring	Birth and rebirth
Fire	South	Summer	Middle age
Water	West	Autumn	Later life

Colour correspondences vary from one tradition to another. In Kabbalah, they vary depending on which of the Four Worlds one is located in. The Four Worlds are Atziluth (Emanation), the divine world; Beriah (Creation) the realm of the archangels; Yetzirah (Formation), the angel realm, also the level of human souls; and Asiyyah (Action), the material universe in which we live.

The most common colour attributions seem to be green for Earth; yellow for Air; red for Fire; and blue for Water. Another system (possibly of Celtic origin) uses white for Earth; black for Air; red for Fire; and green for Water.

Raising power

There are a number of different techniques for raising power in the circle. These can involve dancing, chanting, scourging, energy work, visualisation, and making love.

Dancing is, usually, done deosil (clockwise). However, there are other dances, such as all holding hands and dancing into the centre of the circle and back again; the spiral dance; and if you have five people in your circle, forming a pentagram with interlocking arms makes for satisfying symbolism. Dances can be slow and stately, or fast and frenzied. Eventually, it reaches a climax, when the power is released. Dancing is often accompanied by rhythmic chanting.

The aim of all circle-work is to access the twilight consciousness or non-linear functions of mind, such as trance states or the state known as oceanic consciousness. These were formerly known as right-brain functions, although they do not seem to be restricted to the right hemisphere of the brain. They include rhythm, poetry, awareness of nature, intuition, music, and spatial awareness. These are the keys to a magical level of consciousness.

Once the power is raised, it can be used to work magic of various kinds, such as healing, protection, or divination. Always bear in mind that the power flows through you; do not deplete your own energies by drawing on your personal reserves. Tap into the power of the universe instead, but be careful not to raise more power than you can handle.

Discussion

- Do we need a circle/sphere for our rituals? Why, or why not?
- Why do we call the spirits of the four elements and the four directions?
- What is the significance of performing ritual in a circle?

Practical: Make a simple element shrine

Make a selection of things that you associate with the elements, such as something blue and swirly for water; feathers for air; a bowl of earth; some incense. Divide your altar into four sections (one for each element), perhaps using pebbles. Put the things for each element into the quarters. If you don't have ornaments or whatever, put a candle for Fire, incense for Air, water for Water, and some earth or salt for Earth. Use the altar as a focus for meditating on the elements.

Meditation: the four elements

For each element, imagine yourself entering through a pentagram into the realm of that element. Meditate on the qualities of the element, the places where it may be found, and the creatures associated with it. When you have finished your meditation, leave the elemental realm using the pentagram through which you entered.

If it helps, use dance movements that feel like the way that the element moves (sinuous and flowing for Water, floating and flying movements for Air, rhythmic and pulsing for Fire, stompy and heavy for Earth). For each element, sit facing the direction with which it is associated.

If you have a group of people, it is useful to sit in a circle, and each meditate on the four elements in turn. Start with the element with which you feel the strongest connection, and each sits in one of the four quarters; then move round one place until you have all meditated on all four quarters.

Chapter 3

Gender and sexuality

Gender and sexuality have been major concerns for modern and contemporary Paganisms, ever since the first stirrings of the revival were felt in the 19th century. Two key ideas from the perspective of the women's movement were the reclaiming of the concept of "witch", and the reinstatement of the divine feminine (recently re-popularised by Dan Brown's novel *The Da Vinci Code*). Gay and lesbian practitioners were initially inspired by the idea of sexual freedom in ancient Greece, epitomised for women by Sappho and for men by the god Pan and the satyrs, and later by the discovery that many ancient cultures were accepting of a variety of sexual orientations.

Alex Owen[6] emphasises the importance of the Hermetic Order of the Golden Dawn for the creation of modern occultism, and the centrality of modernist discourse in their views. The Golden Dawn was largely a magical order, but combined so many different forms of mysticism and magic that a wide variety of people got involved. The founder of the Order was married to Moina Bergson, sister of the philosopher Henri Bergson; W.B. Yeats, Arnold Bennett and other well-known figures were members. If you were anyone who was anyone and you weren't in the Golden Dawn, you were probably a Theosophist instead (Oscar Wilde was a member of the Theosophical Society). One of the stated aims of Golden Dawn practice was to achieve psychological androgyny (though this did not necessarily mean they were tolerant of homosexuality). Many of its most enthusiastic members were women (and treated as equals by their male colleagues) and were also prominent in the socialist movement and the suffragette movement, along with members of the Theosophical Society. The Order also created a highly eclectic synthesis of previous magical traditions, which became the basis of much subsequent magical and Pagan practice in the 20th century, including Wicca and Thelema.

In 1899, an unusual book was published: *Aradia, or the Gospel of the Witches*, by Charles Godfrey Leland, who claimed to have discovered a secret witch cult in

---

[6] Owen, Alex (2004), *The Place of Enchantment: British Occultism and the Culture of the Modern*. Chicago: The University of Chicago Press.

Tuscany, worshipping Diana, Lucifer and Aradia (the pronunciation of Herodias in Italian; Herodias was alleged by the Inquisition to have been worshipped by medieval "witches").

Another key source in the development of modern Paganisms is the writer Edward Carpenter (1873 – 1920). Although few remembered him until recently, he is enjoying a revival amongst gay Pagans. He influenced E.M. Forster and D.H. Lawrence, and thereby the wider culture. In 1889, he called for a return of cosmic consciousness to modern "Man":

> "The meaning of the old religions will come back to him. On the high tops once more gathering he will celebrate with naked dances the glory of the human form and the great processions of the stars, or greet the bright horn of the young moon."[7]

Carpenter was a poet who campaigned against air pollution and vivisection, promoted mystical socialism, vegetarianism and rational dress. He was a pacifist, a campaigner for gay rights as early as the 1890s (he lived openly with his partner, George Merrill) and an advocate of Pagan and pantheist ideas.

In 1921, an anthropologist, Margaret Murray, published *The Witch Cult in Western Europe*, expressing the view that pagan witchcraft had survived into the middle ages. This was the beginning of the idea that the witch hunts of the Reformation period had actually been persecuting genuine pagan witches, as opposed to people who were accused by their neighbours of maleficent witchcraft, but were not actually witches at all. This view was very prevalent in popular discourse, and was seized upon with enthusiasm by Gerald Gardner, who used it to great effect in his 1949 novel *High Magic's Aid* and his 1954 non-fiction work *Witchcraft Today*, both founding texts of Wicca. It now appears, from research by Philip Heselton,[8] that modern Wicca was effectively founded as early as the 1920s by three women drawing upon various classical and magical sources, and that Gardner stumbled upon this in the mid-1940s.

Ideas about the persecution of witches and how this linked in with the wider oppression of women fed into feminist discourse and the Goddess movement in the sixties, seventies and eighties.

Many writers (Jessie Weston, Jane Ellen Harrison, and Jacquetta Hawkes among them) influenced by J.G. Frazer's *The Golden Bough* were promoting the idea of a prehistoric cult of the Great Mother Goddess. Whilst this idea has long been discredited in academia, it retained its popularity in popular discourse until quite recently, when the work of Ronald Hutton rendered it an untenable position, as Pagans began to read his erudite, scholarly and beautifully-written books. Hutton is a professor of history at the University of Bristol, a specialist in the history of the English Civil War, and a major historian of the recent revival of Pagan traditions.

The early advocates of the Great Mother Goddess theory were social conservatives. Hawkes, a prominent enthusiast for the theory, believed that women

---

[7] Edward Carpenter (1889), *Civilisation: its cause and cure*, quoted in Ronald Hutton (1999), *The Triumph of the Moon: the rise of modern Pagan witchcraft*
[8] Philip Heselton (2003), *Gerald Gardner and the Cauldron of Inspiration: An Investigation into the Sources of Gardnerian Witchcraft*. Capall Bann Publishing.

and men were fundamentally different and that the role of women was to remain in the home and bring up children. This is rather ironic in view of the theory's next generation of advocates, the separatist feminists of the sixties and seventies. Gardner, the founder of modern Wicca, was influenced by the idea of the Great Mother Goddess. This is apparent from much of the material that he wrote for use in Wiccan ritual. He was also (embarrassingly for most Wiccans who are largely left-leaning) a member of the Conservative Party. However, the women he portrays in his two novels are very feisty and independent characters.

It is not known when the members of the newly-formed Wiccan tradition first became aware of the book *Aradia, or the Gospel of the Witches*. Doreen Valiente began rewriting the Wiccan rituals around 1953, when she became Gardner's High Priestess, and drew upon Aradia for her extensive reworking of Gardner's version of the prose poem, *The Charge of the Goddess*. The piece also draws upon classical texts.

The Charge of the Goddess is a key text in Wicca, as it contains many of its core ideas, especially the line "All acts of love and pleasure are My rituals", which is widely taken to mean that the Goddess approves of all consensual sexual interactions. The Charge also emphasises the nurturing aspect of the Goddess:

> I am the Gracious Goddess, who gives the gift of joy unto the heart of man. Upon earth, I give the knowledge of the spirit eternal, and beyond death, I give peace and freedom and reunion with those who have gone before. Nor do I demand aught in sacrifice; for behold, I am the Mother of all living, and my love is poured out upon the earth.

It explicitly identifies a number of diverse goddesses with the Great Mother, as it begins with the words:

> Listen to the words of the Great Mother; she who of old was also called among men Artemis, Astarte, Athene, Dione, Melusine, Aphrodite, Cerridwen, Cybele, Arianrhod, Isis, Dana, Bride and by many other names.

In 1954, Gerald Gardner's book *Witchcraft Today* was published. It (and his 1949 novel, *High Magic's Aid*) drew heavily upon Margaret Murray's popular work, *The Witch-Cult in Western Europe*. Murray wrote the foreword to *Witchcraft Today*. Many people were attracted to witchcraft by both Murray's and Gardner's work.

Gardner felt safe to publish the book and start publicising Wicca because of the repeal of the 1735 Witchcraft Act, which was replaced by the Fraudulent Mediums Act. The 1735 Act was aimed at people who pretended to have the power to call up spirits, or foretell the future, or cast spells, or discover the whereabouts of stolen goods. The last person to be imprisoned under this act was Helen Duncan, a spiritualist medium, in 1944.

In 1957, Doreen Valiente left Gardner's coven when he produced the "Laws of Witchcraft" (a document that he claimed was ancient, but which he had clearly just written). Among the laws was the statement that a High Priestess must step down when she gets too old and is no longer glamorous. Valiente understandably objected to this Law. She joined the other form of witchcraft available at the time, that of Robert Cochrane, who, like Gardner, was inspired by Robert Graves' book, *The White Goddess*. Cochrane died in an unfortunate accident with some belladonna in 1966.

Gardner handed on his writings to three of his priestesses: Monique Wilson, who went on to found a New York based lineage which has now spread throughout North America; Eleanor Bone, from whom two lineages claim their descent; and Patricia Crowther, founder of another lineage.

Doreen Valiente, Patricia Crowther and Lois Bourne now proceeded to write further books about Wicca, which made it even more widely known.

The witch archetype, the story of the "Burning Times" (the persecution of witches) and the idea of the Great Mother Goddess were enthusiastically advocated by sections of the feminist movement on both sides of the Atlantic, though mainly in America. A parallel development was the growth in popularity of the idea of the divine feminine in Christianity (via the Sophianic tradition, though it may also have been influenced by Goddess-oriented feminism). To demonstrate the centrality of these notions to the identity of adherents of the Goddess movement, Hutton[9] quotes Cynthia Eller, a historian of feminist spirituality:

> "[T]he European witch burnings work both as a persecution history for women and as a symbol of the resilience of women and their goddess-loving religion. As a persecution history, the witch burnings intensify spiritual feminists' sense that they are anathema to the patriarchal powers; it bolsters their conviction that feminism is a question of life and death, of the very survival of women."

Note that this passage refers to the centrality of goddess-religion, the idea that the victims of the witch craze were goddess-worshippers, and the idea that they worshipped a single goddess, not a multiplicity of deities. Fine sentiments (though the reader might feel a little manipulated by the appeal to her sense of persecution paranoia), but based on spurious history.

Spurious history notwithstanding, the idea of the witch is an empowering one for women, as many feel that it represents the aspects of women that are suppressed in patriarchal society: wildness, independence, magic, freedom, power, strength, intellect, intuition, sexuality and cunning.

Sex, gender and sexuality

Psychologically speaking, sex and gender are two different things: sex is your biological characteristics (chromosomes and genitalia) and gender is your psychological role - in which case there are as many genders as there are people. Many Pagan deities do not fit patriarchal gender stereotypes. And now that we are emerging from the era of patriarchy, women and men are finding that they do not have to conform to the narrow and shallow definition of male and female purveyed by patriarchal traditions.

It has been pointed out by some feminists (e.g. Judith Butler) that sex is also socially constructed, given that we do not have to divide the world into the two categories of male and female, and that women's and men's bodies are differently

---

[9] Hutton, Ronald (1999), *The Triumph of the Moon: a history of modern Pagan witchcraft*. Oxford: Oxford University Press.

developed according to gender stereotypes (e.g. men are encouraged to develop their muscles, and women are not).

Lou Hart[10] has explored a variety of models of gender from other societies and concluded that the conflation of sex and gender is a peculiarly Western idea. For example, in some societies, you could be a woman-man (woman living as a man), a man-woman (man living as a woman), cross-gendered (in modern terms, a gender-blender), a man, or a woman.

As we have seen, people's theological stance can affect their views of gender. There are various models available in magical discourse.

One of these is **duality.** As I understand it, duality is the presentation of things as opposites with no shared characteristics (dark and light, evil and good, left and right, etc.) where the different halves of the pairs then become conflated with each other (e.g. left = passive = female = dark = evil, hence the word sinister, literally left).

Another is **polarity**, which I have always understood as being either end of a continuum. The two poles are attracted to each other and a dynamic exists between them. Not only that, but each end of the continuum contains the other within itself (hence the Yin Yang symbol has a black dot within the white half and a white dot within the black half to represent Yin within Yang and Yang within Yin). This is sometimes also called **complementarity.**

A further possibility is **multiplicity**, the idea that there are many different forces and energies in the universe, just as there are many gender roles and many forms of sexuality.

Gender and sexuality in Wicca

In many covens, particularly Gardnerian ones, there is a tendency to work magic by using the polarity of sexual tension; and as the majority of members are heterosexual, this can lead to feelings of exclusion on the part of LGBT members. Some Wiccans are duotheist, that is, believing that "All the Gods are one God and all the Goddesses are one Goddess". As the divine couple are then understood to be lovers, this again excludes LGBT practitioners. It is also a problem for those people of either gender who do not particularly identify with or relate to the predominant archetypes associated with the divine couple. In the past, some Wiccans even went so far as to suggest that because the primary dynamic of the universe was the sexual interaction between the God and the Goddess, this meant that homosexuality was "unnatural". This was counteracted by other people pointing out some words from *The Charge of the Goddess*, "All acts of love and pleasure are My rituals".

According to Dion Fortune (a big influence on Wicca), the female is passive on the outer planes and active on the inner planes, while the male is active on the outer planes and passive on the inner planes (she also emphasises that each of us has both male and female within us). Whilst I do not necessarily find her model of

---

[10] Lou Hart (2005), *Magic is a many gendered thing*,
http://www.philhine.org.uk/writings/flsh_gendered.html

magical dynamics helpful, it is interesting how it imagines the 'male' and 'female' roles to change as you proceed from plane to plane, presumably also to infinity.

The reason usually given for a woman initiating a man (and vice versa) is that it is to ensure a balance of power in the group (e.g. if one gender or one person did all the initiations, they would have an unfair advantage). Generally, I feel that Pagan men are more 'in touch with their feminine side' than most non-Pagan men, so perhaps the original purpose of being initiated by someone of the opposite gender was to awaken one's anima or animus.

Wicca is generally very empowering for women. In the early days of Wicca, it was standard practice for women to lead rituals, and the Goddess was generally viewed as the 'senior partner' of the divine couple. This was heady stuff in the fifties, sixties, and seventies.

Now some men in Wicca are beginning to complain that they do not identify with the Horned God, and that the experience of Wicca has not been as life-changing for them as it has for women. However, it has generally been the case that Wicca for men is about 'discovering their feminine side' and seeking a new model of masculinity. Perhaps one reason why this quest has been less successful is that it is not so widely supported in society at large.

There is also some mention of the divine androgyne in Wicca, and the third degree initiation ritual is about achieving the *hieros gamos*, the internal union of masculine and feminine aspects of the psyche. So there is a resolution of the duality of masculine and feminine.

One of the key ideas in Wicca is the balancing of 'masculine' and 'feminine' aspects of the psyche (the anima and animus identified by Jung). This idea can be seen as problematic if there is a too rigid identification of a gender with specific qualities; but as the idea is to bring all these aspects into balance and achieve psychological androgyny (an idea borrowed from the Golden Dawn and alchemy), perhaps this is not too much of an issue.

It seems to work to some degree, either because people who like the idea of psychological androgyny are attracted to Wicca, or because it makes it easier for practitioners to express the side of themselves that is usually associated with the opposite gender.

Conclusion

In general, Wiccans are very accepting of variation in gender and sexuality, and are very willing to challenge received societal norms on this and many other issues. There is also strong evidence that ancient paganisms tolerated a variety of gender and sexual roles, and a lot of Pagan mythology reflects this. Although there has been some difficulty in Wicca with adapting the rituals to be more inclusive, this can easily be achieved by introducing new versions of traditional forms of words.

Discussion

- What is your understanding of gender and sex?
- How does it interact with your spirituality?

- How can you make your rituals more inclusive?

Practical

- Create a ritual with as many variations of gender and sexuality as you can
- Research gender-variant practices, deities, and symbols from the past
- Research same-sex desire in ancient pagan societies

Chapter 4

Polarity

"POLARITY, or action and reaction, we meet in every part of nature; in darkness and light; in heat and cold; in the ebb and flow of waters; in male and female; in the inspiration and expiration of plants and animals; in the equation of quantity and quality in the fluids of the animal body; in the systole and diastole of the heart; in the undulations of fluids, and of sound; in the centrifugal and centripetal gravity; in electricity, galvanism, and chemical affinity. Superinduce magnetism at one end of a needle; the opposite magnetism takes place at the other end. If the south attracts, the north repels. To empty here, you must condense there. An inevitable dualism bisects nature, so that each thing is a half, and suggests another thing to make it whole; as, spirit, matter; man, woman; odd, even; subjective, objective; in, out; upper, under; motion, rest; yea, nay.

Whilst the world is thus dual, so is every one of its parts. The entire system of things gets represented in every particle. There is somewhat that resembles the ebb and flow of the sea, day and night, man and woman, in a single needle of the pine, in a kernel of corn, in each individual of every animal tribe. The reaction, so grand in the elements, is repeated within these small boundaries. For example, in the animal kingdom the physiologist has observed that no creatures are favorites, but a certain compensation balances every gift and every defect."

- from *Compensation*, Ralph Waldo Emerson (1803 – 1882)

I am left-handed, and I have always been interested in the two (seemingly unconnected) assertions that 10% of the population are left-handed and that 10% of the population are homosexual. It seems to me that the other 90% cannot be totally right-handed, or totally heterosexual. Rather, the left-handed 10% prefer to use their left hand for most things; there is probably another 10% at the other end of the spectrum who can only use their right hand, and the eighty percent in the middle are probably ambidextrous but culturally conditioned to use their right hand. It is the same with sexuality - 10% are homosexual, there is probably another

10% who are completely heterosexual, but the eighty percent in the middle is probably bisexual but culturally conditioned to be heterosexual. Again, there is a continuum between the two polarities, as bisexuals know.

As a child, I was fascinated by the experience of standing between two mirrors, and looking at the room reflected in the mirror, reflected in the other mirror, and so on to infinity. I suggest that polarity is like this. Where does female stop and male begin? The one is reflected in the other, to infinity. The black dot in the middle of the Yang half (and the white dot in the middle of the Yin half) can also be represented as another Yin Yang symbol, which also has its dots in each half, which are even smaller Yin Yang symbols, and so on into infinity.

Psychologically speaking, sex and gender are two different things: sex is your biological characteristics (chromosomes and genitalia) and gender is your psychological role - in which case there are as many genders as there are people – for example, the goddesses Macha and Morrigan do not fit into 'traditional' (Christian and patriarchal) gender stereotypes. However, the society in which they lived would have had no problem accepting them as women, since (apparently) that was what most women were like in those days, to a greater or lesser degree. And now that we are emerging from the era of patriarchy, women and men are finding that they do not have to conform to the narrow and shallow definition of male and female purveyed by patriarchal traditions.

Homosexuality is a natural phenomenon - animals do it, plants do it. Many plants actually have male and female flowers on the same tree; some plants are androgynous; some have no sex at all; some change sex several times during their lifetime. Guppies (a species of fish) can change sex at will in order to breed. Male seahorses carry and give birth to their young, and female hyenas have penises. Anyway, as soon as the pleasure principle enters into a sexual relationship, it ceases to be purely about reproduction. So all those homophobes who think that gay sex is not natural because it doesn't result in reproduction should not be using any form of contraception because it will make them unnatural.

One of the many reasons that I chose to identify as a Pagan and a Witch is that our basic philosophy celebrates love in **all** its forms, including queer love. According to *The Charge of the Goddess*, 'All acts of love and pleasure are My rituals' (rituals of the Great Goddess). There is no implication in any Craft ritual that I have ever seen that all magical acts are about fertility (and even if they were, there's no need to take it literally and assume that it means the fertilisation of an ovum by a sperm, otherwise there would be a population explosion). Gerald Gardner may have been homophobic, but as far as most Wiccans are concerned, his pronouncements are not holy writ - he also wrote that women should stop being High Priestesses when they were no longer young and pretty, which was one of the reasons Doreen Valiente parted company with him.

Incidentally, the reason usually given for a woman initiating a man (and vice versa) is that it is to ensure a balance of power in the group (e.g. if one gender or one person did all the initiations, they would have an unfair advantage). Interestingly, when Oðinn was initiated by the goddess Freyja into the usually female mysteries of Seiðr, he became more transgendered. Generally, I feel that Pagan men are more "in touch with their feminine side" than most non-Pagan men, so perhaps the original purpose of being initiated by someone of the opposite gender was to awaken one's anima or animus.

I think also that 'fertility' should be interpreted in its widest possible meaning, namely fertility of ideas, spirit, etc. rather than just being about physical reproduction. In the folk tale of the Fisher King, it is stated that men's minds were barren as well as women's wombs (so were women's minds and men's balls, presumably) before the coming of the Grail Knight. It is also significant that the King was wounded in his 'thigh' (obviously a euphemism for his penis) and that it is a male knight 'asking the right questions' who restores him to full life, and hence also restores fertility to the land.

Personally, I feel that the 'Great Work' is to awaken the spirit in matter. In some traditions (e.g. Gnosticism), it is believed that spirit is trapped in matter, and must return to the Godhead, the divine source. I believe that the purpose of our existence is to become more conscious at all levels of being and that as our awareness of the Universe grows, it becomes more aware of itself. We have all experienced the feeling that a particular place has a *genius loci* (spirit of place), has greater awareness, and the more we honour it, the more it responds to us.

On a more earthy level, it is a connection to the land which is important. On one of my visits to a forum for LGBT Pagans, I was struck by the depth of people's connection to the landscape (something I have only seen expressed by a few people elsewhere in Paganism). Fertility is important for the land, yes, but so is the full cycle of death and rebirth, the tides of sowing, growing, reaping, and resting. The land is the rocks, the trees, the earth, the wild places, the fields, the rivers – it is not just about making the crops grow. For most of our history, we have been hunter-gatherers (well known for their shamanic activities, including gender-bending). This agricultural preoccupation with crops is almost as new-fangled as Christianity is. Of course, I like food, so I tend to be quite interested in crops growing, but it's not the be-all and end-all of my magical practice.

Problems with polarity

Many Wiccan rituals emphasise the importance of polarity, the idea that for magic to work, there has to be erotic attraction, usually between a man and a woman. Traditionally, a woman had to initiate a man, and a man had to initiate a woman.[11] One of the reasons for this was that Gardner himself was homophobic.[12] The reason usually given nowadays for a woman initiating a man (and vice versa) is that it is to ensure a balance of power in the group (if one gender or one person did all the initiations, they would have an unfair advantage).

Some Wiccans are duotheist, that is, believing that "All the Gods are one God and all the Goddesses are one Goddess." As the divine couple are then understood to be lovers, this again excludes GLBTQ practitioners. It is also a problem for those people who do not particularly identify with or relate to the predominant archetypes associated with the divine couple.

---

[11] Gerald Gardner (1954), *Witchcraft Today*, page 69.
[12] Lois Bourne (2006 [1998]), *Dancing with Witches*. Robert Hale. page 38

Nevertheless, even though polytheist Wiccans see the Horned God and the Moon Goddess (the two deities of the divine couple) as patron deities of Wicca, with a special relationship with the religion, rather than a conflation of a multiplicity of different deities, there is still a great deal of emphasis on duality and polarity in the rituals; and there are still plenty of people who insist that Wicca is a "fertility religion", presumably based on ideas gleaned from J.G. Frazer's *The Golden Bough*. However, Wiccan liturgy does not seem to imply that all magical acts are about fertility. It could also be argued that 'fertility' should be interpreted in its widest possible meaning, namely fertility of ideas and spirit, rather than just being about physical reproduction as a result of heterosexual sex.

However, Wicca as it is practised today is sometimes heterocentric, but very rarely homophobic.

Personally, I do not believe that there are "male energies" and "female energies" only; there is a multiplicity of different types of magical energy (compare the electromagnetic spectrum, which includes radio waves, microwaves, infrared, the visible spectrum of light, ultraviolet, x-rays, gamma rays, and high-energy gamma rays). Gender is far more complex than a simple binary, so reducing it to a simple binary is far too simplistic as a model for understanding it.

Quite often, when advocates of LGBTQ rights talk about "smashing the gender binary", heterosexuals get anxious, as if we were talking about abolishing heterosexuality and cisgender identities. However, the gender binary is the notion that cisgender heterosexual pairs are the norm and that everything in the universe resembles a cisgender heterosexual couple. We need to expand the model to include different genders and sexual orientations. That does not mean that heterosexuals will not be included, it just means that they won't be the only ones represented in mythology, symbolism, and ritual.

Balance and complementarity

In Wicca, darkness does not symbolise evil. The darkness is necessary for rest, growth, and regeneration. Death is not evil, but a necessary adjunct to life. If there was no death and dissolution, there could be no change or growth. The cycle of birth, life, death, and rebirth is part of the interaction of the polarities. Suffering is also part of the process of growth; just as a tree is shaped by the wind, we are shaped by our experiences. It is only by experiencing suffering that we acquire sufficient depth to know the fullness of joy. It is then that the full light of consciousness dawns in us, and we achieve mystical communion with the divine.

But what if we never emerged into the light? What if we were always suffering? This would only be the case if time were linear and not cyclical. In the Wiccan worldview, we go through cycles of birth, death, and rebirth, but not in an endlessly repeating, always-the-same kind of way, rather there is change and growth. The pattern is an ascending spiral, not a treadmill. We pass through light (spring and summer) and descend into darkness (autumn and winter). But just as the seasons are not the same each time, nor are the greater cycles.

The celebration of darkness, which we have been told by mainstream culture is the realm of evil, allows us to transcend boundaries:

> "Darkness requires performance and each of us is called upon to perform, to play across the boundaries of those worlds we have been told are dark and therefore evil or bad or alien."[13]

It also allows us to escape the hierarchical view of the cosmos which is associated with the exclusive honouring of the light:

> "Baldwin and Lorde, each in their distinctive ways, show us that turning to the dark, celebrating darkness, and turning away from dichotomous thinking in which light and dark are opposed—with light as a positive force for conquering the negative dark—offer hope for saving humanity from destructive hierarchies based on supremacies of race, sex and gender. "[14]

Wicca is partly about the interaction of light and darkness, played out in the Wheel of the Year (the cycle of Wiccan festivals). Instead of being opposed, light and darkness interact in a dance or sexual union. This is the basis of the idea of polarity.

One way to make the idea of polarity more inclusive is to regard the primary polarity as being the interaction of self and other, lover and beloved (rather than as male and female). Lynna Landstreet[15] sees the first touch of lightning on the primordial waters as being the "true Great Rite, of which all other enactments, sexual or not, are merely symbolic". (The 'orthodox' definition of the Great Rite in Wicca is the enactment of the union of the masculine and feminine polarities.)

It could be argued that Wicca is inherently queer, but most practitioners are unaware of this. The word *wicca* (Anglo-Saxon for a male witch) apparently derives from an Indo-European root meaning 'to bend' or 'to shape' - and the actions of bending and creativity are both frequently associated with same-sex love. The emphasis on the need to become psychologically androgynous (frequently couched in terms of developing men's feminine side and women's masculine side) and the use of the *Dryghtyn Prayer* add to the feeling of queerness at the heart of the tradition. In addition to this, the figure of the witch, derived in part from the spae-wives and *seiðr*-workers of Northern Europe[16], is often associated with sexual and gender transgression. These ideas may not be very current in Wicca generally, but they are part of the historical discourse about witchcraft.

---

[13] R Hawley Gorsline, (2003), 'James Baldwin and Audre Lorde as Theological Resources for the Celebration of Darkness.' *Theology and Sexuality* 10.1 (2003) 58-72 Available from: Ebscohost. – page 71

[14] R Hawley Gorsline, (2003), 'James Baldwin and Audre Lorde as Theological Resources for the Celebration of Darkness.' *Theology and Sexuality* 10.1 (2003) 58-72 Available from: Ebscohost. – page 71

[15] Landstreet, L (1999 [1993]), *Alternate Currents: Revisioning Polarity Or, what's a nice dyke like you doing in a polarity-based tradition like this?*
http://www.wildideas.net/temple/library/altcurrents.html

[16] Blain, J (2002). *Nine Worlds of Seid-Magic: Ecstasy and Neo-Shamanism in North European Paganism*. London and New York: Routledge. pp 89-110

Discussion

- What does polarity mean to you?
- How do you experience magical energy?
- How many different forms of polarity can you think of? Do you think they map neatly onto male and female, or not?

Practical techniques

Investigate different ways of working with polarity. Try a working with two people born under astrological signs ruled by different elements, such as Aries (ruled by Fire) and Pisces (ruled by Water). Try using the symbolism of darkness and light, up and down, inner and outer, hot and cold, wet and dry, lover and beloved, primordial ocean and lightning bolt.

Play with magnets and experience the pull of magnets of opposite polarity, the repulsion of magnets of the same polarity.

Chapter 5

Spirituality and sexuality

Pagan rituals are performed with the whole body as well as the mind and the heart. They have an erotic quality – not overtly, but sublimated and transmuted. Ritual is sensual and involves all the senses. This erotic aspect of worship is frequently expressed by medieval Christian mystics, Sufis like the poet Rumi, as well as contemporary Pagans.

The mood-swing of Western culture against the body, women and sensuality is said by historians to have begun around 500 BCE and reached its height in about 500 CE. At its worst, it was profoundly anti-women. It had a lasting influence on the Christianity of later centuries.

Bound up with this fear of women, sexuality, and the body was the fear of the dark, which is connected with the feminine, nature, and wilderness and has been denigrated for most of Christian history. In a patriarchal culture, the assertive and sexually active female is regarded as dark, dangerous and malevolent, and characterised as a witch. The passive female is elevated as the model for how women should be: quiet, virginal, and modest. In order for patriarchy to function, female sexuality must be suppressed and controlled, and men must be taught to fear it and abuse it, and the wilderness must be conquered and tamed.

Fortunately for us, the mystics frequently rebelled against this anti-women worldview. Their writings were deeply sensual and erotic, and extolled the dazzling darkness of God, the ultimately unknowable and mysterious aspect of the Godhead.

Judaism, on the other hand, never entirely abandoned its respect for the body and for women, and making love remained an act of worship. It was and is obligatory in Judaism to make love on the Sabbath Eve, because making love reunites the exiled Shekhinah with the Godhead. According to many Jewish theologians, the Shekhinah, who is the immanent feminine aspect of the Divine, is exiled in the material world, and seeks to be reunited with the transcendent male Godhead. We can help her by making love and performing acts of kindness, which are known as *Tikkun Olam*, repairing the world.

Spirituality and sexuality are intertwined. The most profound sexual experiences involve an abandonment of the centrality of the ego and opening up to the beloved other; this can become an opening up to the Divine Beloved. This is reflected in the erotic and spiritual poetry of the Sufis. The Sufis loved the night, which was seen as the time when the soul was most open to the Divine Beloved.

Similarly, the deeply spiritual is also erotic, and opening up and self-abandonment to the Divine can resemble a relationship with a human partner. The ancient Greek story of Eros and Psyche represents the Divine visiting the soul. In India, the story of Krishna pleasuring a thousand cow-girls simultaneously also symbolises the erotic relationship with the Divine. Medieval mystical poetry is full of erotic yearning for the Divine. One meditation on the *Song of Songs* exclaims "Oh that he would kiss me with the kisses of his mouth". In the medieval period, among both Jewish and Christian thinkers, the *Song of Songs* was seen as an allegory of the soul's relationship with God.

So, how can ritual be erotic without being overtly sexual? How do we entice Eros to visit Psyche?

The erotic can be sensual, involving all five senses. There can be visual elements to ritual: magical tools, the altar, flowers, candlelight, jewellery, pictures. In Wicca, there are numerous symbols representing the sexual union of lover and beloved.

Ritual can include scent – the smell of flowers, incense, good moist earth, baking bread, wine, fruit. Smell is the most subtle and evocative of all the senses and smells can transport you instantly to a memory of the past or an intimation of future bliss.

Ritual can include taste – the taste of food, mindfully and appreciatively savoured, shared amongst friends. Many Pagan rituals include the use of food in a ritual context.

Jewish worship in the home includes food, as in the well-known ritual of the Seder (Passover meal) with its various symbolic foods.

Ritual can include touch and movement – hugging, dancing, joining hands, gestures, warming oneself at a fire, anointing with oil and water, ceremonial kissing, the feel of rich earth, planting bulbs, experiencing textures.

Ritual includes sound, but there is not as much singing in Paganism as there could be (presumably a reaction to the singing of hymns in Christianity). The lyrics of Pagan chants are sometimes a bit trite. In Hinduism, however, the classical raga form goes through stages, firstly of yearning for the Divine Beloved, making contact, and achieving union. The erotic aspect of this encounter is clearly celebrated in the music.

The erotic aspects of spirituality are present in Paganism (especially Wicca) but not much talked about, because they are so easily misunderstood. The erotic can be sensual, passionate, tender, mysterious, alluring, mystical; it does not have to be explicit or acted upon.

Our rituals are performed with the whole body, not just with mind and heart. This is how we integrate our spirituality with everyday life. As Mary Oliver so memorably put it, "Let the soft animal of your body love what it loves."

Let us welcome Eros into the bridal chamber of the psyche, for only then can we make the shift from the domination of the ego (the rule of law) to the balance of all aspects of the psyche (the religion of love). Let us descend into our own depths to encounter the darkness and silence, and be dazzled by the unknowable mystery of the Divine.

Creating a culture of consent

In mainstream culture, sexuality and sex are commodified (regarded as a commodity for sale). The body is packaged as an object of desire, and women are regarded as objects for sexual gratification, rather than subjects with our own desires.

The lethal inheritance of the patriarchal system is the view that women's sexuality is dangerous and needs to be controlled; that women's desires are not legitimate; and that a woman is "damaged goods" (a telling phrase) if she is no longer a virgin. The basic idea in this discourse is that women do not want sexual intercourse, and women who do want sex are deviant and must be punished. Therefore (in this discourse) no sexual intercourse can be truly consensual, because only deviant women actually want it, so women must be cajoled or forced into having sex. This is the basis of what many feminists refer to as "rape culture". Curiously enough, the view that women must be either cajoled or forced into sex is embraced by trans-excluding radical feminists, right-wing Christians, so-called men's rights activists, and pick-up artists.

The corollary to this view is the idea that men "need" sex, and cannot control their sexual urges; that's why women are the ones who have to take all the preventive measures against rape, like not dressing "provocatively", not walking home late at night, not getting drunk and incapable. This is horrible slut-shaming nonsense, but it is also grossly unfair to the majority of men who are not rapists.

Sadly, some of this discourse has spilt over into Pagan culture. Pagans have gone a long way towards re-examining the discourses inherited from mainstream culture, especially around the issues of the autonomy and sacrality of women, but perhaps not far enough.

The Pagan movement really took off in the 1960s, with the culture of free love. Sadly, although the sixties affirmed that sex is good, there was also a widespread idea that if someone declined to have sex, they were up-tight and frigid. So consent was not enshrined as a value alongside guilt-free sex.

Being in the same bed as someone does not constitute consent to sexual activity. Consent is continuous and explicit, not merely acquiescing to the sexual act because it is easier than arguing. It does not have to be verbal, but it should be enthusiastic.

Pagans are supposed to be a community that values women, that believes women are the embodiment of the Divine just as much as men, if not more so.

We are a community that celebrates all acts of love and pleasure. Well, let me tell you right now, anything less than enthusiastic consent is not an act of love and pleasure. Love and pleasure are sacred. Rape and abuse are the most horrible violations of the sacred integrity of the human body.

What is enthusiastic consent? It is where sexual partners actively describe what they do and don't desire. It means not just avoiding a No, but actually getting a clear Yes. And not just a yes to sex, but also a yes to all the other activities that surround it. Maybe your partner doesn't like being touched in a particular way, or in a particular place – so don't touch them there, and/or don't touch them like that.

Pagans think that we are immune to the problems of the wider society, including rape culture, because Pagans are ethical, or because high priestesses are very wise and intuitive and supposedly always filter out dodgy people, including rapists and abusers. I am aware of enough cases of sexual harassment, rape, and domestic violence among the Pagan community to know that that just is not true. And besides, some of these people are downright manipulative and can be quite convincingly 'nice'.

So what can we, the Pagan community, do about it?

I have said it before, and I will say it again: we need a safeguarding policy for Pagan communities and Pagan events, and people trained in safeguarding. I do not care how difficult it would be to set up. Of course covens and other groups are autonomous; I know the Pagan community is more of a network than a gathered community; I know it would cost money, and maybe only have partial coverage – but we need to do it. Which would you rather join – a coven/grove/hearth that is signed up to the safeguarding committee, or a coven that isn't?

We really need to have consensus: no more predators, no more rapists. If someone says they don't like someone's behaviour – don't just ignore them, or tell them it's not that serious, or tell them not to rock the boat – bar the perpetrator from the group for a period of time, or permanently, depending on the seriousness of the act.

Don't make excuses for predators and claim that they are "just socially awkward" – that is no excuse. There are behaviours that are unacceptable: commenting on the bodily characteristics of others (just because your tradition practices nudity, does not give you the right to comment on the size of other members' breasts or penises or extra weight); unwanted touching, especially on areas of the body that are considered erotic, is harassment. Everybody knows what makes people uncomfortable, but we are all too polite to challenge these behaviours.

All covens, groves, hearths, moots and groups need to educate their members about consent and enthusiastic consent, and make it clear that violations of consent will not be tolerated. Have a regular talk with your new members, make sure people understand the issues, and that sexual harassment will not be tolerated. If a new person joins your coven, grove or hearth, make sure that they understand about consent.

I can think of a Pagan pub moot that collapsed due to the presence of someone whom everyone considered to be a creeper, and no-one wanted to be in the room with him on their own, and yet no-one asked him to leave, so in the end, the group collapsed, because no-one turned up in case they were alone with the creeper. I can think of a student society where a creeper was asked to leave, and the society flourished.

Quite often, when someone suggests ostracising or banning a predator or an abuser or a rapist, they are told, "Your feelings, your problem", or "we don't really know what happened", or "That's just the way that person behaves; they're a bit weird", or "It's wrong to ostracise people".

Do not tolerate predators. If a person says they have been assaulted, believe them. If a woman objects to sexist behaviour and/or predatory behaviour (e.g. unwanted touching) don't silence her. If you hear someone making misogynist, homophobic, transphobic, or racist comments, challenge them and make it clear that their views are not welcome in the Pagan community. Tell the perpetrator of sexual harassment that that sort of behaviour is unacceptable. We need to do this to make the community safe for everyone.

If we create a loving, consensual, and sacred sexuality; if we embrace and celebrate the erotic, the sensual, and touch, then we can create a culture of consent, of sacred sexuality. If we regard every other person as a manifestation of the Divine, a subject in their own right, with their own desires and dreams, then we can approach each other as equals in the erotic encounter. Then we can truly say that all acts of love and pleasure are rituals of the Goddess.

Discussion

- What are the distinctions between sensuality, sexuality, and the erotic?
- How are spirituality and sexuality connected for you?
- Why do you think so many religions have tried to suppress the connection between the two?
- What is consent? What is enthusiastic consent? Can consent be non-verbal?
- How can we create a culture of consent, and promote a Pagan ethic of sacred sexuality and sensuality, in our communities?

Practical

Do something sensual and self-nurturing, such as going for a facial, a massage, a sauna, or turning your bathroom into a sensualist's paradise and having a long bath with scented oils and candles. Pay attention to what your body needs, and do that.

Practice communication with your lover. Try different forms of consent (verbal and non-verbal) for every aspect of sexual interaction. Practice trust exercises with each other.

Visualisation

You are in a room decorated with pink satin, velvet, gold, and pale marble. The cushions are soft and yielding, and everything has a pearly, iridescent sheen. A soft and diffuse light permeates the room, reminiscent of the rose-gold light of dawn. You are reclining on a very comfortable sofa, and grapes, and sherbet, and wine, and moon-cakes are near at hand. The music of a lute drifts across your awareness.

Languidly, you rise and wander over to the door. It is made of the palest birch-wood and carved and gilded with sinuous curves reminiscent of human breasts and thighs and buttocks.

Softly, you open the door, and it opens into a temple, also decorated with rose-pink, satin, velvet, gold, and marble. Endless pillars stretch away into the distance, and shafts of sunlight illuminate incense drifting through the air. The scent of roses envelops you, and you see that roses are climbing among the pillars, forming a canopy of pink and red and white.

You walk slowly into the temple, and see in front of you a great scallop shell in a circular pool. Lying on the shell is the most beautiful woman you have ever seen; olive-skinned, and with the most beautiful languorous curves. She sleeps with her head pillowed on her arm, her hair spilling out over the shell and into the water. She stretches, yawns, and wakes, and rises in a single graceful sinuous movement to her feet, balancing effortlessly in the middle of the shell. Her hair falls in soft ripples, framing her face, and her breasts rise and fall gently as she breathes. It is the goddess Venus, goddess of love, sensuality, the Earth, and the morning and evening star. She is the source of all loveliness and pleasure, sensuality, and sexuality.

(Silent pause here for adoring and communing with the goddess Venus)

When you feel it is time to leave, return through the door by which you entered, sink softly down onto the very sensual and comfortable sofa, close your inner eyes, return to the space that surrounds you, and open your actual eyes.

Further reading

- T Thorn Coyle, Predators in Paganism, *Numinous and Concrete*, 31 March 2014. http://www.patheos.com/Pagan/Predators-Paganism-T-Thorn-Coyle-03-31-2014

- Kim Dent-Brown, Sex! Witches!!! Nudity!!!!! And yes, ethics...., *Acts of Love and Pleasure*, 18 December 2013. http://actsofloveandpleasure.wordpress.com/2013/12/18/sex-witches-nudity-and-yes-ethics/

- Erin, On the critical hotness of enthusiastic consent, *Feministing*, 27 october 2010. http://campus.feministing.com/2010/10/27/on-the-critical-hotness-of-enthusiastic-consent/

- Mary Gardiner and Valerie Aurora, Conference anti-harassment campaigns do work: Three existence proofs from SF&F, atheism/skepticism, and open source, *The Ada Initiative*, August 2013. http://adainitiative.org/2013/08/conference-anti-harassment-campaigns-do-work-three-existence-proofs-from-sff-atheismskepticism-and-open-source/

- Melissa Harrington, *Wicca and Sex*, http://www.wiccanski-krag.com/wicca_i_sex.html#english

- Christine Hoff Kraemer, Erotic Ethics and Pagan Consent Culture, *Sermons from the Mound*, March 2014.

http://www.patheos.com/blogs/sermonsfromthemound/2014/03/erotic-ethics/

- Brendan Myers, <u>The community statement on religious sexual abuse.</u>
  http://is.gd/9y37cg
- <u>Meet The Predators</u>, *Yes means yes*, 12 November 2009.
  http://yesmeansyesblog.wordpress.com/2009/11/12/meet-the-predators/
- <u>The Myth of the Boner Werewolf</u>, *The Pervocracy*, August 2012.
  http://pervocracy.blogspot.ca/2012/08/the-myth-of-boner-werewolf.html
- *Enthusiastic Consent*, Doctor Nerdlove, March 2013.
  http://www.doctornerdlove.com/2013/03/enthusiastic-consent/
- The Geek Girl Convention Code of Conduct.
  http://www.geekgirlcon.com/code-of-conduct/

Chapter Six

Progressive Wicca

In 1988, Tam Campbell gave a talk at which he launched the concept of progressive Wicca, which he had developed together with Karin Rainbird and David Rankine. There were many covens which already embraced progressive values, and they were articulating a mood within the Craft.

Tam Campbell explains:

> "The world has moved on and there is now a much different Craft. It is no longer necessary to have a distinct movement as most groups have come to develop towards many of the ideals and practices which we advocated at the time.
>
> It was a time when there was a more rigid and hierarchical spirit in the Craft, many of the Gardnerian establishment saw each other as rivals. ... Rituals were often also rigid and repeated year after year. Creativity was stifled and 'rank' and status was all important.
>
> Progressive Wicca saw the individual as a vital part of each coven ... It did not see the movement as separate from the initiatory Craft or as eclectic in itself ... It is fully Initiatory, and a reform movement for covens that participate in the mysteries and lineages of the Craft.
>
> I believe it to be an obsolete term in the 21st Century as the Craft has evolved and is now growing up. Co-operation and the value and voice of all individuals are becoming the norm ... Also, my own views have evolved. I no longer see the need for a pre-Initiation grade as I regard the First Degree to be a learning Degree, in the same way as the Freemason Entered Apprentice Degree is a learning Degree. Nowadays training is often done in an outer court grove leading up to the First, much as Alex Sanders did in his open sessions in the 1960s and 70s. Previously Gardnerians were expected to learn through experiencing the rituals by osmosis so to speak.
>
> Whereas this is a valuable tool and needs to be seen as important in the learning process towards the true Initiation, the Second Degree which should be done after the initiate has experienced at least a whole year

of Seasonal and Full Moon rituals (thereby after a Year and a Day, or more), it must be enhanced by a more formal training regime together with individual study of specialisms. I also believe that the individual and covens should be given *Book of Shadows* material as soon as they reach the appropriate grade. Movement of knowledge and ideas will enrich the Craft for all and enhance the Brotherhood and Sisterhood which should be an important part of the Craft ... The higher the Degree is, the more one is a servant and facilitator to one's brothers and Sisters of the Craft and the Gods, the more one should have appropriate humility and openness to those around one."

In many ways, the inclusivity and openness of covens now would not have happened without the progressive style which was started by Tam, Karin, David and others. It was certainly something that I found inspiring and helpful when I came into the Gardnerian Craft in 1991. "Inclusive Wicca" should not be a splinter group or a separate tradition either; it is just a way of describing what many covens are already doing.

The use of the term 'progressive' came out of a conversation between Karin Rainbird and Tam Campbell in London in the late 1980s. They were discussing the evolution of Wicca in the UK, and the fact that it had changed over the decades, moving beyond the labels of Gardnerian or Alexandrian. They wanted the term 'progressive' to describe a tendency, not a tradition or a lineage, so any coven that is creative in its approach and not limiting itself to Gardner's original *Book of Shadows* is progressive.

In 1988, Tam Campbell gave a talk in London explaining Progressive Wicca (the text of this talk is reproduced in Appendix 3).

In 1991, Karin Rainbird and David Rankine formed a network for covens who subscribed to a more creative view of Wiccan practice, called the Progressive Wiccan Network. This network included covens in Wales, England, Germany and Canada. Around thirty witches from six different covens met at Lammas 1991 in South Wales. This developed into an annual gathering in Cornwall which met for some years.

In 1992, David Rankine became the editor of the magazine *Dragon's Brew*, which became the magazine of the Progressive Wiccan movement. *Dragon's Brew* was created by Chris Breen in 1990, originally as the house magazine for the Silver Wheel Coven.

In 1992, the magazine included a statement about Progressive Wicca:

> Progressive Wicca is a movement which spans the traditions and emphasises networking, closeness to nature, personal growth and co-operative development. Personal experience of other paths is welcomed and integrated into covens, and we do not slavishly follow a *Book of Shadows*, as we see Wicca as an ever growing religion and the *Book of Shadows* changes and grows with each new Witch.

Progressive Wicca was also very involved in eco-pagan protest, and many members were involved in the Dragon Environmental Network, which protested at Oxleas Wood and other road protests.

By 1994, Progressive Wicca was well-known throughout Europe. David Rankine gave talks at events such as the Talking Stick Meet the Groups conference in 1994, and at various University Pagan Societies.

To avoid conflict and confusion caused by the term "Progressive" in the Wiccan community, the term was changed from "Progressive Wicca" to Progressive Witchcraft in 1993. At the same time, Karin Rainbird and David Rankine set up the Progressive Witchcraft Foundation.

In 1994, Karin Rainbird and David Rankine started running correspondence courses on natural magic based on much of the (non-oathbound) Progressive Witchcraft material. This material was to form the basis for their book *Magick Without Peers: A Course in Progressive Witchcraft for the Solitary Practitioner*.

One of the key aspects of Progressive Wicca was that it emphasised creativity and evolving tradition, and each witch having a personal *Book of Shadows* with a record of rituals attended, rather than copying out their initiator's book by hand.

The coven I joined in 1991 was not 'officially' part of the progressive Wicca tendency, but my High Priestess did not expect coveners to copy material out by hand. She also wrote rituals which gave parts to all the participants, and invited coveners to write rituals too (whereas some of the other covens I encountered around that time performed rituals where the high priestess and high priest performed the ritual, and the coven was the audience; and they did not invite coveners to write rituals). She was also inclusive towards LGBT people, as were Progressive Wicca covens. I was never 'officially' part of the Progressive Wicca grouping either, but the way I have run my covens is heavily influenced by their style. Hence my assertion that there was a mood of change, and the progressive tendency were articulating that mood.

Progressive Wicca is creative, blending eclectic elements with traditional elements of ritual. Members of progressive covens were among the first to do same-sex initiations. They were innovators and explorers. They developed new ritual styles and experimented with different techniques. They were more concerned with personal growth, interpersonal dynamics, and more politically engaged than some of their peers.

The success of Progressive Wicca is indicated by the fact that many people now take these things for granted and regard them as the norm, and are not necessarily aware that there was ever a movement for change within Wicca. This again backs up the idea that it was a set of ideas whose time had come.

Progressive Wicca emphasised the spiritual development of the individual on all levels – psychological, spiritual, mental, social, and magical. It encouraged the development of skills in all these areas, and a non-hierarchical approach to ritual. It encouraged people to take it in turns to cast the circle, call the quarters, and run a complete ritual. None of these ideas was unique to Progressive Wicca, but they were its core features.

Chapter Seven

Inclusive Wicca

Wicca is not by its nature excluding. It is inclusive as it is practised by most people. So inclusive Wicca is not a movement or a new grouping within Wicca, it is simply a label for a pre-existing set of ideas. It is similar in many ways to progressive Wicca as formulated by Tam Campbell and Karin Rainbird. It is about including different perspectives, sexual orientations, levels of ability, and understandings of the world; not erasing these differences, but celebrating them and working with them.

Wicca is an initiatory religion for people who want to become priestesses and priests of the old goddesses and gods of Nature (however you conceptualise them). So it is not for people who do not want to be priestesses and priests, or for people who don't want to follow an initiatory path. Trying to be all things to all people is a recipe for disaster, as the old folktale of the two men and the donkey illustrate. Wicca is what it is – skyclad, initiatory, transgressive.

However, it should not exclude anyone who genuinely wants to be a priest/ess and witch. If there are barriers to inclusion of people of colour, lesbian, gay, bisexual, transgender (LGBT), disabled, or dyslexic people, we need to remove those barriers.

Copying out the *Book of Shadows* by hand is very difficult for people with dyslexia. This is because dyslexia is not, as is commonly thought, a difficulty with reading, but a problem with transferring information from one medium to another. This is because the working memory of a person with dyslexia (the bit you use to remember a list of drinks to get from the bar, for example) has less capacity than most people's. So trying to remember the sentence you want to copy from one book to another is really difficult for a person with dyslexia.

People with dyslexia often have really amazing abilities, such as spatial awareness. I was in a room once with two people with dyslexia, and they were talking about where the sun would strike the wall at a particular time of year and time of day. They could mentally track it through the sky. I asked how they knew, and one of them said to me, surely you must know where the sun will be at a particular time of day and year, and I replied that I had no idea – it is one of their special abilities. They are also good at other right-brain functions, and of course, right-brain functions are very useful for magic. I know that the hemisphere theory of brain function is disputed, but the categories are still useful. We might call these functions "twilight consciousness" instead – things like awareness of rhythm, space, metaphor, and so on.

I do not consider copying the *Book of Shadows* by hand to be a core part of Wiccan practice. Other people feel that it is, because they say that it instils respect for the material contained therein. I would argue that Wicca is not a religion of the book, like Islam, Christianity, and Judaism, so why are we so focussed on a book? Wicca should be experiential and about connecting with Nature, not about copying out texts.

Another interesting group of people is the ones who cannot visualise. You ask them to form a picture in their mind, and they can't. So now, I always start with a simple visualisation such as an orange, asking people to visualise it, smell it, and taste it. If they can't, then I know they are probably a non-visualiser, in which case, I adapt my guided visualisations accordingly, building in more information about feelings, spatial awareness, and other non-visual elements. I also ask them what would help them to feel included in this activity.

In early Wicca, people with physical disabilities were often excluded from covens. This would not happen now, I hope, and many Wiccans have expressed revulsion at the notion that one must be "physically perfect" to be a priest or priestess. However, many Wiccan practices need adapting for an ageing and infirm population. Standing for long periods of time, dancing, and kneeling (all of which are involved in Wiccan practice at various times) are all difficult for people with physical disabilities. I once had a nasty graze on my knee, and there was a bit of the ritual that involved kneeling, so I asked for a cushion to be placed on the floor.

One of the most culturally transgressive aspects of Wicca is that it is practised in the nude, known as working skyclad. I consider working skyclad to be one of the core aspects of Wicca, but what do you do if someone says they have difficulty with this? What if someone was raped and has difficulty trusting others as a result? What if someone has scars that they are uncomfortable with showing to others?

My personal response to this would not be to give up on working skyclad, but to try to assist the person with working through their issues about it. Working skyclad is such a beautiful and empowering thing, and an expression of love and trust among the participants, so it would be a shame to lose this practice. But issues like rape, body image, and so on are hard problems and the person should probably be encouraged to seek counselling (not specifically for their inability to work skyclad, but for the after-effects of the trauma).

There are situations where it is just not possible to work skyclad; for example, people with poor circulation may be unable to work skyclad out-of-doors at night, because it is too cold; a person with eczema that is triggered by sunlight may not be able to work skyclad if the ritual is during the day. If a woman is menstruating, the usual practice is for her to wear a sarong in circle, or just keep her knickers on – whatever she feels comfortable with.

Another difficult aspect of Wicca for some people is the practice of scourging. Many shamanic practices include the use of pain in order to achieve altered states. Many people have difficulty with scourging because they associate it with punishment. However, it is not about that at all. Again, I think people should be encouraged to work through their issues about this, rather than giving up on what is potentially a transformative and empowering practice. Scourging is a core part of Wiccan practice as far as I am concerned. Being inclusive does not involve taking away all the aspects of the tradition that might upset people – if we did that, we would end up with something bland and boring – rather, it involves putting support structures in place to enable access, and adapting our rituals to be more inclusive, where this enhances them and does not dilute their power and beauty.

Where our rituals are heterocentric, for example, I feel that they do need adapting. This would give a truer picture of reality, because the gender binary is not an adequate model of gender, and the ultimate polarity is not male and female, it is manifest and unmanifest. Gender is a spectrum. Being more inclusive would be empowering for cisgender[17] and heterosexual people as well as LGBT people. There is a huge range of gender expression within cisgender and heterosexual people which is often not acknowledged, as well as the variation of gender expression and sexual orientation among LGBT people.

Another group that often gets forgotten is people who practice polyamory. There are quite of number of polyamorous people in Wicca, and hurtful assumptions are often made about them. Just because someone is in a polyamorous relationship, does not mean they are available for sex with everyone who asks. The relationship may be a closed one. Polyamorous people are just as committed to their relationships as monogamous people are. They also have as much right to privacy as anyone else, and are not obliged to answer questions about their relationship.

Polyamorous relationships may be a web (a group of people who are having a relationship with each other, but not with everyone in the group; people who are in the web that are not having a relationship with each other are known as metamours). Other polyamorous relationships may be a triad (three people who are all having a relationship with each other), a vee (one person who is having a relationship with two others, who are not in a relationship with each other), or a larger closed group. They are different from open relationships, which are more fluid. Polyamory is not the same as cheating on your partner, because it is done with the knowledge and consent of all concerned.

It would be interesting to adapt the ritual of Cakes and Wine for a polyamorous triad or vee (for example). Normally this is done by two people (usually a woman and a man, but there is no reason why it can't be done by two people of the same sex). A polyamorous triad or vee could have two of the partners adoring the third, or take it in turns to be adored, for example.

It is a well-known fact that some people consider Wiccan practice to be heterocentric, and thereby excluding of lesbian, gay, bisexual, transgender, and queer (LGBTQ) people. If you are not yourself LGBTQ, you may not even have noticed, but you might have heard from your LGBTQ friends that it is excluding.

---

[17] Cisgender means someone who identifies with the gender that matches the physical sexual characteristics they were born with. *Cis* just means "this side" as opposed to *trans*, meaning "the other side" (as in Cisalpine and Transalpine).

What if your coven consists entirely of straight people? Why bother to modify your practice at all? Well, it will make you more aware that gender is an artificial construct and that sexuality is fluid. It will make you less likely to assume nonsensical things like men don't knit, boys don't cry, ladies don't fart, blokes don't like flowers, men drink pints and women drink halves, and so on, and that boys and girls always settle down together and make babies. Of course, you don't think any of those things, right? Right? But there are other gender stereotypes in Wicca which could usefully be questioned — like warrior gods and flowery goddesses of love. And there are stereotypes of sexual orientation too — the assumption that Beltane is about heterosexual love; that the God and the Goddess are a heterosexual couple. We also tend to assume that all deities are cisgendered (that their gender identity matches their biological sex) but as deities don't have biological sex, because they don't have biology, as far as we know, why restrict ourselves to cisgender deities? Why not transgender deities?

And when you do get that first LGBTQ coven member - you'll be practising inclusive Wicca already, so it won't seem forced when you do things in an inclusive manner; and we won't have to ask you to make your practice more inclusive. It's rather like making your office premises accessible to all comers without waiting for someone to ask.

Historical background

It does not matter that Gerald Gardner shared the homophobic attitudes of many of his contemporaries, because whilst Gardner is respected as the founder of modern Wicca, his views on many issues are seen as a product of his time. Gardner does not have the same status in Wicca as Jesus of Nazareth does in Christianity. He is not believed to be some kind of messiah figure. Wiccan practice and tradition is not about Gardner, it's about magic and Nature.

There are some practices in Wicca that are heterocentric, but many people are changing these to be more inclusive of LGBT people. If the coven you are in is not changing to include you, there are other covens that might be more flexible. There's also the option to start your own coven.

These heterocentric practices may have been started because of Gardner's homophobia, or just because he was heterosexual and heterocentric, so in that sense it is still relevant, but for heavens' sake, Wicca is less than a century old, so it's perfectly possible to change things. Tradition is not set in stone; it evolves.

In the 1970s and 1980s, Wicca and other forms of witchcraft attracted many second-wave feminists, interested in reclaiming the negative stereotype of the witch (an embodiment of female and "deviant" sexuality) and celebrating women's power, and the nurturing qualities of darkness and nature.

Also in the 1970s, Dianic witchcraft (which is mostly women-only and honours a single Goddess) was founded. It attracts women of all sexual orientations.

In 1975, a group for gay men, called the Minoan Brotherhood, was formed in New York. The founders had decided there was a need for a specifically gay or queer spirituality, as the culture of Wicca at the time was mainly centred on heterosexual ideas.

Wicca became much more eclectic and open to innovation in the 1990s, when people began to experiment with different and more inclusive forms, including same-sex initiations and more polytheistic rituals. This trend has continued into the twenty-first century.

So, which practices might be considered heterocentric, and what are the alternatives?

Alternate boy-girl-boy-girl in circle

This drives me crazy. It isn't even necessary. Just don't even bother with it. Polarity does not have to be male and female, it can be all sorts of other things. Dark and light, yin and yang, active and passive — none of these qualities maps directly onto male and female. The ultimate polarity is not male and female — it transcends gender.

And you know, when passing the cakes and wine around, it still doesn't have to be boy-girl-boy-girl — it won't turn you gay to kiss a member of the same sex on the lips; and coven members who are in a same-sex relationship might like the opportunity to kiss their significant other.

Calling the quarters

If you are one of those people who calls the "Lords of the watchtowers of the [direction]," this could be amended to "Guardians..." or "Lords and Ladies..." Personally I just say "Mighty ones of the [direction], Powers of the [element]."

Consecrations

I generally like the fact that consecration of men is done by a woman, and consecration of women by a man, as it emphasises that neither gender has all the authority to consecrate. But it doesn't have to be done like this every circle. You could sometimes get an LGBT person to consecrate all the straights, and *vice versa*. Or even a blonde person to consecrate all the brunettes and gingers, and a brunette to consecrate all the blondes. Or a person born under an astrological fire sign to consecrate everyone with incense, and a person born under a water sign to consecrate everyone with water. Be creative!

Invocation

This does not always have to involve a man invoking a goddess on a woman, and a woman invoking a god on a man. Women can invoke on other women; men can invoke on other men; you can invoke a god onto a woman, and a goddess onto a man. And you can invoke gender-neutral deities too. Get a hold of the excellent book, Cassell's *Encyclopedia of Queer Myth, Symbol and Spirit*, which has a vast compendium of LGBTQ deities. Question gender stereotypes - does a god have to be a hunter and a warrior? There are female deities of architecture, cities, and mathematics. Of course, you can still do the more traditional form of invocation, but you don't have to do it every time.

Cakes and wine

Traditionally, this involves a man kneeling at the feet of a woman. This is a powerful counter-symbol to the prevailing "patriarchal" paradigm. But again, it doesn't have to be done the same every time.

One very simple way to make it more inclusive, is to say "As the cup is to the beloved, so the athame is to the lover".[18] I have been doing this ever since I first heard it (previously I had been using a different form of words which was also non-gendered: "As the cup is the inner, so the athame is to the outer").

Another way is to have two women consecrate the wine by pouring it from one chalice into another. (I invented this in about 1995.) The idea is based on the *Temperance* card in the Tarot.

A third way is to make the polarity symbolism primordial, as suggested by Lynna Landstreet:

> "But ultimately, for me at least, polarity transcends sexuality completely. Sex can be a manifestation of it, but it is not inherently based on sex, or even on deity in an anthropomorphic sense. If I had to choose one image that most embodied, for me, the primal act of creation I see embodied in the wine blessing, ... That moment of lightning striking the primeval sea to create the first living organism is what I see when the athamé touches the wine.
>
> All Craft sexual symbolism is at its deepest level merely that: symbolism. The athamé does not represent a penis, nor the chalice a vagina; they represent forces of nature which can also be represented by those organs -- but don't necessarily have to be."[19]

I sometimes do a preamble to the cakes and wine which emphasises this symbolism, and it works really well.

Festivals

It has been suggested that the round of Wiccan seasonal festivals represents the stages in the relationship between the God and the Goddess. However, there is much more depth and symbolism and mythology to the festivals than this. There is the Grail symbolism associated with Midsummer; there is the legend of Lugh and Tailtiu at Lughnasadh; there is the legend of the Fomorians and the Tuatha de Danaan at Samhain. There are numerous deities whose symbolism can be associated with a particular festival and explored.

I once went to a public Beltane ritual (not a Wiccan one, I am thankful to say) which made no mention of same-sex love at all. I was pretty shocked. Yes, I could have mentioned same-sex love, but I just ceased to feel a part of the ritual at all, and became an observer rather than a participant. Now, if it had been a private

---

[18] Devised by a group of European Wiccans.

[19] Lynna Landstreet (1999 [1993]), *Alternate Currents: Revisioning Polarity: Or, what's a nice dyke like you doing in a polarity-based tradition like this?* available from
http://www.wildideas.net/temple/library/altcurrents.html

ritual consisting entirely of heterosexuals, the omission would not have been so problematic. But it was a public expression of Paganism, and as such, should have been inclusive.

Initiation

The reason usually given nowadays for a woman initiating a man (and vice versa) is that it is to ensure a balance of power in the group (if one gender or one person did all the initiations, they would have an unfair advantage).

However, there is no particular reason why you can't have same-sex initiations. If the power is transmitted through sexual attraction (as is sometimes claimed), then it would make more sense for gay and lesbian Wiccans to be initiated by a member of the same sex; and perhaps for bisexuals to be initiated by two people, or by a member of the gender they are most strongly attracted to.

Many covens do not accept same-sex initiations as valid, but are otherwise inclusive; so it is best to consider this before deciding to go ahead with a same-sex initiation. In the UK, most people do not ask about your lineage anyway, so it may not be that much of an issue. Another possibility might be to have an initiation where both the High Priestess and the High Priest of the coven initiate the candidate, thereby satisfying the traditionalists who feel that initiations should be cross-gender, and creating the right polarity for the initiate.

Celebrating darkness and Nature

Wicca and other contemporary Pagan traditions celebrate our existence in this world and attempt to gain spiritual insight from nature and the world around us. Wicca also honours the qualities of darkness and the powers of the Moon. These are themes that are particularly prominent in queer spirituality and attractive to LGBTQ adherents of Wicca.

Darkness represents the aspects of life that are repressed by civilisation – spirituality, sexuality, the body, dreams. It can also represent people of colour, many of whom are excluded by the symbolism of darkness as evil in other religions. In Wicca, darkness is celebrated as representing the feminine, yin, instinctual side of life.

The Wiccan celebration of Nature may also have a special appeal for LGBTQ adherents. Early gay rights pioneer Edward Carpenter was an enthusiastic advocate of Nature as a place of freedom. Following him, his friend E.M. Forster made the hero of his novel *Maurice* (written in 1913) feel "at one with the forests and the night" as soon as he had made the decision to adopt an actively gay lifestyle. Harry Hay, founder of the Radical Faeries, who was a Carpenter enthusiast, also stressed the importance of communing with nature.

Many Wiccans believe that the celebration of darkness, which mainstream culture regards as the realm of evil, allows us to transcend boundaries and to recover lost and repressed aspects of the psyche, and to honour the ideas associated with them. It may also allow us to escape the hierarchical view of the cosmos which is associated with the honouring of the light.

The divine androgyne

There is also in Wicca a tradition of the Divine Androgyne (inherited from the Western mystery tradition), a being who includes both genders and perhaps even transcends gender.

The emphasis on the need to become psychologically androgynous (frequently couched in terms of developing men's feminine side and women's masculine side, and found in many spiritual traditions) and the use of the *Dryghtyn Prayer* add to the feeling of queerness at the heart of the tradition.

In addition, the figure of the witch, derived in part from the spae-wives (fortune tellers) and *seiðr*-workers (practitioners of a type of shamanism that included men-loving men) of Northern Europe, is often associated with sexual and gender transgression. These ideas may not be very current in Wicca generally, but they are part of the historical discourse about witchcraft.

It's really not difficult to make Wicca more inclusive - and it would actually make it more interesting for everyone. Why not give it a try?

Just as Wiccans and other contemporary Pagans have similarly reclaimed the word "witch" to mean a shaper, a changer of consciousness, and a radical, so LGBTQ people have reclaimed the word "queer" as a badge of resistance to heteronormativity and as a tool for liberation. With a strong strand of ecological, political, and sexual radicalism in Wicca and its variant traditions, there is much overlap with the interests and concerns of the LGBTQ community.

Including people with a disability

Most practices can be modified for people with a disability. Dancing may be difficult for people with mobility issues; dancing in a circle is difficult for people who get dizzy easily, such as those with labyrinthitis or Meniere's disease. Kneeling down and standing for long periods may be difficult for older coven members. I generally alternate activities between sitting, standing, and lying down (some people like to lie down for meditations and visualisations; others prefer to sit on a chair or a cushion or a meditation stool). Working skyclad may be difficult for people with poor circulation or eczema. Copying out a *Book of Shadows* may be difficult for people with dyslexia (though not everyone with dyslexia necessarily has a problem with this, as some have copied out a *Book of Shadows* quite happily). A person with ME (myalgic encephalomyelitis) or CFS (Chronic Fatigue Syndrome) may find long rituals exhausting.

The key to making sure that people with a disability are included is to listen to their needs, and actively encourage them to specify what they need, and make sure that everyone accepts that it is a genuine need.

What about tradition?

Tradition is something that grows and evolves. It is not set in stone, but is more like a discourse; if you start with a particular set of premises, ideas and values, you will get further ideas and practices that are consistent with the initial set of ideas. Religious traditions evolve according to social, cultural, and political circumstances. For example, a Catholic community in India had the tradition of having a procession in honour of the Virgin Mary. It was a particular honour to carry a special flag in the procession, and to raise and lower the flag on the special flagpole. This meant that more people wanted to have the honour than could be accommodated by a single flag and a single raising of the flag. So more flags were added to the procession, and more occasions of raising and lowering the flag were added, till over the years, the original custom was elaborated by considerable additional flags and flag-raising. There's an example of a tradition evolving.

Some people think that tradition is rigid and unchanging (or that it ought to be so), but this is not the case. Some people also think that saying "because it's traditional" is sufficient reason for doing a thing. But because tradition evolves in response to circumstances, and because customs can sometimes be harmful, saying "because we've always done it that way" is not a sufficient reason for doing something. First we need to consider why it was done that way in the first place. If the reason for doing it that way is still valid, then that's not a problem. But if there is a new group of people to be taken into consideration (who weren't considered when the custom was first devised), then we may need to adapt or drop the custom in order to accommodate them.

Folklorists pay attention to the transmission and context of a tradition, as well as to its content. The means of transmission is also important in Pagan traditions. In Wicca, the validity of an initiation is important (it has to be done by someone who is already initiated, and it must be done according to certain criteria). In reconstructionist and polytheist traditions, some people think it is important to have a cultural or ethnic connection to the religion being reconstructed; others derive the legitimacy of their practice from ancient texts about their religion, mythology and deities. Before a new insight (an Unverified Personal Gnosis) can be more widely adopted by practitioners, it needs to be compared to textual evidence, and/or substantiated by comparison with insights from other contemporary practitioners. It then becomes a substantiated personal gnosis.

In Native American religion, the transmission and context of tradition are incredibly important. They would argue that you cannot take their traditions out of the context of people, language, and land where they arose. It is certainly true that when these traditions are taken out of their context and borrowed indiscriminately, with little understanding of what they mean, it is usually cultural appropriation, which erases the identity of the keepers of the original tradition, and can be actively harmful.

That is not to say that you can never adopt a tradition that does not relate to your ethnic background; it does mean that in order to be respectful towards that tradition, you need to study it in depth and respect its original sources and context. If it is possible to receive transmission of that tradition from one of its keepers, then so much the better.

However, if an aspect of the tradition that you have received is actively harmful, then it is legitimate to change it, in my view. An obvious example is the tradition of marriage. In the past, the definition of marriage included polygamy. Some people regarded this as injurious to the individuality of the additional wives, and so polygamy became widely frowned-upon. Past definitions of marriage also included a woman being required to marry a man who raped her; this was obviously harmful, so the practice has been discontinued in most cultures. Until the early twentieth century, it was extremely difficult to obtain a divorce, which meant that many people were trapped within failed marriages; again, this was regarded as harmful, so marriage was redefined as something that could be terminated. Currently, many same-sex couples are harmed by their exclusion from the possibility of being married, so they want the law changed so they can get married. Some have argued that this is a redefinition of marriage; maybe it is, but marriage has been redefined many times before, and it's still popular. The story of the evolution of marriage shows that it is possible to modify a custom to include more people, or to reduce the harm that it may cause, without changing the basic features of the tradition.

Discussion

- How far can you change a tradition before it becomes something else?
- To what extent should we adapt a tradition to our own needs, and to what extent should we adapt ourselves to suit the tradition?
- What do you regard as the core ideas and practices of Wicca?
- What aspects of your ritual practice have you changed for what reasons since you started?
- What aspects of the rituals do you find include you or exclude you in some way? Why?
- Should you change to a more inclusive style before any LGBT people join your coven?
- What aspects of Wicca do you think reinforce heteronormativity and cisnormativity, and which celebrate diversity?

Chapter Eight

Queer Paganism

Various people have sought to define queer in a variety of ways – as "resisting normativity" and as a verb meaning "to spoil or interfere", and as a tool for liberation (Goss, 1999: 45-46).   Irshad Manji[20] defines queer as 'being unpredictable', rather than 'rigid and absolute, and frankly dull'.   Queerness is a metacategory which includes various non-normative sexual identities. 'Queer' is also a very different term from 'gay'.   Being gay or lesbian has meant fitting into a specific identity:

> "Gay identity can be as confining as 'closetedness' in its minoritization and elision of the social-cultural differences of same-sex desire."[21]

The concept of queer defies categorisation and resists normativity:

> "Queer is often understood as critically non-heterosexual, transgressive of all heteronormativities and, I would add, gay normativities. 'Queer' turns upside down, inside out, and defies heteronormative and gay normative theologies."[22]

Some LGBT (lesbian, gay, bisexual, transgender and transsexual) people contest the appropriateness of the term 'queer'; trans* people say that a lot of their experience does not fit into the queer paradigm;[23] others have complained that trying to define a specific LGBT or queer spirituality is essentialist[24] — in this

---

[20] Summerskill, B (2006), ed. *The Way we are now: Gay and Lesbian Lives in the 21st Century.* London and New York: Continuum. page 62

[21] Goss, RE (1999). 'Queer Theologies as Transgressive Metaphors: New Paradigms for Hybrid Sexual Theologies.' *Theology and Sexuality*, 10: pp 43-53. Available from Ebscohost. page 45

[22] Goss, RE (1999). 'Queer Theologies as Transgressive Metaphors: New Paradigms for Hybrid Sexual Theologies.' *Theology and Sexuality*, 10: pp 43-53. Available from Ebscohost. page 45

[23] Prosser, J. (1998). *Second Skins: The Body Narratives of Transsexuality.* New York, Columbia University Press. page 59

[24] Ali, S, Campbell, K, Branley, D and James, R (2006). 'Politics, identities and research.' In: Seale, C, ed. (2006), *Researching Society and Culture*. London: Sage. page 30

context, the idea that gay people are more, or differently, spiritual than others because of their liminal status,[25] either as marginalised people, or as "intermediates".[26]

Charges of essentialism notwithstanding, because of the marginalisation of LGBT people, a separate culture has developed to a certain extent in the enclaves and safe spaces created by LGBT people.

Because of the marginalisation of women and LGBT people, many people have concluded that they need a separate form of spiritual expression from the patriarchal and heteronormative mainstream.[27] Some of these people have also assumed that there is something different about the spirituality of women or gay men that necessitates this separatism.[28]

Strategies for queering Paganism – or rather, recovering the queer aspects of ancient paganisms – have partly involved mining ancient mythologies for feminist and queer imagery, and partly around simply creating new mythology.[29]

Many queer and LGBT people have found a spiritual home in Paganism, and there are specific groups catering for their interests, such as the Radical Faeries, the Modern Gallae, the Temple of Antinous, the Minoan Brotherhood, and so on. However, not everything in the Pagan garden is rosy. Some Pagans are homophobic, and many are somewhat heterocentric. I once attended a public Beltane ceremony where all the references to love were couched in heterosexual terms; this was all the more noticeable since our coven ritual the previous night was inclusive and gender-bending.

The heroes of queer spirituality are those who have struggled for gay liberation by being out (openly gay), acting up (engaging in political activism, particularly around the issue of AIDS), and exploring new possibilities for political and spiritual identities. Such heroes are celebrated on the LGBT Religious Archives Network website, for example. They include Harry Hay (founder of both the Mattachine Society and the Radical Faeries); the eight founders of the Daughters of Bilitis; Edward Carpenter; and many others. These heroes are still remembered today for their pioneering struggle for liberation. They are both shapers of queer spirituality, and a distinctive feature of it.

The experience of AIDS heightened the sense of community and spirituality among gay men[30] as they cared for each other, and devised new spiritual strategies

---

[25] Stemmeler, ML (1996). 'Empowerment: the Construction of Gay Religious Identities.' *In*: Krondorfer, B, ed. (1996). *Men's Bodies, Men's Gods: Male Identities in a (Post-) Christian Culture.* New York and London: New York University Press. page 100

[26] Owen, Alex (2004), *The Place of Enchantment: British Occultism and the Culture of the Modern.* Chicago: The University of Chicago Press. page 109

[27] Conner, Randy P., Sparks, David Hatfield, and Sparks, Mariya (1997), *Cassell's Encyclopedia of Queer Myth, Symbol and Spirit.* London and New York: Cassell. page 173

[28] Ibid, page 105

[29] Reid-Bowen, P (2007). *Goddess as Nature: Towards a Philosophical Thealogy.* London: Ashgate Publishing. pp 33-34

[30] Stemmeler, ML (1996). 'Empowerment: the Construction of Gay Religious Identities.' *In*: Krondorfer, B, ed. (1996). *Men's Bodies, Men's Gods: Male Identities in a (Post-) Christian Culture.* New York and London: New York University Press. page 105

for coping with the trauma of the untimely deaths of friends and lovers, such as the memorial AIDS quilt, and numerous caring organisations and activities. The experience of having AIDS oneself has been likened to alchemy by Robert Arpin:

> "Pain and suffering and sickness is like fire. It can refine people into gold or reduce them to ash. In the AIDS epidemic, gay people have begun refining their lives into gold… It refines them into beautiful examples of the meaning of life… and love."[31]

The spiritual practices that arose in response to AIDS included: healing techniques drawn from a variety of religious traditions; the role of the psychopomp (a being who assists a dying person to make the transition from life to death); celebratory and upbeat funerals; making altars for the dead; the search for inner peace, coming to terms with death; and an outpouring of art, poetry and drama.[32]

Arguably the impact of AIDS has also led to less radical sexual practices in the gay community, and more conformity to heterosexual norms. Some queer-identified thinkers are critical of the introduction of same-sex marriage, in that they see it as just taking on the trappings of heterosexual marriage and the norms of monogamy[33], though most LGBT people feel that it is a very positive development.[34]

The tribe

Some gay people, particularly the Radical Faeries, see the gay community as a tribe.[35] This is partly because they draw inspiration from Native American concepts such as 'two-spirit'.[36] The idea of a gay tribe seems to be unique to LGBT Pagans.

Christopher Penczak entitled one of his books *Gay Witchcraft: Empowering the Tribe*, clearly referencing this tradition.

The concept of the tribe is quite popular among other Pagans, especially druids (many British druid groves are named after ancient Celtic tribal groupings and lands), so in this respect queer spirituality could be seen as similar to the 'mainstream' of Paganism.

However, Irshad Manji, a queer Muslim, criticises tribalism[37], as it can lead to

---

[31] Conner, Randy P., Sparks, David Hatfield, and Sparks, Mariya (1997), *Cassell's Encyclopedia of Queer Myth, Symbol and Spirit*. London and New York: Cassell. page 45

[32] Conner, Randy P., Sparks, David Hatfield, and Sparks, Mariya (1997), *Cassell's Encyclopedia of Queer Myth, Symbol and Spirit*. London and New York: Cassell. page 46

[33] Tatchell, P (2001). *Equality is Not Enough*. http://www.petertatchell.net/Equality%20-%20Limits%20and%20Deficiencies/equality%20is%20not%20enough2.htm

[34] Summerskill, B (2006), ed. *The Way we are now: Gay and Lesbian Lives in the 21st Century*. London and New York: Continuum.

[35] Rodgers, B (1995), 'The Radical Faerie Movement: A Queer Spirit Pathway'. *Social Alternatives*, 14:4 pp 34-37. Available from Ebscohost, Academic Search Elite

[36] Conner, Randy P., Sparks, David Hatfield, and Sparks, Mariya (1997), *Cassell's Encyclopedia of Queer Myth, Symbol and Spirit*. London and New York: Cassell. page 172

[37] Summerskill, B (2006), ed. *The Way we are now: Gay and Lesbian Lives in the 21st Century*.

conformism, reductionism, and a form of fundamentalism. She suggests that instead, people should focus on shared values and individual integrity. She recounts how she met a white gay man who complained that she wasn't lesbian enough, implying that she should conform to the way other lesbians were, otherwise she was a 'sell-out'. She, therefore, identifies herself as queer, to emphasise the multiplicity of her identities. The queer rejection of standard models of gender and sexual identities undermines the idea of a group identity.[38]

Coming Out and Acting Up

Coming out, it has been suggested, is an act of resistance to the surrounding heteronormative culture and a radical affirmation of the gay self.[39] It is also an act of honesty and clarity:

> "When I come out, to any degree I do so to make a relationship more real not in order to talk about my sex life. It may be painful yes, maybe a relief, maybe at the risk of violence, but coming out shines a very intense light on our relationships. The person I am talking with has a chance to get to know who I am."[40]

According to Saadaya,[41] coming out allows self-expression, and should be celebrated as a rite of passage, which initiates the quest for love, spirit and self. It releases "archetypal potential" and can be experienced joyfully. It is a declaration of independence and individuality.

Some Pagans, fearing discrimination, remain closeted about their religion; revealing it is known as 'coming out of the broom closet', a reference to the gay experience. Similarly, Pagan Pride events were inspired by Gay Pride events.[42] The experience of being closeted and the potential consequences of being out, as well as a sense of relief when one no longer has to avoid mentioning a significant part of one's life, are similar to the LGBT experience.

Wahba[43] says, however, that coming out is not a single act, but a process, a gradual revelation. The LGBT person has to come out in each new social

---

London and New York: Continuum. pp 70-71
[38] Goss, RE (1999). 'Queer Theologies as Transgressive Metaphors: New Paradigms for Hybrid Sexual Theologies.' *Theology and Sexuality*, 10: pp 43-53. Available from Ebscohost. page 48
[39] Stemmeler, ML (1996). 'Empowerment: the Construction of Gay Religious Identities.' *In:* Krondorfer, B, ed. (1996). *Men's Bodies, Men's Gods: Male Identities in a (Post-) Christian Culture.* New York and London: New York University Press. pp 98-99
[40] Nathan Foster (1997), "A prayer in the dark", *The Independent*
http://www.independent.co.uk/life-style/a-prayer-in-the-dark-1250740.html
[41] Saadaya (undated). *Coming Out as a Rite of Passage.*
http://www.angelfire.com/journal/saadaya/ComingOut.html
[42] Dewr, C (1998). *Why Pagan Pride?* [online] Available from:
http://www.paganpride.org/what/why.html
[43] cited in Stemmeler, ML (1996). 'Empowerment: the Construction of Gay Religious Identities.' *In:* Krondorfer, B, ed. (1996). *Men's Bodies, Men's Gods: Male Identities in a (Post-) Christian Culture.* New York and London: New York University Press. page 46

situation; unless we choose to make our queer identity obvious by 'acting up'.

Acting up is a radical assertion of queer identity, being so out of the closet that no-one needs to ask; it is getting involved in political activism[44] and refusing to accept heteropatriarchal norms. Acting up is an expression of righteous and transforming anger against injustice. It is saying, "We're here. We're queer. Get used to it."[45]

Given that 'mainstream' Paganism is heteronormative, coming out and acting up, as radical affirmations of the gay self, are clearly different from the 'mainstream'; although declaring oneself to be Pagan in a generally hostile context is similar in some ways to the experience of coming out for queer people, the queer Pagan has to come out as both queer and Pagan, thereby increasing his or her sense of difference.

Gender-bending and Androgyny

The third wave of feminism is characterised by a decrease in emphasis upon separatist strategies and by an increased awareness of women-loving women and women of colour and the problematisation of the concept of gender.[46] This development was reflected in theology and the study of religions by feminist scholars engaging with queer theory.

Queer theory offers a critique of gender, regarding it as a performance or a political formulation and a product of discourse.[47] Gender is firmly entrenched in Pagan discourse.[48]

Some queer Pagans have emphasised the fluidity of gender identity. Lou Hart presents an overview of gender fluidity throughout history, and its implications for contemporary Pagan practice. Queer Pagans have criticised Pagan descriptions of 'polarity' (the notion that the primary dynamic of the universe consists of 'the masculine principle' and 'the feminine principle') on the grounds that it does not include their experience of gender and sexuality (Hine, 1989). Hence my (and others') reformulation of polarity to something more inclusive.

Religions have generally sought to impose gender roles, and although contemporary Paganisms are much less prescriptive in this regard, many Pagans still talk about gender in essentialist ways (the idea of feminine and masculine

---

[44] Hawley-Gorsline, R. (2003). 'James Baldwin and Audre Lorde as Theological Resources for the Celebration of Darkness.' *Theology and Sexuality* 10.1 (2003) 58-72 Available from: Ebscohost. page 136

[45] Stemmeler, ML (1996). 'Empowerment: the Construction of Gay Religious Identities.' *In:* Krondorfer, B, ed. (1996). *Men's Bodies, Men's Gods: Male Identities in a (Post-) Christian Culture.* New York and London: New York University Press. page 97

[46] Juschka, Darlene M., ed. (2001), *Feminism in the Study of Religion: a Reader.* London and New York: Continuum. page 568

[47] Sawyer, D. (2004). 'Biblical Gender Strategies: The Case of Abraham's Masculinity.' *In:* King, U. and Beattie, T. (2004), *Gender, Religion and Diversity: Cross-Cultural Perspectives.* London and New York: Continuum. pp 163-164

[48] Hart, L (2005). *Magic is a many-gendered thing.* [online] Available from: http://www.philhine.org.uk/writings/flsh_gendered.html

energies, for example; or the idea that goddesses are nurturing and gods are warriors; or 'Mother Earth' and 'Father Sky' – now thankfully quite a rare concept, but I have heard it said within the last decade). Whilst having a deity or deities that include the female gender is helpful in some ways, it does not necessarily follow that this will lead to greater gender equality in society, as women are still regarded as the source of corruption in Hinduism,[49] even though it has goddesses. Will it, therefore, be helpful to find queer deities?

Many people choose a Pagan path because of issues around gender[50] and sexuality. Either they are looking for a more inclusive image of the divine, or for a religion that celebrates sexuality in all its forms, and honours both genders. They find in contemporary Paganism some helpful aspects (such as the role of priestess and the honouring of goddesses and women) and some unhelpful ones (such as the widely prevailing essentialist view of gender among Pagans, and the existence of homophobic Pagans). Thomas Michael Ford [51] says that "Gay men have frequently been left out of Wiccan thought because we don't seem to fit neatly into the notions of male-female polarity" and that he frequently encountered homophobic Wiccans.[52]

Occultists at the end of the nineteenth century regarded psychological androgyny as the ultimate aim of the Adept,[53] partly because of a belief that humans were androgynous before the Fall, and partly because of a belief in the androgyny of the divine.[54] As Wicca draws in part on the Western Mystery Tradition, it has inherited these ideas, which are expressed in the *Dryghtyn Prayer*, which is addressed to an entity that is "male and female, the original source of all things".[55] I interpret this entity as the Divine Androgyne.

The Radical Faeries also place great importance on androgyny:[56]

> "The concept of androgyny was taken on by the Faeries and given a distinctly spiritual bent. Rather than referring to an asexual or omni-sexual state, androgyny for the Faeries means radically juxtaposing elements of the masculine and feminine in psychological as well as physical formulations. The relationship of the archetype of the Androgyne to figures in myth and history has become a spiritual imperative for many Radical Faeries seeking a tradition to reclaim[.]"

---

[49] Seneviratne, T and Currie, J (2001). 'Religion and Feminism: A Consideration of Cultural Restraints on Sri Lankan Women.' *In:* Juschka, Darlene M., ed. (2001), *Feminism in the Study of Religion: a Reader.* London and New York: Continuum. page 206

[50] Hutton, Ronald (1999), *The Triumph of the Moon: a history of modern Pagan witchcraft.* Oxford: Oxford University Press. pp 341-344

[51] Ford, Thomas Michael (2005), *The Path of the Green Man: Gay Men, Wicca and Living a Magical Life.* New York: Citadel Press. page 42

[52] Ibid, page 43

[53] Owen, Alex (2004), *The Place of Enchantment: British Occultism and the Culture of the Modern.* Chicago: The University of Chicago Press. page 212

[54] Ibid, page 110

[55] Bourne, Lois (1979), *A Witch Amongst Us.* London: Satellite.

[56] Rodgers, B (1995), 'The Radical Faerie Movement: A Queer Spirit Pathway'. *Social Alternatives*, 14:4 pp 34-37. Available from Ebscohost, Academic Search Elite

The author goes on to quote Thompson:

> "The role of the fool, the trickster, the contrary one capable of turning a situation inside out, is one of the most enduring of all archetypes. Often cross dressed or adorned with both masculine and feminine symbols, these merry pranksters chase through history, holding up a looking glass to human folly. "

Another interesting example of Pagan gender-bending is the contemporary practice of *seiðr*. This is a revived form of an ancient "shamanic" practice. In heathen myths, male *seiðr*-workers were referred to as *ergi* (a term which may mean the receptive partner in a relationship between two men). Many contemporary *seiðr*-workers are gay men, and heterosexual male practitioners have found that they need to adjust their gender performance to accommodate this practice, because it involves openness to being entered by spirits.[57] Many conservative Heathens reject the practice of *seiðr* because of these associations.[58]

The celebration of androgyny is not unique to queer spirituality, but the emphasis upon it is far greater within queer spiritual groups than in other groups. There are a number of queer Pagan groups which specifically celebrate the divine androgyne, such as the Modern Gallae, the Brotherhood of the Phoenix, and the Radical Faeries.

The Sisters of Perpetual Indulgence defy classification as any one tradition, as they profess many different traditions, but they too are interested in gender-bending, and spreading joy and beauty whilst dispelling guilt and shame.

Darkness, Nature and Vulnerability

Further common themes across expressions of LGBT spirituality are the concepts of darkness, nature and vulnerability. Darkness and Nature are seen as refuges from homophobic society. In *De Profundis*, Oscar Wilde[59] speaks of the nurturing and non-judgmental qualities of Nature:

> "Society, as we have constituted it, will have no place for me, has none to offer; but Nature, whose sweet rains fall on just and unjust alike, will have clefts in the rock where I may hide, and secret valleys in whose silence I may weep undisturbed. She will hang the night with stars so that I may walk abroad in the darkness without stumbling, and send the wind over my footprints so that none may track me to my hurt: she will cleanse me in great waters, and with bitter herbs make me whole."

Edward Carpenter advocated Nature as a place where people could be free,[60] and inspired by his ideas, his friend EM Forster made the hero of his novel *Maurice*

---

[57] Wallis, RJ (2003). *Shamans / Neo-shamans: Ecstasy, alternative archaeologies and contemporary Pagans*. London and New York: Routledge. pp 230-233

[58] Blain, J (2002). *Nine Worlds of Seid-Magic: Ecstasy and Neo-Shamanism in North European Paganism*. London and New York: Routledge. page 122

[59] Wilde, Oscar (1996 [1905]), *De Profundis*. New York: Dover Publications, Inc. page 90

[60] Hutton, Ronald (1999), *The Triumph of the Moon: a history of modern Pagan witchcraft*. Oxford: Oxford University Press. page 27

feel "at one with the forests and the night" as soon as he had decided to run away with his male lover.[61] Harry Hay, founder of the Radical Faeries, and a fan of Carpenter, also emphasised the importance of communing with Nature.[62]

Queer deities

Gay artists have created numerous images of the queer divine. The French photographers Pierre et Gilles have produced numerous images of Christian saints, Hindu deities, and classical deities, and many of them are gay icons in one way or another. The series of photographs of saints begins in 1987 with an image of Saint Sebastian, looking remarkably calm as he is transfixed with arrows, lashed to a tree-stump with garlands of roses. Sebastian has been a symbol of same-sex love at least since the Renaissance,[63] hence Derek Jarman's remarkable film of the same name, and Pierre et Gilles created two more images of him in 1994 (*Sébastien de la Mer*) and 1996 (*Le martyre de Saint Sébastien*). Pierre et Gilles also depicted Joan of Arc (in 1988 and 1997), presumably chosen for her gender-bending activities and possible lesbianism.[64] They also produced an image of Sainte Affligée, known in English as Uncumber or Wilgefortis, a legendary figure who grew a beard to avoid marriage. There are numerous other saint pictures, some of which seem to have homoerotic connotations, but mostly seem somewhat randomly selected. However, a lot of their models are LGBT people, so perhaps the artists are making a statement by portraying them as saints.

Pagan deities that they have depicted include Adonis (1992), Amphytrite (1989), Bacchus (1991), Medusa (1990), Orpheus (1990), Venus (1991, 1992 and 2000), Adonis (1992 and 1999), Eros (2003), Mercury (2001), Ganymede (2001), and Diana (1997). Medusa is sometimes seen as a lesbian icon.[65] Orpheus chose male lovers after failing to retrieve Eurydice from the underworld, and it was for this that the Maenads tore him apart; legend has it that his friend Sappho buried his head.[66] Adonis was the *eromenos* (lover) of Dionysos.[67] Eros was also a symbol of same-sex love in ancient Greece,[68] among the Lacedaemonians and the Athenians for example. In alchemical texts, Mercury was frequently depicted as an androgyne; in Pierre et Gilles' 2001 work, he appears as a graceful and muscular youth. Ganymede is well-known as the *eromenos* of Zeus, [69] and according to mythology, Diana shunned the company of men and preferred the company of women. It would seem from this brief survey that the association of the deity or saint with same-sex love or gender-bending is a factor in their selection by Pierre et

---

[61] Ibid, page 50
[62] Conner, Randy P., Sparks, David Hatfield, and Sparks, Mariya (1997), *Cassell's Encyclopedia of Queer Myth, Symbol and Spirit*. London and New York: Cassell. page 173
[63] Ibid, page 297
[64] Ibid, page 190
[65] Ibid, page 229
[66] Ibid, page 258
[67] Ibid, page 43
[68] Ibid, page 132
[69] Ibid, page 155

Gilles as a subject.

Thomas Michael Ford[70] has created a series of short stories about the encounters of the Green Man (the symbol of his tradition) with various deities, including a sexual encounter with Pan. For others, the recovery of ancient queer myth seems as important as the discovery of new queer deities.

Many lesbian Pagans find the idea of a single Goddess attractive, sometimes because they have been molested by men,[71] sometimes because they do not feel the need for 'balance'.[72] Other lesbian Pagans try to work within existing models, but often find that they perceive them differently from the way heterosexuals do.[73]

Queer spiritual roles

Christian de la Huerta (founder of Q-Spirit) has suggested that queer people fulfill ten spiritual roles.[74] These are: catalytic transformers; outsiders and mirrors of society; consciousness scouts; sacred clowns and eternal youth; keepers of beauty; caregivers; mediators or in-between people; shamans, priests and sacred functionaries; the divine androgyne (drawing on Carpenter's ideas); and gatekeepers. Some of these draw on ideas about gay people being essentially a particular type of person - more caring, more instinctual, more spiritual, having a better sense of humour, and so on. Some of them are predicated on the idea that because gay people are 'neither male nor female' in terms of gender role, then they are also good intermediaries between the material and spiritual worlds (which in turn is based on an assumption that the material and spiritual worlds are separate). However, if we lived in a society where gender roles were less fixed, and the category of biological sex was not so important, these ideas might have been irrelevant, as everyone would be free to play whatever role they desired without having it assigned to a particular gender category.[75] LGBT people flourish in environments where gender categories are more fluid:

> "It is not an accident that music and the arts were always a tolerant environment for gay men. It was a world where appreciation for the 'feminine' was not seen as a weakness, and where strength did not have to manifest itself in violence and coarseness. ... It was the perfect place

[70] Ford, Thomas Michael (2005), *The Path of the Green Man: Gay Men, Wicca and Living a Magical Life.* New York: Citadel Press.

[71] Foltz, TG (2000). 'Sober Witches and Goddess Practitioners: Women's Spirituality and Sobriety.' *Diskus*, 6: 1. [online] Available from: http://web.uni-marburg.de/religionswissenschaft/journal/diskus/foltz.html

[72] "Mama Rose" (undated). *Why go Dianic?* http://www.iit.edu/~phillips/personal/philos/dianic.html

[73] Landstreet, L (1999 [1993]), *Alternate Currents: Revisioning Polarity Or, what's a nice dyke like you doing in a polarity-based tradition like this?* http://www.wildideas.net/temple/library/altcurrents.html

[74] Moon, T (2005). 'Spirit Matters IV: Ten Queer Spiritual Roles.' *San Francisco Bay Times.* [online] Available from: http://www.sfbaytimes.com/index.php?sec=article&article_id=3772

[75] Juschka, Darlene M., ed. (2001), *Feminism in the Study of Religion: a Reader.* London and New York: Continuum. page 238

in which to indulge a sense of the extravagant and exuberant, as well as offering ideal camouflage. A mask, a costume, an affecting melody, a graceful leap were all perfect alibis for those whose affections danced to a different tune."[76]

Subject-SUBJECT consciousness

Harry Hay suggested that a defining feature of gay men is Subject-SUBJECT consciousness,[77] and this idea was enthusiastically adopted by the Radical Faeries.[78] It is the idea that heteropatriarchal relationships are characterised by the man regarding himself as a subject and women as objects, whereas gay men regard their partners as fellow subjects. Carrie Pemberton[79] says that:

> "Of course the subject is always subject in her own eyes when not objectified and displaced by the gaze and the analytical grid of the other. Subjects speak, think, act, love, cry, scream, ululate, make love, feel fear, carry history, dream dreams. They do this best in a radical inter-subjectivity."

This radical inter-subjectivity seems similar to Hay's subject-SUBJECT consciousness. Clearly, in order to move away from the hierarchical and exploitative nature of the current heteropatriarchal paradigm, there needs to be a radical shift towards an awareness of the subjectivity of everyone; this is similar to the ideas of queer theory, which argues that identity is fluid and shifting, and that each of us is "a subject whose gender identity is purely performative, the product of a compulsory set of rituals and conventions, which conspire to engender retroactively the illusion" that our gender is "natural and innate".[80]

Discussion and activities

- Look at Christian de la Huerta's ten queer spiritual roles. Do you identify with any of them?

- Review the various models of gender and sexuality – where do you fit on the spectrum?

---

[76] Summerskill, B (2006), ed. *The Way we are now: Gay and Lesbian Lives in the 21st Century.* London and New York: Continuum. page 210

[77] Conner, Randy P., Sparks, David Hatfield, and Sparks, Mariya (1997), *Cassell's Encyclopedia of Queer Myth, Symbol and Spirit.* London and New York: Cassell. page 172

[78] Rodgers, B (1995), 'The Radical Faerie Movement: A Queer Spirit Pathway'. *Social Alternatives*, 14:4 pp 34-37.

[79] Carrie Pemberton (2004), 'Whose face in the mirror? Personal and postcolonial obstacles in re-searching Africa's contemporary women's theological voices'. Ed Ursula King and Tina Beattie *New Studies in Religion and Gender*. Concilium.

[80] Moore, SD (2001). *God's Beauty Parlor and other queer spaces in and around the Bible.* Stanford: Stanford University Press. pp 177-178

- Review your coven's practices and see what you could change or adapt in order to make your practice more inclusive and/or radical.
- Explore queer deities and write rituals about them

Chapter Nine

Deities and spirits

"He sees no stars who does not see them first
of living silver made that sudden burst
to flame like flowers beneath an ancient song,
whose very echo after-music long
has since pursued. There is no firmament,
only a void, unless a jewelled tent
myth-woven and elf-patterned; and no earth,
unless the mother's womb whence all have birth."

~ JRR Tolkien, *Mythopoeia*

"Once every people in the world believed that trees were divine, and could take human or grotesque shape and dance among the shadows, and that deer, and ravens and foxes, and wolves and bears, and clouds and pools, almost all things under the sun and moon, and the sun and moon, were no less divine and changeable. They saw in the rainbow the still bent bow of a god thrown down in negligence; they heard in the thunder the sound of his beaten water jar, or the tumult of his chariot wheels; and when a sudden flight of wild ducks, or of crows passed over their heads, they thought they were gazing at the dead hastening to their rest; while they dreamed of so great a mystery in little things that they believed the waving of a hand, or of a sacred bough, enough to trouble far off hearts, or hood the moon with darkness."

~ W.B. Yeats

What are deities and spirits?

Deities can be personifications of natural forces; deified humans; or spirits of a particular locality. Some people believe in them as literal entities; others see them more as an emergent phenomenon of Nature; some people see them as metaphors.

My personal view is that deities are a product of our interaction with the underlying energy of the universe. The particular deity forms emerge as a result of our interactions with sacred places and the forces of Nature, and are shaped both by their environment and by the culture that envisages them in a particular form. So they are real, but not immutable and fixed (just as people are not immutable and fixed).

It is a great idea to get to know your local deities, so that you can connect with the landscape in your local area. Local deities are embodiments of the land in a particular place, and guardians of its ecosystems and sacred places. They are expressions of the land-forms, geology, local vegetation, mythology and folklore of the region. Connecting with them shows respect for your local landscape, and also means that you can really put down roots and create connections.

How should we interact with deities?

I do not *worship* deities; as far as I am concerned our relationship is one of mutual benefit. I get to access their expanded, non-local, timeless consciousness, and they get to access my finite, local, time-bounded and focussed consciousness. Not all spirit beings are necessarily following an agenda that is the same as that of life on planet Earth; just as humans often don't take other species' needs into account, sometimes spirit beings don't either. I think we can align our agenda with the 'moral arc' of the universe, for the benefit of all life; but we must listen very carefully, not just blindly obey because another entity (human or spirit) tells us to do something. In fact, I am always deeply suspicious of anyone or anything *telling* me to do something. Remember that 'I was only obeying orders' doesn't cut any ice with war-crimes commissioners. I don't believe that obedience is a virtue. It is sometimes necessary in situations of extreme danger (such as in battle, or when a child is about to stick their fingers in an electrical socket and you tell them not to) but it must usually be accompanied by trust. Well, you might say, in the realm of the deities we are potentially like a child blundering about, unaware of the rules of engagement. Perhaps; so we should proceed with caution; but the procedure in that case is to learn the way that world works, just as a child learns how the world works and gradually ceases to be reliant on adults. So, if the analogy works, the deities should be helping us to operate independently and explaining what's going on, not telling us what to do and expecting us to obey blindly.

The nature of belief

As Wicca is such an experiential religion, concentrating more on the mysteries than on dogma, it can accommodate a wide spectrum of beliefs within it, from polytheism to duotheism to humanism. This question arose for me whilst reading the chapter entitled *'Living with Witchcraft'* in Ronald Hutton's book *Witches, Druids, and King Arthur,* in which he discusses the impact of Tania Luhrmann on Wicca. The thing that set me thinking was her concept of interpretive drift, which is her explanation of how witches and magicians come to believe in magic. As Ronald points out, there were a number of occasions when she almost believed in the efficacy of the magical rituals she had participated in, but then drew back to her rationalist-sceptical stance. He quotes Luhrmann (on p262) saying "the process of becoming involved in magic makes the magic believable, and makes explicit belief in magical theory quite tempting unless there is a strong disincentive against it" (which in her case there was, namely the knowledge that she had an academic career to carve out, and no desire to be tainted with the label of witch).

Luhrmann answered her question of "how can apparently rational people come to believe in magic?" with the notion of interpretive drift – the idea that as you get more involved, your interpretation of phenomena you have experienced drifts from a rational one to a magical one.

However, her model presupposes that the universe is a rational place, consisting of Euclidian space (discrete points separated from each other by empty space) across which no magical influence could permeate. But what if she's wrong? Then magical thinking would be a *better* explanation of the universe.

Personally, I am a polytheist, and I believe that consciousness is distributed throughout matter, and just as the distribution of matter in the universe is "clumpy", so is the distribution of spirit. Different kinds of consciousness may arise, and be transformed from one kind to another. According to C.G. Jung, the whole universe is striving towards consciousness. There seem to be two kinds of consciousness, that which dwells in linear space-time, and that which dwells in cyclical space-time (more traditionally known as "time" and "eternity"). We can become part of cyclical space-time briefly by spirit travel, astral projection, and the like. When we die, we become part of that reality. Both realities are mutually enfolded, and the separation between the two is really a difference of perception. It is also possible to have as many deities and pantheons as you like in this system, as the local forms of various deities are different "frequencies" at which you can tune in to a divine being (as it were), but may also be individual entities in their own right. Personally, I like to pick and choose between different pantheons, taking various personal deities (the household gods, if you like). This may sound terribly eclectic, but it works.

Coming to know

So, how do we arrive at whatever we believe? In the Pagan paradigm, belief develops from a mixture of received ideas and experience. We approach new knowledge with a healthy mixture of scepticism and open-mindedness – not dismissing it automatically, but not accepting it without question either.

A typical path might be a childhood experience of Nature, a sense of awe and wonder at the beauty of the natural world, coupled with reading the right sort of books (C.S. Lewis, J.R.R. Tolkien, Rudyard Kipling, Kenneth Graeme, and Ursula Le Guin, etc. I'm sure everyone could add to this list), followed by a teenage realisation that sexuality is a divine gift, and that life and pleasure should be celebrated. Then a search for the right spiritual path, eventually culminating in the feeling of coming home on encountering Wicca (or whichever path is chosen). I asked some twenty-somethings if the Internet had made it easier to find Paganism, and they said, actually it has made it harder because there are so many rubbishy sites on there. And in a roomful of about thirty students (the majority of whom were doing science degrees), all of them described a path similar to the above in discovering that they are Pagans.

Once one has been initiated into the Craft, the process of discovery, of experiencing the mysteries, intensifies. This is the bit that Luhrmann labelled as "interpretive drift", I suppose; maybe we originally believed in the gods as internal psychological constructs, valuable archetypes in the process of self-actualisation, but then shifted towards an idea of them as real entities as we experienced more of the mysteries. If one is rigidly rationalist, one will approach the process with a preconceived idea of the universe as a purely material phenomenon, where any spiritual realm is necessarily external.

Pagans like to balance the rational with the mystical; scepticism with open-mindedness; the inner realms with the outer realms. And this is not merely a static balance, but a dynamic one, as experience and theory intertwine to produce something new.

Tradition develops like this as well; growing from ancient (or not-so-ancient) roots, it gets pruned by the process of forgetting, watered by the process of remembering, and fertilised by new circumstances and ideas, then puts forth the leaves and fruit of new ceremonies.

The various types of Pagan belief can be formally defined as follows:

- belief in the deities as internal psychological constructs
- belief that the multiplicity of deities come ultimately from one divine source (monism)
- belief in "All the gods are one god, and all the goddesses are one goddess" (duotheism)
- belief that the divine is immanent in everything (pantheism)
- belief in a multiplicity of deities and spirits, and if there is an ultimate divine source, it is unknowable (polytheism)

All of the above shade into each other, with variations and gradations in between. The spectrum of beliefs within Paganism and Wicca is vast, and this is a good thing.

So rather than describing the shift from purely inner interpretations of the numinous to ones that include outer manifestations of it as "interpretive drift", I think a better metaphor would be that of a tree growing; its roots are in our experiences, but its branches and leaves are our interpretation of them. And every tree in the forest is different, because it is growing in a different place.

Wiccan cosmology

Most Wiccans regard the cosmos as consisting of the seen and the unseen. How these are seen as interacting varies from one Wiccan to another.

Is Wicca polytheistic?

It is commonly held in popular discourse and books that Wicca is duotheistic, that is, worshipping only two deities, the Horned God and the Lady of the Moon, or Cernunnos and Aradia. Popular books on (non-initiatory) Wicca have expanded these two deities to become the universal masculine principle and the universal feminine principle, with all other deities as "aspects" of these two. Even some Wiccan initiates[81] have started to talk about "the God" and "the Goddess".

This position is highly problematic for a number of reasons, not least of these being that the liturgy and "founding literature" of Wicca does not support it. This spurious duotheistic doctrine also affects LGBT people adversely, since if it is assumed that the primary dynamic in the universe is the interaction of masculine and feminine, this would render same-sex relationships "unnatural" in the eyes of those who follow this doctrine; and indeed some groups adopted this position. It is also problematic for men and women of whatever sexual orientation who do not identify with the archetypes associated with the Horned God and the Great Mother. Last but not least, many people do not find that it fits in with their actual experience of deities.

Some "hard" polytheists have asserted that Wiccans are "soft polytheists", in other words, that they say they are polytheists, but that when questioned closely they turn out to believe that all deities are aspects of the One.

I personally find the distinction between "hard" and "soft" polytheism to be a spurious one; that is, as far as I am concerned, someone who believes that all deities are aspects of a single divine entity is not a polytheist at all, therefore there is no need for the distinction to be made. They are actually monists.

The actual view expressed by many Wiccan polytheists (and by some polytheists from other traditions) is that there is an underlying divine consciousness in the universe, which has various names in various traditions (the Pleroma in Gnosticism, the Tao in Chinese thought, and *Dryghtyn* in Wicca), that the whole universe is infused with this consciousness, and that we are all (deities, humans, animals, spirits of place, etc.) manifestations of this consciousness – distinct identities in a sea of consciousness. We know ourselves to be a person, an identity, but we can also communicate from one mind to another, both within and between species. Hesiod (*Works and Days*, line 108) tells us "how the gods and mortal men sprang from one source." This text is quoted in Wiccan liturgy in a passage which emphasises the limited magical powers of humans, but also aims to show that we can communicate with the gods.

Polytheist Wiccans generally view Aradia and Cernunnos as the patron deities of Wicca who exist among many other deities, not as the "masculine principle" and the "feminine principle".

Many Wiccans are animists as well as polytheists, believing that everything has a spirit. Most also believe that deities are immanent in the world.

So, where did the assumption that Wicca is duotheistic come from? It seems that it initially came from the Eleusinian Mysteries via Dion Fortune (a writer who is very popular with Wiccans), who famously said (in her novel *The Sea Priestess*) "All the gods are one god, and all the goddesses are one goddess". Presumably she

---

[81]NB – this book is mostly about initiatory Wicca (referred to in the USA as British Traditional Wicca). Where eclectic Wicca is mentioned, it is by way of contrast with the original initiatory form.

based this assertion on the account of the vision of Isis in Lucius Apuleius' *The Golden Ass:*

> "Behold Lucius I am come, thy weeping and prayers have moved me to succour thee. I am she that is the natural mother of all things, mistress and governess of all the Elements, the initial progeny of worlds, chief of powers divine, Queen of heaven! the principal of the Gods celestial, the light of the goddesses: at my will the planets of the ayre, the wholesome winds of the Seas, and the silences of hell be deposed; my name, my divinity is adored throughout all the world in diverse manners, in variable customs and in many names, for the Phrygians call me the mother of the Gods: the Athenians, Minerva: the Cyprians, Venus: the Candians, Diana: the Sicilians Proserpina: the Eleusians, Ceres: some Juno, others Bellona, others Hecate: and principally the Aethiopians which dwell in the Orient, and the Egyptians which are excellent in all kinds of ancient doctrine, and by their proper ceremonies are accustomed to worship me, do call me Queen Isis." (William Adlington translation, 1566)

Certainly this list reads similarly to the list of Goddess names in Doreen Valiente's *The Charge of the Goddess:*

> Listen to the words of the Great Mother; she who of old was also called among men Artemis, Astarte, Athene, Dione, Melusine, Aphrodite, Cerridwen, Dana, Arianrhod, Isis, Bride, and by many other names.

So the urge to syncretise (conflate different deities into one) goes back to ancient times, and perhaps there are some deities who have different names in different cultures (e.g. Oðinn, Woden, Wotan). However, the conceptual leap from syncretising some deities who are similar to each other, to conflating all goddesses into one goddess, and all gods into one god, is rather too great for a lot of people.

Syncretism often occurs when one religion encounters another. Examples include the encounter between Hellenistic paganism[82] and early Christianity, when late classical paganism became more monotheistic, and early Christianity became more polytheistic in response to each other.[83] The encounter between Islam and Hinduism resulted in an artificial syncretic religion, Din-i-Ilahi, largely created by Akbar the Great. Similarly, when Hindus encountered Christians for the first time, there was considerable mutual influence, particularly among Deists. Syncretism appears to be a result of people's desire for a unified theory to explain the nature of things; they meet someone with a different world-view, and immediately try to reconcile it with their own. The attempt by some late classical pagans to create a synthesis of Christian and pagan ideas was a desperate last-ditch attempt to

---

[82]I am using 'pagan' to refer to pagans in antiquity, since they did not necessarily identify themselves as such, and 'Pagan' to refer to modern Pagans, since they do identify as such. This usage was proposed by Ronald Hutton in *The Triumph of the Moon: a history of Modern Pagan Witchcraft.* Oxford Paperbacks, 2001.
[83]G. W. Bowersock (1990). *HELLENISM IN LATE ANTIQUITY, Thomas Spencer Jerome Lectures.* Ann Arbor: The University of Michigan Press.

prevent paganism from disappearing altogether.

> Everything is full of gods. Whatever men worship, it may fairly be called one and the same. We all look up to the same stars; the same heaven is above us all; the same universe surrounds every one of us. What does it matter by what system of knowledge each one of us seeks the truth? It is not by one single path that we attain to so great a secret.
>
> – Quintus Aurelius Symmachus[84]

The late classical pagan apologists were in a tight cleft. Christianity was in a period of unstoppable ascendancy and expansion. They wanted to carry on being pagan, but the social and intellectual climate was against them. Similarly, many American Pagans, who live in a country where the vast majority are practising Christians, and Christianity is an all-pervading influence in public life, find it difficult to embrace polytheism. Hence the proliferation of the duotheistic view of Wicca, and in some cases, a monotheistic view, where the divine feminine and the divine masculine become aspects of a single divine being.

The duotheistic view is problematic in many respects, however. The view that the primary dynamic of the universe is an interaction of a masculine principle and a feminine principle represents a peculiarly Western view of gender. There is a tendency in Western thinking to conflate sex with gender; that is, to assume that one's biological sex equates with one's gender identity. In other cultures, the view of gender is much more complex, allowing for one's gender identity to be different from one's biological sex.[85] These cultures often correspondingly believe that there are many gods and goddesses, with different social and gender roles, and therefore different gender identities and sexual orientations are much more likely to be accepted.

Duotheistic models of the divine tend to assume that heterosexual sex is the norm because that is what "the God" and "the Goddess" do. They also tend to assume that the primary role of a woman is mothering and nurturing, because they regard "the Goddess" as the Great Mother. Although she is held to be a triple goddess, with maiden, mother and crone aspects, undue emphasis is placed on the mother aspect, and the other archetypes associated with adult women scarcely get a look in. Ronald Hutton has shown that the idea of the Great Mother was initially promoted by Jacquetta Hawkes, a conservative archaeologist who believed that women were intrinsically different from men and should stick to the divinely ordained role of mothering.[86] Polytheism, however, should be able to accept all variations of gender and sexuality, because there are so many divine role models to choose from. Many polytheistic cultures have more complex models of gender

---

[84] Quintus Aurelius Symmachus (A.D. c. 340–402) was a Roman senator. Letter, written 384, to the Christian Emperor Valentinian II, pleading for the continuation of Pagan ceremonies. In RM Ogilvie (1969), *The Romans and their gods.*

[85] Lou Hart (2005), *Magic is a many gendered thing,*
http://www.philhine.org.uk/writings/flsh_gendered.html

[86] Ronald Hutton (2001), *The Triumph of the Moon: a history of Modern Pagan Witchcraft.* Oxford Paperbacks.

than the West. Indeed, many gay men have embraced modern Heathenry, partly because of this, and partly because of the historical precedent of *ergi* men taking part in *seiðr*.

People of both genders and all sexual orientations have found it difficult to identify with the archetypes[87] of the Horned God and the Great Mother. It has been suggested that this is one reason why Wicca is more popular with women than with men, because the Great Mother is quite a strong image, but the Horned God is usually referred to as her consort, implying a secondary role. He is sometimes also described as having a dual aspect (the King of the Waning Year and the King of the Waxing Year, based on Robert Graves' *The White Goddess*) but this is a conflation with another deity, the agricultural dying and resurrecting god, who is not the same as the Lord of Animals type deity which Cernunnos seems to be.[88]

The problem of not being able to identify with or connect with deities does not occur in polytheistic covens, because there are plenty of deities to choose from, and Cernunnos is not regarded as the consort of Aradia, because they come from two different pantheons.

In much populist discourse, there is undue emphasis on the literal interpretation of fertility (that is, the idea that witchcraft is a fertility cult, primarily aimed at making the crops grow, preferably by engaging in heterosexual sex among the furrows). Apart from the fact that this is based on an outdated understanding of the development of folk customs,[89] it also creates a narrow understanding of fertility, which should not only be understood as bodily fecundity, but also mental and spiritual creativity.[90] Nor is it just about making the crops grow; fertility is important for the land, certainly, but so is the full cycle of death and rebirth, the tides of sowing, growing, reaping, and resting.

However, there is room in Wicca for a variety of perspectives on the nature of deity, as long as no-one tries to impose their views on anyone else. How does this work? It works because Wicca is an orthopraxy rather than an orthodoxy (it has a consistent body of practice, rather than a consistent body of doctrine). In fact, this is true of many religions; if you delve very far below the surface of individuals' beliefs within a supposedly single tradition, you can often find quite radical variations of belief.[91] As Elizabeth I said, she would "open no window into men's souls."

Looking back at what Gerald Gardner intended to create, however, we can see two things: he often referred to 'the gods', implying many gods, and he never intended there to be orthodoxy. He told his initiates to keep what they liked of the

---

[87]When I refer to archetypes, I do not mean that deities are archetypes, but that sometimes they can present an archetypal face to us (just as we sometimes project archetypes onto other people), though obviously they are more complex than that.

[88]Yvonne Aburrow (1993), *The Sacred Grove: Mysteries of the forest*, Chieveley: Capall Bann

[89] Bob Trubshaw (2002), *Explore Folklore*, Explore Books, an imprint of Heart of Albion Press.

[90]Yvonne Aburrow (2000), **Between Mirrors**, *Queer Spirit*, issue 13.

[91]Douglas A Marshall (2002), **Behavior, Belonging and Belief: A theory of ritual practice** in *Sociological Theory* 20:3, 3 November 2002, pp 360-380

written material that he gave them, and substitute other material for the bits they didn't like.[92]

Several sections of the first degree initiation refer to the gods in the plural, including the Wiccan Rede poem at the end, and in some versions of the ritual, there is the quote from Hesiod mentioned above, which also refers to the gods in the plural. Indeed, even the ostensibly syncretistic *Charge of the Goddess* has the Goddess saying "Before my face, beloved of gods and men..."

The third degree enacts the mystery of the *hieros gamos* or divine union of the *anima* and *animus*, to produce the Divine Androgyne; a being we don't hear much about in modern Wicca, but who was once an important part of the Western Mystery Tradition.[93] The Divine Androgyne represents a synthesis of the masculine and feminine principles within the soul. So even within the initiatory structure, there is a hint of a resolution of the dichotomy of male and female.

However, despite the ambivalence of a lot of Wiccan ritual towards the exact nature of the divine, there are some changes to practice that polytheist Wiccans tend to adopt.

One is that, when calling the quarters, it is considered more respectful to ask than to command. I try to avoid references to 'the Goddess' or 'the God' unless it is clear that it means 'the patron deities of the Craft'. When practising theurgy, we refer to the deity being invoked only as one deity, not conflating several deities into one invocation. Also, when the deity is invoked, we give them time to speak; we don't just recite some poetry and regard that as their utterance. This is very important to me.

Libation is an important aspect of Wiccan practice; after cakes and wine, a portion is always saved for the gods and spirits, and poured onto a sacred place.

Probably the biggest reason for the resurgence of polytheism within Wicca is that people have started to have encounters with deities as individuals. Janet Farrar and Gavin Bone have written that they have developed personal relationships with individual deities,[94] partly because of personal encounters with them, and partly because of their explorations of other traditional religions. Many other Wiccans have also established relationships with individual deities from various pantheons, often because those deities have contacted them. I have heard of a number of Wiccan priestesses who have felt called by Oðinn, and others who have felt called by deities from other traditions. Several Wiccans have been contacted by Voudun *orishas*.

One of the joys of Wicca is that it is a set of mystical and magical practices within which deities from any pantheon may be honoured. The deities who have contacted me over the years have come from a range of different pantheons (Hindu, Saxon, Roman, Sumerian and Celtic), so I couldn't restrict myself to only one of the ancient pagan traditions.

---

[92]Frederic Lamond (2004), *Fifty Years of Wicca*, Green Magic

[93]Alex Owen (2004), *The Place of Enchantment: British Occultism and the Culture of the Modern*, University of Chicago Press.

[94]Janet Farrar and Gavin Bone (2004), *Progressive Witchcraft: Spirituality, Mysteries & Training in Modern Wicca*, New Page Books.

It can be seen then, that Wicca was originally polytheistic, but its outer form became ostensibly duotheistic, partly because of the social milieu in which it took root. However, most people find it difficult to conform to a duotheistic belief system, because it is incompatible with their experiences of deities, sexuality and gender.

Whilst Wiccans prefer not to probe too deeply into each other's beliefs, because Wicca is an orthopraxy rather than an orthodoxy, it is becoming increasingly apparent that a significant number of initiated Wiccans are polytheistic.

Discussion points

- How does the Divine / deities relate to the Universe?
- What is the main dynamic of the Universe?
- What is the purpose of consciousness?
- Does the Universe have a beginning and an end? Or has it always existed?
- Is the divine realm inside or outside the Universe?
- Is our Universe only one of many parallel universes?
- What can traditional ideas tell us about cosmology?
- Look at Yggdrasil (Norse world tree, Ets Chayyim (Kabbalistic tree of life), Hindu creation myth, Celtic cosmology, etc.
- What are deities – energies, thought-forms, powerful land-wights, consciousness of natural phenomena....?
- How can we account for the existence of good and evil in a world that is not fallen?
- Is the dynamic of the Universe multiplicity, duality, polarity, Yin and Yang, dark and light, or what? How do you see it?
- How much of the Universe is conscious? How does this consciousness manifest?
  Can we relate to it?

Chapter Ten

The nature of truth

Truth is everywhere

Pagans don't believe in universal revelation. There are no prophets, and no sacred writings are regarded as infallible or canonical. If the truth is out there, it should be available and everywhere – it should not require special revelation. It is true that truths are revealed gradually to initiates, but it is possible to discover these truths through life experience, because life itself is an initiatory process. The primary purpose of initiations is to create a connection between the initiate and the gods and goddesses.

What is truth?

It depends on your perspective. Each of us has a unique view of life, coloured by our experiences, our dreams, and so on. Each of us aspires to different aims in life, and this diversity is good. Monocultures are dry and brittle; they fall apart and the centre cannot hold. Similarly, the idea of a single and absolute truth which holds true for everyone through all time seems unlikely. We all see things differently, depending on where we're coming from. But truth is relational (it relates in a nested way to everything around it), not relative (where all points of view are regarded as equally valid).

I've always adopted a simultaneously open-minded and sceptical view of any phenomena that I might encounter - I allow all possible interpretations to simmer gently on the back burner of my mind until I arrive at a multi-faceted understanding of the phenomena. But I usually have a preferred interpretation; like most people, I tend to have an emotional investment in my view of the world; and my point of view stems from who I am and where I am situated in the dynamic landscape of ideas and experiences.

Levels of truth

There are many different levels of truth: metaphorical truth (a metaphor that describes accurately a state that is otherwise difficult to describe); personal or local truth (true for me); cultural truth (accepted by a whole culture); and global truth (true for everyone). Some principles are universal – for example, every religion has an injunction not to harm others, but to treat them well. Maybe there is absolute truth, but if there is, how would we recognise it? Our position with regard to it cannot be objective, but is necessarily relational; it relates to other views of the truth, and other truths that we can perceive. To see the "whole" truth, you would need to be able to see from all perspectives at once, and then you would be unable to see it from any one individual's point of view. But even then, you would not be able to identify all the causes of a situation, as there are so many strands woven together in the web of wyrd. It is hard enough to find out *what* happened and *where* it happened, but when you start to try to establish *why* it happened, the task becomes even more difficult – and everyone has their own pet theory. Consider any event with fairly complex causes and you will see what I mean.

Truth depends on your perspective. There's a Chinese story in which a man first loses a horse, which is generally considered unlucky, but he reacts with equanimity. But then it returns from the wild with a number of other horses, which is generally considered lucky. Once more he shows little reaction, saying "Maybe so, maybe not". Then one of his sons breaks a leg whilst breaking in the wild horses; again people see this as unlucky, but the man shrugs it off in the same way. Finally soldiers arrive in the village to conscript all the young men for a war, but the son with the broken leg is not conscripted. Again people regard this as lucky, but the man says, "Maybe so, maybe not." And apparently the story is still going on.

Scientific truth?

What about science? Isn't that objective and therefore truthful? Certainly it strives to find out the truth, but quite often it turns out that it is just plain wrong, even recently. This is because it has a vested interest in defending the *status quo*, until it becomes indefensible and collapses, and then you get a paradigm shift.

Professor Frank Pajares[95] sums it up beautifully:

> "A scientific community cannot practice its trade without some set of received beliefs. These beliefs form the foundation of the "educational initiation that prepares and licenses the student for professional practice". The nature of the "rigorous and rigid" preparation helps ensure that the received beliefs are firmly fixed in the student's mind. Scientists take great pains to defend the assumption that scientists know what the world is like... To this end, "normal science" will often suppress novelties which undermine its foundations. Research is therefore not about discovering the unknown, but rather "a strenuous and devoted attempt to force nature into the conceptual boxes supplied

---

[95]Frank Pajares (2004) *'The Structure of Scientific Revolutions' by Thomas S. Kuhn, A Synopsis from the original*, Philosopher's Web Magazine,
http://www.emory.edu/EDUCATION/mfp/kuhnsyn.html

by professional education".

A shift in professional commitments to shared assumptions takes place when an anomaly undermines the basic tenets of the current scientific practice. These shifts are what Kuhn describes as scientific revolutions - "the tradition-shattering complements to the tradition-bound activity of normal science". New assumptions –"paradigms" - require the reconstruction of prior assumptions and the re-evaluation of prior facts. This is difficult and time consuming. It is also strongly resisted by the established community."

Uncertainty in science has been growing over the last century, not diminishing. The scientific method of enquiry and experiment works well up to a point, but the problem with it is that it separates the subject of the experiment from its context, creating a fixed frame of reference – a box – which ceases to resemble the real context from which the content was extracted. So the results of the experiment only predict what will happen in another similar closed system (or fixed frame of reference), *not* what will actually happen in the real world. Also, the scientific method, usually, works by manipulating variables which affect the thing under observation, as if these variables were separable forces acting on an inert object.

Postmodernism has attempted to do away with the contradictions inherent in rationalism by dissecting everything with discourse analysis and asserting that nothing is true, or that truth is relative. Another tenet of postmodernism is the "death of the self" - the idea that we are all merely intersections of overlapping domains of discourse, and our identities have no intrinsic reality.

So if neither science nor postmodernism are reliable guides, how *do* we know what we know? Often it is because it "rings true" - that is to say, it resonates with inner truth. This is why we need to practice attunement with the divine, so that we know that the promptings of inner truth are not merely self-delusion. Quite often we mistake our own selfish desires for inner truth, and then things can go badly wrong. For example, deciding that just because you fancy someone, it is the will of the universe that you get to sleep with them (whereas they might have entirely different ideas).

However, making mistakes, learning by experience, is the beginning of wisdom. In a way, you could define wisdom as 'knowing how much we don't know'. It is this awareness of not knowing that seems to me to be a sign of a truly wise person, one who can act from uncertainty and still be attuned to Wyrd, or Tao, or the dynamic of the universe. In the ordinary cock-a-hoop world of the rationalist, wisdom is often seen as foolishness. In a traditional Welsh story, *The Three Blows*,[96] a faery woman marries a human man, bringing a dowry of magical cattle. She tells him that she will remain with him as long as he does not strike her more than three times without a cause. He protests that he would rather cut off his own hand than do such a thing, but her father just smiles. One day they are invited to a wedding and she asks him to go back to the house for her gloves. On his return she is sitting very still on her horse, so he playfully flicks her with the gloves and says, "Go, go." That is the first causeless blow. Some years after they

---

[96]*The Lady of the Lake,* http://www.sacred-texts.com/neu/celt/wfb/wfb03.htm

are at a christening, and whilst everyone else rejoices, she weeps. Her husband slaps her on the shoulder and asks why she weeps; she tells him that it is because the child's life will be full of sorrow, and that that is the second causeless blow. Not long after the child dies, after a short life of suffering, and at the funeral she laughs. Her husband strikes her, shocked at her behaviour, and she explains that she was laughing because the child is now free of its suffering. And she tells him that that was the third causeless blow, and she returns to the lake, taking her faery cattle with her.

symbolic or mythological truth

In her novel *Always Coming Home*, Ursula le Guin[97] divides Western narrative modes into three main areas, fact, fiction, and propaganda. The first two rows of the table refer to our contemporary divisions of narrative, and the last row is the fictional Kesh equivalent.

Fact: non-fiction						Non-fact: fiction							
Report	Description	Journalism	Biography	Annals	History	Myth	Legend	Folk tale	Parable	Tale	Story	Novel	Propaganda
What happened						**Like what happened**							**Lies, jokes**

In the story, the metaphorical and conceptual framing of the world by the Kesh culture is completely different from present modes of thinking, and hence their culture is completely different from ours. They divide the world into nine "houses", four of which are Sky houses (the unborn, the dead, the imaginary, and those in the wilderness) and five of which are Earth houses. The whole of society is divided into exogamous clans or moieties based on these houses, and animals and birds and plants are also regarded as being in one of the five Earth houses. The symbolic scheme makes sense and provides a coherent framework for the society to function. Similar systems can be found in many tribal societies.

Mythological or metaphorical truisms are deeply embedded in our culture, and constantly influence the way we think. Sometimes these metaphorical constructs can be used to great effect to transform the psyche; at other times they may be used cynically to manipulate people. This is perhaps why the word myth has acquired a rather pejorative connotation, as in "It's only a myth" - implying that it's not true. This category of myth should, I feel, be properly referred to as legend, by which I mean a story with some basis in historical fact, but which has acquired mythical connotations. Frequently people embellish or alter stories to make them

---

[97]   Ursula K Le Guin (1985), *Always Coming Home*, Grafton Books, London. ISBN: 0586073833

more exciting. Ronald Hutton describes this process in *"How Myths Are Made"*, a chapter in *Witches, Druids and King Arthur*. He searched high and low for genuine folk memories handed down through the generations from the English Civil War. He found many legends, but only three factual stories that could be corroborated with historical evidence. Anthropology has demonstrated that the oral tradition is reliable for a maximum of 120 years (usually in pre-literate societies). However, what is contained in these folk legends is an indication of what people are interested in, whether it be ghosts or treasure or whatever, as these are the details they embellish.

However, myths and folktales appeal to us because they ring true – they contain many useful insights into life, as can be seen from the Taoist story cited above, and the Welsh story, *The Three Blows*. Traditional stories also contain archetypes, which interact and develop through the story, and may bring about transformation in the listener. It is said that in India, psychiatric care consisted of giving the mad person a traditional tale to meditate on.

Metaphor

It is necessary to take great care to check your assumptions when working with metaphors, however; as George Lakoff says, "Metaphors can kill." He points out that much of American foreign policy is based on the metaphorical notion that nations are people.

> "The Nation As Person metaphor is pervasive, powerful, and part of an elaborate metaphor system. It is part of an International Community metaphor, in which there are friendly nations, hostile nations, rogue states, and so on. This metaphor comes with a notion of the national interest: Just as it is in the interest of a person to be healthy and strong, so it is in the interest of a Nation-Person to be economically healthy and militarily strong. That is what is meant by the "national interest."

In the International Community, peopled by Nation-Persons, there are Nation-adults and Nation-children, with Maturity metaphorically understood as Industrialization. The children are the "developing" nations of the Third World, in the process of industrializing, who need to be taught how to develop properly and to be disciplined (say, by the International Monetary Fund) when they fail to follow instructions. "Backward" nations are those that are "underdeveloped." Iraq, despite being the cradle of civilization, is seen via this metaphor as a kind of defiant armed teenage hoodlum who refuses to abide by the rules and must be 'taught a lesson'."[98]

The theories of George Lakoff and others with regard to metaphorical constructs framing the way we think are known as **cognitive linguistics**; it is a very useful approach to understanding how myths – both positive and negative – work.

---

[98]George Lakoff (18 March 2003), *Metaphor and War, Again*, AlterNet, http://www.alternet.org/story.html?StoryID=15414

In their ground-breaking book, *Metaphors We Live By*, Lakoff and Johnson pointed out the underlying metaphors used in many figures of speech. For example, the underlying metaphor "Argument is War" has us talking about winning an argument, wiping the floor with our opponents, and so on. Imagine how different arguments might be if the underlying metaphor was "Argument is Dance". Another example they give is "A Relationship is a Ship", where we talk about marriages foundering, being on the rocks, and breaking up.

Similarly, in *The Inner Reaches of Outer Space: Myth as Metaphor and as Religion*, Joseph Campbell explored some of the bodily metaphors underlying religious symbolism and mythology.

Metaphors are a very powerful thing. They can dictate how we see the world, and therefore how we behave. They can constrain our expectations of what will happen, and how it will happen. The metaphorical connotations of an idea shape and limit what can be said about it.

I have written in the chapter on gender and sexuality in Wicca about the limitations and negative effects of the gender binary in much of our mythology. I have also argued for a more nuanced view of gender.

In Hinduism and Buddhism, there is an ancient practice of stripping away metaphors until you are left with questions and uncertainty; this is a very good thing. It is known in Christianity as apophatic theology or the *via negativa*, and it is a very important part of my spirituality. I think we need more apophatic theology in Paganism. However, according to Matthew Fox, there are four ways to engage with spirituality, of which the *via negativa* is only one. The others are *via positiva*, *via creativa* and *via transformativa*.

However, saying something is "only a metaphor" is a bit disingenuous, because we live by metaphors and they shape our thoughts.

There is hope, though, because the power of metaphors is such that if you create a new metaphor to live by, you can create a new reality. For instance, many Pagans have adopted the eightfold wheel of the year (eight seasonal festivals), and this metaphor, which expresses sacred time, has shaped our relationship with the cosmos and with Nature. So if we want to change the binary model of gender, we could create a more powerful metaphor to replace the gender binary. We can use the examples of sexual, reproductive, and gender diversity in Nature as a metaphor for the diversity we wish to celebrate in human sexuality.

Stories are very powerful. Many years ago, I saw a made-for-TV film which had the resounding slogan "Folklore can kill". In the film, weird things start happening to a folklorist who is investigating urban legends – the legends are happening right in front of him, but he is in denial, insisting that folklore can't come true… but it does.

If you attend a Wiccan gathering, there will very likely be stories. What will be the bit you remember? The talks and workshops you attended, or the stories (either enacted in ritual, or told around the campfire)? I can guarantee that the thing you will remember will be the stories. Stories speak directly to both hemispheres of the brain, and that's probably why they are remembered. Jack Cohen has suggested that *Homo sapiens* should be renamed *Pan narrans*, the storytelling ape.[99] People like stories.

Archetypes and narrative

Archetypes are "Forms or images of a collective nature which occur practically all over the earth as constituents of myths and at the same time as autochthonous, individual products of unconscious origin."[100]

Jung says that there are three levels of symbolism: personal symbolism (where one thing represents another only in the mind of one person); cultural symbolism (where one thing represents another across a whole culture); and archetypal or universal symbolism (where one thing represents another for the whole of humanity). This universal symbolism, he thought, is found in the collective unconscious – that part of our minds which we share as part of our common heritage of humanity.

Archetypes of the feminine	Archetypes of the masculine
• Muse / Femme Fatale	• Businessman / Traitor
• Amazon / Gorgon	• Protector / Gladiator
• Mystic / Betrayer	• Hermit / Warlock
• Daddy's Girl / Bitch	• Ladies' Man / Seducer
• Earth Mother / Terrible Mother	• Saviour / Punisher
• Matriarch / Scorned Woman	• Artist / Abuser
• Messiah / Destroyer	• King / Dictator
• Damsel-in-distress / Troubled Teen	• Fool / Tramp

(source: Victoria Lynn Schmidt (2001), *45 Master Characters, Writer's Digest Books ISBN: 1582970696*)

Each archetype has both a positive and a negative aspect. The archetypes are frequently used in constructing narratives. There is a kind of narrative imperative in the writing of history and journalism; we always want to make it a story, with an intelligible plot and characters. By fitting people into the frame of an archetypal figure, we can make the story more appealing, as described by Lakoff:

> "One of the most frequent uses of the Nation As Person metaphor comes in the almost daily attempts to justify the war metaphorically as a "just war." The basic idea of a just war uses the Nation As Person metaphor plus two narratives that have the structure of classical fairy tales: The Self Defense Story and The Rescue Story.
>
> In each story, there is a Hero, a Crime, a Victim, and a Villain. In the Self-Defense story, the Hero and the Victim are the same. In both

---

[99] Jack Cohen & Ian Stewart, *The Science of Discworld.*
[100] C G Jung, *Psychology and Religion*, Collected Works, Vol. 11.

stories, the Villain is inherently evil and irrational: The Hero can't reason with the Villain; he has to fight him and defeat him or kill him. In both, the victim must be innocent and beyond reproach. In both, there is an initial crime by the Villain, and the Hero balances the moral books by defeating him. If all the parties are Nation-Persons, then self-defense and rescue stories become forms of a just war for the Hero-Nation.

In Gulf War I, Bush I tried out a self-defense story: Saddam was "threatening our oil-line." The American people didn't buy it. Then he found a winning story, a rescue story – The Rape of Kuwait. It sold well, and is still the most popular account of that war. "[101]

Terry Pratchett uses the idea of the narrative imperative to great effect in *Witches Abroad*, when the villainess tries to use the power of story to gain control of a kingdom. He calls it the theory of narrative causality:

"[which] means that a story, once started, takes a shape. It picks up all the vibrations of all the other workings of that story that have ever been. This is why history keeps on repeating all the time."

"All witches are very conscious of stories. They can feel stories, in the same way that a bather in a little pool can feel the unexpected trout.

Knowing how stories work is almost all the battle."

Wisdom and truth

Wisdom is generally regarded as being more important than knowledge. It is broader, deeper, and has more perspective.

"Insights and acts that are widely considered wise tend to:

- arise from a broad (not narrow-minded) perspective,

- serve life in some broad or deep way (not just narrow self-interest)

- be grounded in but not limited by the past (experience, history, etc.) and the future (likely consequences)

- be informed by multiple forms of intelligence – reason, intuition, heart, spirit, etc..

Because of its expanded perspective, wisdom is also often associated with humility, compassion, composure, and being able to laugh at oneself. Many liberals would argue a tolerance for dissonance, paradox, nuance, ambiguity, uncertainty is also important."[102]

Wise people know that we cannot know everything, and base their progress through life on a sense of integrity and openness. They do not act from selfish motives, but from an intuitive understanding of the community dynamic. They realise that the individual perspective is limited, and try to holographically include

---

[101]George Lakoff (18 March 2003), *Metaphor and War, Again*, AlterNet, http://www.alternet.org/story.html?StoryID=15414
[102]http://en.wikipedia.org/wiki/Wisdom

others' perspectives, whether from tradition or from current thinking. At the same time they trust their instincts, acting from the heart, using the gift of discernment. They are connected to the great well of Unknowing, the Tao, the source. This concept is found in various metaphorical guises in all traditions.

> "Destroy the world, you men of the atoms, and Unknowing will retain the pattern. 'Trust that which belongs to the universe itself,' says the Tao. 'From that there will be no escape.'
>
> Unknowing, if one can be open and vulnerable, will take us down to the very deeps of knowing, not informing the mind merely but coursing through the whole body, artery and vein – provided one can thrust aside what the world calls common sense, that popular lumpen wisdom that prevents the emerging of the numinous.
>
> Unknowing needs that a man be in a certain state of grace, playful, artless, inwardly acquitted of opinion, not at all as children are but rather as fools or saints."
>
> (P.L. Travers[103])

Absolute truth?

So can there be any such thing as absolute truth? If there was, would it be knowable from our finite human perspective? If there is an Absolute, could it be manifest in the Universe at all?

Jung, in his *Septem Sermones Ad Mortuos* (Seven Sermons to the Dead), thought not.

> "A thing that is infinite and eternal hath no qualities, since it hath all qualities. This nothingness or fullness we name the Pleroma. Therein both thinking and being cease, since the eternal and infinite possess no qualities. In it no being is, for he then would be distinct from the pleroma, and would possess qualities which would distinguish him as something distinct from the pleroma. In the pleroma there is nothing and everything. It is quite fruitless to think about the pleroma, for this would mean self-dissolution."

He then goes on to say that God (the *summum bonum*, or sum of all good) and the Devil (*infinum malum*, or total evil) are very close to the Pleroma, since they subsume all other pairs of qualities in themselves, but they are not the Pleroma, because they are *creatura* (created beings). In the Gnostic world-view (which Jung is explaining here), there is a higher god, Abraxas.

> "God and devil are distinguished by the qualities of fullness and emptiness, generation and destruction. EFFECTIVENESS is common to both. Effectiveness joineth them. Effectiveness, therefore, standeth above both; is a god above god, since in its effect it uniteth fullness and emptiness. This is a god whom ye knew not, for mankind forgot it. We name it by its name ABRAXAS. It is more indefinite still than god and

---

[103]Pamela L. Travers (1993), *What the Bee Knows: Reflections on Myth, Symbol and Story*, London: Penguin Arkana. ISBN 0140194665

devil. That god may be distinguished from it, we name god HELIOS or sun. Abraxas is effect. Nothing standeth opposed to it but the ineffective; hence its effective natyre freely unfoldeth itself. The ineffective is not, therefore resisteth not. Abraxas standeth above the sun and above the devil. It is improbable probability, unreal reality. Had the pleroma a being, Abraxas would be its manifestation. It is the effective itself, nor any particular effect, but effect in general. It is unreal reality, because it hath no definite effect. It is also creatura, because it is distinct from the pleroma. The sun hath a definite effect, and so hath the devil. Wherefore do they appear to us more effective than indefinite Abraxas. It is force, duration, change."

It strikes me that Abraxas (and the concept of unknowing described by Travers) are both very similar to the concept of Dryghtyn, the "original source of all things" which is also like the Tao, the source of the Ten Thousand Things, or the manifest universe. When I first heard *The Dryghtyn Prayer*, I saw Dryghtyn as an enormous serpent, the kundalini of the universe. But it is also the Pleroma, the Tao, the unknowable; in order to be knowable, to be manifest, to have distinctive qualities, differentiation must arise from it.

Platonic forms

However, Plato proposed the notion of ideal forms which existed beyond the physical world, such as beauty, truth, goodness, and so on. Christian philosophers took up this notion and regarded the Platonic forms as being angels. The ideal forms can be regarded as an abstract standard by which we judge things – an absolute. The argument for Platonic forms suggests that if we see something beautiful, how do we know it is beautiful unless we have an abstract concept of beauty by which to judge it? But if Jung is right, these ideal forms also have their counterparts:

"When we strive after the good or the beautiful, we thereby forget our own nature, which is distinctiveness, and we are delivered over to the qualities of the pleroma, which are pairs of opposites. We labour to attain the good and the beautiful, yet at the same time we also lay hold of the evil and the ugly, since in the pleroma these are one with the good and the beautiful. When, however, we remain true to our own nature, which is distinctiveness, we distinguish ourselves from the good and the beautiful, therefore, at the same time, from the evil and ugly. And thus we fall not into the pleroma, namely, into nothingness and dissolution."

So we must be aware that the beautiful thing is not beauty itself; it is only one of many manifestations of beauty. When we strive after the good, seeking to destroy that which is bad, we only bring about dissonance and destruction. That is why we need the quality of mercy.

To become wise, we must be aware that what we know is like a dream floating on the surface of the void – it is subject to change; only the unmanifest is changeless. As Jung says, "[Abraxas] is force, duration, change."

Personally, I do not believe in Platonic forms – the idea that a perfect version of things exists outside the physical realm, which we should all strive after, can lead to imbalance, as Jung suggests with his idea of the opposites that exist within the Pleroma.

Implications for Wiccan theology

The uncertainty of truth and the primacy of experience have profound implications for our view of theology. We do not know what the ultimate nature of the deities and/or the Divine is. We do know that we can measure what is good by whether it contributes to the sum of human happiness, the wellbeing of our planet and of the other species with whom we share it. We cannot be certain that there is life after death; we can be certain that there is life *before* death, and try to make it the best life it can be for everyone.

Because we are not certain about the existence or the nature of deities, it is good to allow for a diversity of views, including atheism, agnosticism, monism, pantheism, duotheism, polytheism, polymorphism, and so on. Many Wiccans hold more than one of these beliefs at the same time, or change their minds about the nature of the deities; and it is quite possible to have people with different theological perspectives in a circle at the same time, provided they respect each other's beliefs. Wiccan rituals often focus on a god and a goddess, but polytheist Wiccans regard them as individual patron deities of the Craft and/or the coven; atheist Wiccans regard them as archetypes or metaphors; pantheist and monist Wiccans regard them as aspects of the universe; duotheist Wiccans regard them as the God and the Goddess, and so on. If other deities are invoked, polytheist Wiccans regard them as distinct beings; duotheist, monist, and pantheist Wiccans regard them as aspects; atheist Wiccans regard them as archetypes, and so on.

Wicca is primarily an experiential religion, so there is no real imperative for everyone to agree on theology. It is also good to consider that my understanding may be wrong, and allow for the possibility of changing my views in response to experiences. Encountering the mysteries in a ritual setting and allowing yourself to be transformed by them is the main aim of Wiccan ritual, it seems to me, so whilst it is important that our beliefs are consistent with reason and experience, they are not the most important thing in the Wiccan circle. Much more important is the love and trust between the participants in the ritual.

Your mountain is not my mountain and that's just fine

Metaphors for religion are tricky things, especially when we try to stretch them and make them work too hard by trying to turn them into analogies. One very popular metaphor for explaining religious diversity is the idea that we are all walking different paths up the same mountain. However, many people are coming to believe (myself included) that we are in fact all walking up different mountains.

The title of this section is inspired by the saying in the kink community, "Your kink is not my kink, but that's OK" – in other words, diversity is acknowledged and celebrated.

I wonder if we actually each have our very own mountain – not just a different mountain for each tradition and religion and denomination, but personal mountains. Maybe our mountains are on the same mountain range, or on the same continent; maybe they are on different continents. And of course continents move around as the tectonic plates shift; new mountain ranges are created, new continents formed. The Pagan continent (like the mythical Atlantis) was submerged for a while, but now it has re-emerged, and we can explore it again, with its polytheist mountain range, its monist mountain range, its pantheist mountain range, and other geological formations. The Pagan continent also has magic portals or bridges to the Quaker realm, the Unitarian Universalist realm, the Taoist realm, the Buddhist realm, the Hindu realm, etc, or maybe whole regions of CUUPs people and Quaker Pagans, and Jewitches. Of course, being a Pagan sacred landscape, there are no centres, or centres everywhere, and no periphery (unless you want a bit of liminality). And there's nothing to stop you exploring the other continents, or even settling for a while on one of them, as long as the inhabitants are friendly.

Indeed, who's to say we are all climbing up mountains? Maybe some of us are exploring lush valleys, hanging out in the forest, taking a dip in the ocean, building a beautiful eco-village, or whatever takes your fancy. You can define your own journey, you can walk (or run or hop whilst whistling Dixie) on a predefined path, or discover your own bit of the lush Pagan continent. There is room for all. If I choose to decorate my sacred landscape with shrines to Oðinn, Ishtar, Shiva, and Shakti, and someone else decorates theirs with shrines to the Neoplatonic Divine Source, that's all good.

And if you don't like this metaphor for Pagan religions, it's only a metaphor, so pick another one, or invent your own.

Discussion and activities

- Draw a mindmap of your concepts of truth. What concepts do you relate to truth?

- Is truth universal, or a matter of perspective?

- How do you think science and religion relate to each other? Are they complementary world-views, or mutually exclusive?

- Describe your theology – first write down your beliefs or theories about gods, goddesses, spirit, matter, etc, and then try to see if they fit any pre-existing categories (don't worry if they don't, this is something that happens a lot)

- Explore theology with your fellow coveners (using techniques like active listening and non-violent communication is a good idea for this)

Meditation

Contemplate an idea which you believe to be good and true. Consider its many forms, both perfect and imperfect. Consider its opposite, and its many manifestations. Can the idea and its opposite both exist? Is the opposite of your chosen idea good, bad, or neutral?

Contemplate an idea which you believe to be problematic. Consider its many forms, however they may manifest. Consider its opposite, and its many permutations. Can the idea and its opposite both exist? Is the opposite of your chosen idea good, bad, or neutral?

Examples of ideas which you might contemplate: many deities; one deity; the gender binary; the idea of fertility; the concept of polarity; heteronormativity; absolute truth; relative truth; contextual truth.

How to draw a mindmap

Start with the concept you want to explore, such as truth, write it in the centre of a large piece of paper (at least A4), and draw an oval around it. Identify four or five key subcategories, and draw branches from the central oval. The idea behind the branching structure is that it resembles neurons in the brain. Write a word (not a phrase) identifying the subcategory along each branch. The inventor of mindmaps, Tony Buzan, explains that you need to write the words along the branches so as not to block the flow of your thoughts. You also write only one word per branch, because if you find yourself tempted to write a phrase, you have probably identified a further subcategory, which can then be added to a further branch (e.g. if the phrase "mass production" came to mind, you might then realise you had two further categories under production, "mass" and "craft"). Divide the branches into further sub-branches as much as you want.

Chapter Eleven

Wicca and science

The beliefs and practices of Wicca are not incompatible with science, but there are a number of different ways of accommodating the magical and spiritual worldview with the scientific one. The Wiccan approach to belief is to form a **working hypothesis** about a situation, and to **test all assumptions** against experience – in other words, an **empirical approach**. Many Wiccans are cautious about attributing magical causes to events, and prefer to assume physical causes first. We also adopt a position of "it might be preternatural, or it might not" – a sort of ambivalence towards apparently magical events.

Many Wiccans are atheist, agnostic, or non-theist. Most theist Wiccans take the view that the deities are allies, rather than beings to be blindly obeyed. Some take the view that deities are metaphorical, or archetypes, or energies. Communications from deities are tested against ethics and experience, not accepted uncritically. There is no conflict in being a Wiccan atheist; it just means that you don't literally believe in deities, but work with the symbolism instead. Most Pagans, including Wiccans, believe that deities are immanent in the universe, not transcendent or outside it.

My theory is that consciousness is an emergent property of complex systems, and the universe is a sufficiently complex system to allow for the possibility of consciousness emerging from it. However, that consciousness is not evenly distributed throughout the universe, but rather forms in places where there is extra complexity, either in the form of natural phenomena, or where humans have evoked it by communing with it. I also think there is something which supports consciousness existing outside the brain – perhaps the same complex systems that give rise to spirits of place, deities, and so on.

The best explanation of how this process might work is offered in Terry Pratchett's novel *Small Gods*. A tiny particle of free-floating consciousness gets lodged in someone's brain, acquires more consciousness as a result, and starts communicating with its host, who then becomes the prophet of a new religion.

Polytheism and monotheism are entirely different explanations of the relationship of the divine to the universe. Monotheism usually assumes an all-powerful supernatural creator deity; polytheism does not necessarily assume a creator deity, and often views the origin of the universe as unimportant – often assuming that there is a cycle of creation and destruction, with new universes being born after several ages have passed. More importantly, polytheist deities are not assumed to be all-powerful, as they only have jurisdiction over certain aspects of existence (or they are personifications of competing natural forces such as wind and waves).

Theoretical models

There are various ways of accommodating Pagan views within a scientific worldview. Various authors identify different discursive positions which may be adopted. Their conclusions often depend on their own perspective, and whether they are examining Pagan views, or those of other religious groups.

Tania Luhrmann[104] identifies four possible positions which magical practitioners take in justifying their views to sceptics. The first is **realism**, the idea that 'there is a knowable objective reality and that magic reveals more of it than science'. The second position that she identifies is the **two worlds** view, that 'the objective referent of magical claims is unknowable within the terms of an ordinary, scientific world'. The third position is **relativism**, which 'defines all truth as relative and contingent' (which Luhrmann finds to be quite a common view). The final position is the **metaphorical** view, that magic is metaphorical and is probably objectively not true, but is nevertheless a creative and enjoyable practice. Luhrmann[105] says that she rarely encountered this position except among those who had come to magic through political concerns such as environmentalism and feminism.

Luhrmann[106] states that the four positions are not mutually exclusive; she senses that 'most magicians will give most of these arguments at some time during their magical career'. These views are clearly discursive positions.

Bienkowski[107] also identifies four possible belief positions: **materialism**, the belief that only the material plane exists (this is similar to Naturalism, atheism, and humanism); **idealism**, the belief that the material plane is illusory; **dualism**, the belief that both material and spiritual realms exist, but are separate (similar to Luhrmann's two worlds view); and **animism**, the belief that the spiritual world is immanent in the material world. He uses these to explain how these beliefs could inform attitudes to human remains, but they are also applicable to the broader relationship between religious and scientific discourse, because they are different ways of viewing reality. The ideas discussed are very broad in scope, however, as

---

[104] Luhrmann, T. (1989) *Persuasions of the Witch's Craft: Ritual Magic in Contemporary England.* Cambridge, MA: Harvard University Press.pp 285-293

[105] Ibid, page 293

[106] Ibid, page 284

[107] Bienkowski, P. (2006) 'Persons, things and archaeology: contrasting world-views of minds, bodies and death', *Respect for Ancient British Human Remains: Philosophy and Practice.* [online] Manchester Museum,
http://www.museum.manchester.ac.uk/medialibrary/documents/respect/persons_things_and_archaeology.pdf

they are intended to represent a range of religions and philosophies, and something more specific is needed to identify the nuances of Pagan discourse.

In contrast, Richard Dawkins[108] identifies seven possible belief positions on the existence of God, from strong theism to strong atheism, with agnosticism in the middle. However, these are not very useful for the purpose of this discussion, because they only relate to the existence of a supernatural creator deity, and not to the possible ways in which the spiritual and material realms could interact. Belief in a creator is largely irrelevant to Pagans, since we are more interested in relating to Nature.[109]

A more subtle approach is offered by Nuyen,[110] who discusses realism and antirealism in religion. **Religious realism** (like Luhrmann's realist position) asserts that there is an external referent of religious language, a real thing that it is describing; **religious antirealism** asserts that 'there is no transcendent being or reality to which religious languages and practices refer and that the source of religious meaning and value lies in us, human beings'.[111] This antirealism is very similar to Luhrmann's metaphorical position.

Folse[112] describes the classic scientific realist position as holding that at least some terms in theoretical statements correspond to the properties of entities to which these terms refer. Another form of realism is 'the quest for knowledge about the reality producing the phenomena we experience', which does not necessarily insist that that reality is entirely comprehensible. This is comparable to religious realism, which also asserts that descriptions of deities have objective external referents.

Muller and Livingston [113] describe scientific antirealism as the view that scientific terms are merely 'terminological abstraction(s) designed to account for the… results of a particular set of experiments' and do not necessarily have any objective referents. They note that much of the debate between realists and antirealists hinges on the Copenhagen interpretation of quantum mechanics, which posits that the observer affects the observed, thereby calling into question the notion of an objective external reality. Magicians often quote this in defence of the 'relativist' position;[114] it is interesting because it implies that some scientists

---

[108] Dawkins, R. (2006) *The God Delusion*. London: Bantam Press. page 50

[109] Harvey, G. (1997) *Contemporary Paganism: Listening People, Speaking Earth*. New York: New York University Press.page 145

[110] Nuyen, A.T. (2001) 'Realism, Anti-Realism, and Emmanuel Levinas.' *The Journal of Religion*, 81 (3), pp. 394-409 [online] Available from: http://www.jstor.org/stable/1206402

[111] Ibid, page 394

[112] Folse, H.J. (1986) 'Niels Bohr, Complementarity, and Realism'. *Proceedings of the Biennial Meeting of the Philosophy of Science Association*, 1, pp. 96-104 [online] Available from: http://www.jstor.org/stable/193111

[113] Muller, A. and Livingston, P. (1995) 'Realism/Anti-Realism: A Debate'. *Cultural Critique*, No. 30, The Politics of Systems and Environments, Part I, pp. 15-32 [online] Available from: http://www.jstor.org/stable/1354431

[114] Luhrmann, T. (1989) *Persuasions of the Witch's Craft: Ritual Magic in Contemporary England*. Cambridge, MA: Harvard University Press.page 291

understand their descriptions of reality to be metaphorical.

The various positions available in both scientific and religious discourse show that the debate is not simply happening *between* science and religion, but also *within* both those discourses, and so it is not accurate to talk about either discourse as if it were a monolithic entity engaged in a titanic struggle for truth and authority with the other discourse; the whole picture is far more complex.

Historical context of the Pagan revival

Contemporary Paganism has emerged in the context of scientific rationalism[115] and, at least in part, from the Romantic movement,[116] which sought to re-enchant the world, and asserted that reason alone was not enough to understand the world, but must go hand-in-hand with imagination and intuition.[117]

Serena Roney-Dougal[118] is a parapsychologist who explores mystical language and experience in terms of Western science. Her observations on the Pagan revival are interesting. She points to the high point of materialism and logical positivism, the behaviourist school of psychology, where consciousness was deemed not to exist because it could not be measured,[119] and says that the most harmful form of magic is to 'deny that there is "godness" in the world, that there is spirit in a tree, a brook, a person';[120] clearly a 'realist' position, because she is assuming that spiritual phenomena are tangible and testable.

She then compares this with the culture that seems to be emerging:

> "Everyone is highly spiritual in a non-religious sense; that is, there is a recognition and a respect for the spiritual aspect of life, but there is as yet no clear form, each individual finding their own way through the plethora of teachings... they are finding the Divinity within their own selves and are becoming self-responsible."[121]

Here she presents Pagan spirituality as still finding its way, but seeks to orient the reader towards finding the source of authority in the self. This echoes the thoughts of Andy Letcher,[122] Louise Bregman[123] and others, that the 'spiritual revolution'[124] is about creating a personal assemblage of meaning from the

---

[115] Ibid, page 279

[116] Hutton, R.E. (1999) *The Triumph of the Moon: A history of modern Pagan witchcraft.* Oxford: Oxford University Press.pp 43-44

[117] Partridge, C. (2004) *The Re-enchantment of the West, Volume 1: Alternative Spiritualities, Sacralization, Popular Culture and Occulture.* London and New York: T & T Clarkpage 72

[118] Serena Roney-Dougal (2010), *Where Science and Magic Meet,* Green Magic Books

[119] Ibid, page 199

[120] Ibid, page 204

[121] Ibid, page 238

[122] Letcher, A. (2006) *Shroom: A cultural history of the magic mushroom.* New York and London: Harper Perennial.page 68

[123] Bregman, L. (2006) 'Spirituality: a glowing and useful term in search of a meaning.' *Omega,* 53 (1-2), pp. 5-26. [online] Available from Ebscohost: Academic Search Premier, AN 21808441. page 15

[124] Heelas, P. and Woodhead, L. (2005) *The Spiritual Revolution: Why Religion is Giving Way to*

smorgasbord on offer; since the hegemony of organised religion has been removed by the onslaught of science and secularisation, people are free to create their own spiritual meanings. It also accords ultimate spiritual authority to the individual self. Serena Roney-Dougal[125] is hopeful that this is a sign of an emergent paradigm where an animistic and pantheistic worldview informs our thinking about the relationship of spirit and matter.

With the triumph of the scientific worldview, many commentators thought that religion would fade away as society became more and more secular. The decrease in the power of religion is known as secularisation. However, since 2001, religion has arguably made a bit of a come-back, with the rise of fundamentalism in various parts of the world, but also the spiritual revolution – the increase in the number of people who declare themselves to be "spiritual but not religious" and who are often opposed to "organised religion". The increase in interest in the spiritual and the move away from materialism is known as re-enchantment.

Indeed, some commentators have proposed that science itself is being re-enchanted; Whitehead[126] notes a significant increase in research on consciousness, arguing that the nature and origin of consciousness is a 'Hard Problem' for Western science, which challenges its very roots, because it is unclear how consciousness can arise from purely physical processes. Whitehead also points out the re-enchanting possibilities of quantum mechanics, which many Pagans use to explain magic, possibly drawing on popular science authors such as Gary Zhukav. Letcher[127] shows how others have drawn on the neo-shamanic discourse of Terence McKenna, Michael Harner and Carlos Castaneda to fulfil their quest for a theory of magic, and many of these authors use the language of science to lend credence to their theories.

Graham Harvey[128] also sees a connection between science and Paganism, and is critical of mainstream religions:

> "Modern Western consciousness, especially religious consciousness, requires considerable alteration if it is to celebrate the Earth. The resources are available among other "listening peoples" and include secular scientists' careful observations of the ecology of the planet, anthropologists' careful observations of other societies, historians' careful descriptions of past agrarian cultures, and the traditions, songs, techniques and visions of existing shamanic practitioners."

Here he presents Pagans and scientists as being 'on the same side' and wants to orient his audience towards greater respect for the Earth, towards becoming a 'listening people'. Harvey, Starhawk, Clifton and Landstreet all advocate allowing

Spirituality. Oxford: Blackwell.

[125] Serena Roney-Dougal (2010), *Where Science and Magic Meet*, Green Magic Books – page 242

[126] Whitehead, C. (1998) 'The Re-enchantment of Science'. *Anthropology Today*, 14(5), pp 20-21. [online] Available from JSTOR. pp 20-21

[127] Letcher, A. (2006) *Shroom: A cultural history of the magic mushroom*. New York and London: Harper Perennial. pp 216, 266, 298

[128] Harvey, G. (1997) *Contemporary Paganism: Listening People, Speaking Earth*. New York: New York University Press. page 124

scientific knowledge and insights to inspire Pagan practices and metaphors, and Roney-Dougal appears to want magical insights to inform science.

Frisk[129] goes one step further; she also suggests engaging with nature through science, but is highly critical of the Pagan preoccupation with the magical and symbolic qualities of things over their real substance. She further highlights the problem inherent in much use of magic in Paganism – if we are using magic to affect the outcome of events, is that not too much like the domination of nature exercised by patriarchal religion and science? But, she argues, if Pagans embrace environmentalism, myth and symbol can provide the motivation to save the planet from ourselves. She criticises both science and traditional religion for their claims of infallibility, since, she argues, both have damaged the environment and the human psyche.

In her study of British magicians and witches, Tania Luhrmann seeks to understand the process of becoming involved in magic; how people brought up in a rational-scientific world can adopt magical beliefs. She refers to this process as 'interpretive drift':

> "[T]he slow shift in someone's manner of interpreting events, making sense of experiences, and responding to the world. People do not enter magic with a set of clear cut beliefs which they take to their rituals and test with detachment. Nor is their practice mere poetry, a new language to express their feelings. Rather, there seems to be a slow, mutual evolution of interpretation and experience, rationalized in a manner which allows the practitioner to practise."[130]

On the other hand, in a study of New Zealand feminist witches' beliefs about how magic works, Kathryn Rountree[131] finds that their definitions of magic exhibited 'an unequivocal rejection of the magic versus science dichotomy'. She criticises the Tylorian view of magical thinking:

> "[T]he idea that magic is a primitive substitute for science is particularly nonsensical in any analysis of these magicians, all of whom are thoroughly familiar with scientific modes of thinking and acting, and some of whom are scientists themselves."

The Tylorian view is that people formerly explained natural phenomena as the work of supernatural beings; this view strongly influenced many other theorists such as J.G. Frazer. Tylor's view also presupposes that the sole function of myth is explanatory, and that mythological explanations are always unscientific.[132] However, many contemporary Pagans enthusiastically embrace the scientific

---

[129] Frisk, T. (1997) 'Paganism, Magic, and the Control of Nature.' *Trumpeter: Journal of Ecosophy*, 14 (4). [online] Available from:
http://trumpeter.athabascau.ca/index.php/trumpet/article/viewFile/169/206
[130] Luhrmann, T. (1989) *Persuasions of the Witch's Craft: Ritual Magic in Contemporary England.* Cambridge, MA: Harvard University Press.page 12
[131] Rountree, K. (2003) 'How Magic Works: New Zealand Feminist Witches' Theories of Ritual Action.' *Anthropology of Consciousness*, 13(1), pp. 42-60.
[132] Segal, R. A. (1999) Theorizing about myth. Amherst: University of Massachusetts Press.page 20

worldview, yet still enjoy mythology as metaphor; the function of myth is to re-enchant the world, not to explain it.[133] Faye Ringel notes that some Pagans are interested in science fiction, and discusses the literary sources which interested them in Paganism (which also included a hefty proportion of fantasy fiction).[134] However, interest in science does not preclude non-scientific ideas, and Pagans often espouse concepts which many scientists would regard as incompatible with science. These ideas are, however, arrived at by a gradual process, rather than a sudden revelation, as Luhrmann points out:

> "[P]eople entered magic with a dim notion that it involved a different, and science-like, theory of reality. They soon got involved with a range of spiritual and emotional experience to which the ideas were largely irrelevant, and they came to treat their practice like a religion – in that they spoke of gods and spiritual experience – rather than like a theory-laden science, and to value it more for its spiritual, symbolic experiences than for the truth of its magical theory."[135]

The Pagan revival

As the Pagan revival has emerged from the occult revival, which occurred in the era of science and capitalism,[136] Pagans seek to negotiate their own meanings and values within the context of consumer culture[137] and the rational-scientific worldview.[138]

Many Pagans are scientists or are interested in science; Margot Adler,[139] a Pagan journalist and author who carried out an extensive survey of Pagan beliefs and lifestyles, found that 35 out of a sample of 193 people had science-related jobs. Similarly, I noticed, in 2003, 2004 and 2005 that the majority of student members of the University of Bristol Pagan and Earth Religions Society were studying science subjects (27 out of 30 one year, and 30 out of 33 the following year).

Perhaps because of the number of Pagans interested in science, many Pagan

---

[133] Harvey, G. (1997) *Contemporary Paganism: Listening People, Speaking Earth*. New York: New York University Press.page 174

[134] Ringel, F. (1994) 'New England Neo-Pagans: Medievalism, Fantasy, Religion.' *Journal of American Culture*, 17(3) pp. 65-68. [online] Available from Ebscohost: Academic Search Elite, AN 9501170957.

[135] Luhrmann, T. (1989) Persuasions of the Witch's Craft: Ritual Magic in Contemporary England. Cambridge, MA: Harvard University Press.   page 10

[136] Ibid, page 279

[137] Coco, A., and Woodward, I. (2007) 'Discourses of Authenticity Within a Pagan Community: The Emergence of the "Fluffy Bunny" Sanction.' Journal of Contemporary Ethnography, Vol. 36(5), pp. 479-504 [online] Available from: SAGE Publications http://jce.sagepub.com/cgi/content/refs/36/5/479 DOI: 10.1177/0891241606293160

[138] Luhrmann, T. (1989) Persuasions of the Witch's Craft: Ritual Magic in Contemporary England. Cambridge, MA: Harvard University Press, page 272

[139] Adler, M. (1986) *Drawing Down the Moon: Witches, Druids, Goddess-Worshippers, and Other Pagans in America Today*. Boston: Beacon Press. page 446

meditations 'resemble a sensible marriage between science and sacrality'.[140] However, some people would characterise all religion as irrational, because

> "[T]he willingness to accept some kind of "revelation" as a legitimate source of knowledge creates a fatal gap in the barricades that ought to be maintained against irrationality as such."[141]

It seems to me that this includes an assumption that such a barricade ought to be maintained, and that all religion is revelatory, but because the scientific discourse values rationality, it seems that many scientists see a conflict between holding 'irrational' views and 'scientific' views. Pagans are generally non-dogmatic,[142] but we do make claims that many scientists would consider irrational, or non-empirical. However, much of the discourse around this issue seems to conflate empiricism with rationalism; for example the BBC pages on atheism state that:

> "Rationalism is an approach to life based on reason and evidence.
>
> Rationalism encourages ethical and philosophical ideas that can be tested by experience and rejects authority that cannot be proved by experience."[143]

This conflation is ironic, since rationalism often appeals to innate ideas,[144] whereas empiricism holds that we are born with a 'blank slate'.[145] Empiricism is the idea that "truth arises from reflection within the mind on what the human faculties experience through sense perception";[146] in contrast, rationalism is the belief that 'all truth has its origins in human thought, unaided by any form of supernatural intervention or an appeal to the experience of the senses'.[147]

So how do Pagans reconcile our views with an interest in science? Luhrmann[148] characterises magic as "the romantic rationalist's religion"; it satisfies the romantic's yearning for meaning and magic in the world without violating the rationalist's distrust of belief and authority. The magicians in her study hold that truth is subjective and each person has a unique perspective on the world, which

---

[140] Harris, G. (2005) 'Pagan Involvement in the Interfaith Movement, Exclusions, Dualities, and Contributions'. *Crosscurrents*. [online] Available from Ebscohost: Academic Search Premier, AN 16501005.

[141] Levitt, N. (2007) 'What a Friend We Have in Dawkins.' *Skeptic*, 13(2), pp. 48-51. [online] Available from Ebscohost: Academic Search Premier, AN 25486037.

[142] Adler, M. (1986) *Drawing Down the Moon: Witches, Druids, Goddess-Worshippers, and Other Pagans in America Today*. Boston: Beacon Press. page 13

[143] BBC (2006) 'Atheism.' Religion and Ethics. BBC. [online] Available from: http://www.bbc.co.uk/religion/religions/atheism/types/rationalism.shtml

[144] McGrath, A. E. (1999) *Science and Religion: An Introduction*. Oxford: Blackwell Publishing.page 58

[145] Porter, R. (2001) *Enlightenment: Britain and the Creation of the Modern World*. Harmondsworth: Penguin.pp 60-61

[146] McGrath, A. E. (1999) *Science and Religion: An Introduction*. Oxford: Blackwell Publishing.page 62

[147] Ibid, page 58

[148] Luhrmann, T. (1989) *Persuasions of the Witch's Craft: Ritual Magic in Contemporary England*. Cambridge, MA: Harvard University Press.pp 337-343

may be a total reality for them, but is different from others' perceptions; this is seen as good, because whatever the ultimate reality may be, it is infinitely complex and varied. Magicians (including Wiccans) tend to be ambivalent about the reality of magic:

> "The first books that newcomers will buy are full of intellectual vacillation, asserting the claim that the magical forces are clear and effective alongside a justification of the practice even if the claims should prove to be false."[149]

This ambivalent attitude to belief may help to explain why many Pagans do not pass their religion on to their children, although we also feel that it is unethical to constrain another's will, and therefore wrong to indoctrinate children in a religion. This is confirmed by a 2005 survey by the Covenant of the Goddess (an American Pagan organisation), in which 49% of respondents indicated having no children, and of the remaining 51%, only 27% (i.e. approximately 13% of the total sample) said that they were bringing their children up as Pagans. 52% of those with children said they were bringing them up in a multi-faith environment; 9% said 'another faith'; and 12% said 'none'. Even those brought up as Pagans might not choose to practise a Pagan tradition as adults. This is interesting, as one of Dawkins' criticisms of religion[150] is that people indoctrinate their children into it; clearly this is not happening with Paganism.

However, the Pagan revival is a growing phenomenon, but what is driving this growth? Is it disillusionment with scientific materialism, or with mainstream religions? Is it a concern for ecology and interest in immanence and the divine feminine?

Lee[151] describes the New Age movement as drawing upon traditional beliefs such as ancient Eastern and pagan religions, in the hope of bringing about radical cultural change and rediscovering the holistic dimension of human experience. By contrast, Letcher[152] points out that much of the Pagan revival draws on feminist critiques of scientific hegemony. However, whilst contemporary Pagans are sometimes critical of scientific materialism, they do not dismiss rationality and empiricism, and the Pagan revival is often playful, ironic, sceptical and self-mocking.[153]

The Pagan revival is a bricolage of individual choices, which can yet be identified as Pagan, because of a shared ethos.[154] Bregman[155] notes that most

---

[149] Ibid, pp 341-342

[150] Dawkins, R. (2006) *The God Delusion*. London: Bantam Press.page 260

[151] Lee, R. L. M. (2003) 'The Re-enchantment of the Self: Western Spirituality, Asian Materialism'. *Journal of Contemporary Religion*, 18(3), pp. 351–367 [online] Available from Ebscohost: Academic Search Premier, AN 11234629.

[152] Letcher, A. (2003) '"Gaia told me to do it" - Resistance and the Idea of Nature within contemporary British Eco-Paganism.' *Ecotheology*, 8(1), pp. 61-84. [online] Available from Ebscohost: Academic Search Premier, AN 12446132. page 69

[153] Luhrmann, T. (1989) *Persuasions of the Witch's Craft: Ritual Magic in Contemporary England*. Cambridge, MA: Harvard University Press.page 356

[154] Letcher, A. (2003) '"Gaia told me to do it" - Resistance and the Idea of Nature within contemporary British Eco-Paganism.' *Ecotheology*, 8(1), pp. 61-84. [online] Available from

spiritualities in a secularised context are characterised by eclecticism; people are free to pick and choose because of the declining authority of religion.

One of the key themes of the Pagan revival is our relationship with Nature, which also draws on some older ideas such as reading the book of Nature, which can be traced back to the Renaissance,[156] the roots of the Pagan revival in the Enlightenment, and the upsurge of interest in the occult and Nature occasioned by Romanticism. Another core idea is the authority of the self, which has its roots in conflicts of authority which go back to the early modern period. These streams have all fed into Pagan culture. Debates about the relationship of Christianity and science can also spill over into Pagan discourse, such as the assertion that most educated people are atheists, and discussions about the nature of reality.

Discursive positions

The science and religion debate has elicited various discursive positions from those engaged in it. The NOMA (non-overlapping magisteria) position, put forward by Stephen Jay Gould, is that science and religion deal with two different domains, and therefore share no common ground for either agreement or argument; science deals with empirical matters and religion deals with 'questions of ultimate meaning'.[157] Dawkins disagrees with NOMA because he argues that a universe with a creator deity would be a very different place to a universe without one, and therefore discussion of this does fall within the domain of science.[158] The POMA (partially overlapping magisteria) position is that there is some overlap, and that they are two complementary ways of viewing the world[159]. Naturalists argue that only the physical realm exists, and phenomena such as consciousness are emergent properties of complex biological systems.[160] Theists are believers in God – usually the God of the Abrahamic faiths, since this debate is primarily framed in terms of the conflict between science and Christianity.[161] Atheists are those who do not believe in any deity, though Dawkins[162] identifies seven possible positions between strong atheism and strong theism, with agnosticism in the middle. According to the British Humanist Association,[163] humanists celebrate humanity and human potential, and are 'ethically concerned but non-religious'.

Ebscohost: Academic Search Premier, AN 12446132. page 68

[155] Bregman, L. (2006) 'Spirituality: a glowing and useful term in search of a meaning.' *Omega*, 53(1-2), pp. 5-26. [online] Available from Ebscohost: Academic Search Premier, AN 21808441.

[156] Porter, R. (2001) *Enlightenment: Britain and the Creation of the Modern World.* Harmondsworth: Penguin.

[157] McGrath, A. E. (2007) *The Dawkins Delusion?* London: SPCK.

[158] Dawkins, R. (2006) *The God Delusion.* London: Bantam Press.page 55

[159] McGrath, A. E. (2007) *The Dawkins Delusion?* London: SPCK. Page 19

[160] Naturalism.org (2001) 'Spirituality Without Faith.' *The Centre for Naturalism.* [online] Available from http://www.naturalism.org/spiritual.htm

[161] Dawkins, R. (2006) *The God Delusion.* London: Bantam Press.page 18

[162] Ibid, page 50

[163] British Humanist Association (undated), 'About the BHA'. [online] Available from: http://www.humanism.org.uk/site/cms/contentChapterView.asp?chapter=333

Other possible discursive positions on science and religion include deep ecology, the view that the human order is not separate from the natural order, which implies that all life is sacred. [164] This is similar to the animism proposed by Graham Harvey, who advocates an embodied awareness and 'listening neighbourliness' towards other species.[165] The Gaia Hypothesis goes further than this, arguing that the entire planet is such a complex system that it should be regarded as a living organism.[166] Both of these views can be found in Pagan views of relationship with Nature.

Pagans' relationship with Nature

One of the key factors in the increasing popularity of Paganism is the rise of environmentalism and feminism. In the 1970s, James Lovelock formulated the Gaia Hypothesis, and Oberon Zell formulated Gaea Theology. Many Pagan writers became very interested in the Gaia Hypothesis, and popularised it among Pagans as evidence for the Goddess.

However, the Gaia Hypothesis does not make any mention of the self-regulatory system of the planet being conscious, though it does refer to the Earth as a living system.[167] Nevertheless, Lovelock flirted with Goddess religion, vacillating over whether to court the acceptance of the scientific community by denying that he viewed Gaia as a conscious entity, or whether to relax and enjoy the poetic imagery of the Goddess,[168] so it seems entirely understandable that many Pagans might assume that he was talking about a living entity. Otter Zell (a prominent American Pagan) entered into correspondence with James Lovelock, comparing their views.[169] Starting in 1971, Zell had already written a series of articles proposing the idea that the aim of life on earth was to progress towards 'total telepathic union' (an idea borrowed from Teilhard de Chardin), the awakening of planetary consciousness as the organism called Gaea; Lovelock's hypothesis seemed to fit neatly into Zell's ideas. Harvey[170] says that "the Gaia hypothesis is particularly attractive to Pagans". He says that, whatever scientists may have intended by attaching the name of a goddess to their hypothesis, the

---

[164] Livingstone, D. N. (2002) 'Ecology and the Evironment.' In: Ferngren, G. B., *Science & Religion: a historical introduction*. Baltimore and London: Johns Hopkins University Press.page 347

[165] Harvey, G. (1997) *Contemporary Paganism: Listening People, Speaking Earth*. New York: New York University Press.page 141

[166] Livingstone, D. N. (2002) 'Ecology and the Evironment.' In: Ferngren, G. B., *Science & Religion: a historical introduction*. Baltimore and London: Johns Hopkins University Press.page 347

[167] Harvey, G. (1997) *Contemporary Paganism: Listening People, Speaking Earth*. New York: New York University Press.page 146

[168] Hutton, R.E. (1999) *The Triumph of the Moon: A history of modern Pagan witchcraft*. Oxford: Oxford University Press. pp 352-354

[169] Adler, M. (1986) *Drawing Down the Moon: Witches, Druids, Goddess-Worshippers, and Other Pagans in America Today*. Boston: Beacon Press. page 303

[170] Harvey, G. (1997) *Contemporary Paganism: Listening People, Speaking Earth*. New York: New York University Press.page 145

imagery of the Earth as a living organism or self-regulatory system resonates strongly with ecologically-minded Pagans. The link between the Gaia Hypothesis and Goddess religion was also suggested by Farrar and Farrar in *The Witches' Goddess: the feminine principle of divinity*, a widely-read book among Pagans.

The idea of reading 'the book of Nature' goes back to Renaissance natural philosophy, and the writings of Francis Bacon[171] and Thomas Tymme,[172] and descends to us via the nineteenth-century Transcendentalism of Thoreau and Emerson, which advocated coming closer to the Divine through a closer relationship with nature, in which it was held to be immanent[173] (Hutton, 1999: 351). Similarly, Carl Sagan (1994) said that:

> "A religion, old or new, that stressed the magnificence of the Universe as revealed by modern science might be able to draw forth reserves of reverence and awe hardly tapped by the conventional faiths. Sooner or later, such a religion will emerge."[174]

Both Paganism and pantheism have been claimed to be that religion. Indeed, many Pagan writers draw on scientific imagery to express spiritual insights. For example, Landstreet regards the lightning striking the primordial waters (an image she drew from a science text) as the primary polarity, of which the Wiccan Great Rite is an echo or representation; here she is clearly getting inspiration from science. She is, however, strongly critical of the desacralised worldview of scientific materialism, pointing out that it is specific to our culture, and ultimately emergent from the Christian worldview, because first the Divine was displaced to a force beyond the world, and then regarded as non-existent, whereas she regards it as immanent.

A conflict of authority?

Since we are living in a post-Enlightenment, scientific age, Chas Clifton argues, we should be using science as the basis of our spirituality and our connection with nature:

> "If you would practice "nature religion" or "earth-centered spirituality," learn where you are on the earth and learn the songs of that place, the song of water and the song of wind. Yes, Western science is flawed, but it is our way of knowing, so take what it offers: its taxonomy, its lists, its naming. Start there--then build a richer spirituality from that point."

Clifton's Pagan views do not seem to conflict with science, since he is advocating engagement with nature through science. Although he seems oriented towards according authority to science here, he seems to be advocating moving

---

[171] Porter, R. (2001) *Enlightenment: Britain and the Creation of the Modern World*. Harmondsworth: Penguin.page 56
[172] Debus, Allen George (1978), *Man and Nature in the Renaissance (Cambridge Studies in the History of Science)*, page 14
[173] Hutton, R.E. (1999) *The Triumph of the Moon: A history of modern Pagan witchcraft*. Oxford: Oxford University Press. page 351
[174] Sagan, C. (1994) *Pale Blue Dot: A Vision of the Human Future in Space*. Ballantine Books.

beyond it into the metaphorical; accepting the current status quo, but seeking to build something from it.

Starhawk does not think there is any conflict between Paganism and science; in her 'On Faith' blog at *The Washington Post*, she writes:

> "From a Pagan point of view, there's no contradiction between religion and science. Our Goddess is immanent in the earth and the cycles of nature, and the more we understand about the earth, the deeper is our sense of awe and wonder. .... one of the spiritual stories I draw strength from is the story of evolution, the amazing and miraculous account of the earth's birth in fire, of life coming into being and overcoming crisis after crisis with creativity, invention and cooperation. This view of evolution draws heavily from the Gaia theories of James Lovelock and Lynn Margulis, that reveal the importance of cooperation and interdependence in evolution, not just competition."[175]

Starhawk expresses awe at the wonders revealed by science, and seeks to derive spiritual meaning from natural processes and thereby to re-enchant a scientific understanding of the world by using myth as metaphor. The metaphorical and symbolic nature of religious and spiritual explanations is one that is constantly emphasised in Pagan writing.

Does magic work?

Many Pagans do not find their magical beliefs to be incompatible with science. Chris Keating, a Wiccan physicist, writes:

> "Magic is part of Wicca, but the term 'magic' is very different in Wiccan usage than in common usage. The everyday use of the word means something supernatural, beyond the realm of science. The Wiccan usage is completely opposite. Magic in this usage means the use of the natural forces, many of which are explained by science and others that science may still be investigating."[176]

Keating appears to think that all of magic will one day be explained by science, in the sense that magic makes use of natural forces, some of which are already understood by science, and some of which are still being investigated. This passage corresponds to the *'realist'* position identified by Luhrmann; it is trying to justify magic as a scientific endeavour. As Arthur C. Clarke famously said, "Any sufficiently advanced technology is indistinguishable from magic".[177] Keating's view suggests that the religio-magical discourse of Wicca overlaps with science, and will eventually merge with it.

---

[175] Starhawk (2007) 'Pagans embrace science.' [online] Available from: *On Faith*, http://newsweek.washingtonpost.com/onfaith/starhawk/2007/10/pagans_embrace_science.htm

[176] Keating, C. (2008) 'The Wiccan What?' *The Wiccan Scientist* (blog) [online] Available from: http://thewiccanscientist.blogspot.com/2008/02/wiccan-what.html

[177] Collins, G.P. (2008) 'Remembering Sir Arthur C. Clarke, 1917-2008. Graham Collins reflects on meeting the famous author in New York City'. *Scientific American*. http://www.sciam.com/article.cfm?id=remembering-sir-arthur-c

Similarly, on a 'Pagan Science' forum on PaganSpace.net, a small group of Pagans who are interested in science, or who are scientists, discussed whether or not the two worldviews are in conflict; the majority view was that they are complementary, or even converging. The first contributor says that 'in many ways, psychology confirms paganism, magic, and our beliefs'. [178]

Another contributor suggested that science and magic are overlapping and converging; possibly alluding to the magical origins of science in the Renaissance, when science and magic were both seen as attempts to connect with the Divine, and alchemy and chemistry were a single discipline.[179] Physics and chaos theory are here seen as the new magic, and the world is re-enchanted by their mysterious qualities.

A non-theist Pagan on PaganSpace.net indicates that there is no conflict for her, and agrees that

> "Magic and science are one and the same. But, what was once magic is now science because of logical explanations with evidence to back it up."[180]

Her position seems broadly the same as Naturalism. Another, who introduces herself as 'just a plain old Pagan Witch', regards science and Pagan magic as complementary. A further contributor agrees, but qualifies this by adding, 'if both sides just shut up and get along'. This implies that they are non-overlapping magisteria (Luhrmann's 'two worlds' position), because it implies that they can only co-exist if they do not communicate with each other, because their languages are mutually incomprehensible.

However, the majority saw science and magic as complementary ways of viewing the world, and agreed that magic (however it is defined) does work. The idea of complementarity is similar to Luhrmann's 'metaphorical' model, where magical views are regarded as metaphors for scientific understanding.[181] The relativist view, by contrast, posits that magical and scientific views are both regarded as metaphors for an unknowable underlying reality.[182]

The nature of reality

Harvey[183] says that Pagans are "usually happy to assent to scientific accounts

---

[178] PaganSpace.net (2007) 'Who are we?' *Pagans and science.* [online] Available from http://www.paganspace.net/group/paganscience/forum/topic/show?id=1342861%3ATo pic%3A90790

[179] Debus, Allen George (1978), *Man and Nature in the Renaissance (Cambridge Studies in the History of Science),* page 14-16

[180] PaganSpace.net (2007) 'Who are we?' *Pagans and science.* [online] Available from http://www.paganspace.net/group/paganscience/forum/topic/show?id=1342861%3ATo pic%3A90790

[181] Luhrmann, T. (1989) *Persuasions of the Witch's Craft: Ritual Magic in Contemporary England.* Cambridge, MA: Harvard University Press.page 293

[182] Ibid, page 290

[183] Harvey, G. (1997) *Contemporary Paganism: Listening People, Speaking Earth.* New York: New York University Press.page 145

of the origins of life" and points out that Pagan deities, because they are immanent in nature, are "far too involved and implicated in the world to be responsible for its creation". He says that "Pagans do not entertain dogmas that assert a divine first cause of the cosmos"; perhaps seeking to present Paganism as non-dogmatic and not in conflict with science. He observes that that "even Pagan theologies in which there is a transcendent deity do not dissent from scientific narratives which claim to explain the origins of time and space"; instead they usually regard creation myths as metaphorical. This is a cautious and partial re-enchantment of the world, where scientific explanations are still seen as important, and spiritual interpretations are seen as metaphorical.

Harvey[184] argues that Paganism is experimental, and that Pagans are engaged in a search for *'what works'* (again, a use of semi-scientific language to validate Pagan practices, which tends to support the secularisation hypothesis that authority is vested in science and not religion).

If both science and Paganism are looking at nature, and Paganism is concerned with the divine immanent in Nature, and science is concerned with the physical properties of nature, then their domains must overlap. So they cannot be 'non-overlapping magisteria'. Tania Luhrmann[185] found that most magicians view other planes as entangled with the physical universe, or as different ways of viewing the same phenomena.

Peter Berger, theorist of secularisation and re-enchantment, predicted that 'cosmology becomes psychology';[186] this seems to be confirmed by the metaphorical views of many Pagans and Wiccans, and the popularity of Jungian terminology among magicians.[187] Instead of mythology being taken literally, it becomes a representation of internal states; this perhaps happens as a result of there being many mythological cosmologies available to contemporary Pagans, but also because we accept the scientific account of cosmology.

The attempt to make magical and spiritual discourse seem scientific has a long pedigree. It began in the 1840s and 1850s with spiritualism, and talk of 'odyllic force' and 'electro-biology'. Nowadays it is usual to claim that magic works because of quantum mechanics, which sounds impressive, but the truth is, we just don't know.

The rise of occult discourse continued in the 1870s with Theosophy and the Hermetic Order of the Golden Dawn, and the foundation of the Society for Psychical Research. Much of the magical discourse in use today can be traced back to these organisations, because 'modern magic first emerged in a world torn by the

---

[184] Ibid, page 124

[185] Luhrmann, T. (1989) *Persuasions of the Witch's Craft: Ritual Magic in Contemporary England.* Cambridge, MA: Harvard University Press.pp 274-276

[186] cited in Gallagher, E.V. (1994) 'A Religion without Converts? Becoming a Neo-Pagan'. *Journal of the American Academy of Religion*, 62(3), pp. 851-867. [online] Available from JSTOR

[187] Luhrmann, T. (1989) *Persuasions of the Witch's Craft: Ritual Magic in Contemporary England.* Cambridge, MA: Harvard University Press. page 281

struggles between science and religion'.[188] This could be argued to be the first stirrings of re-enchantment in a world disenchanted by the Reformation, the Enlightenment, and scientific rationalism. The next important development was the rise of Jungian psychoanalysis, with its concept of the collective unconscious, which is reified in magical discourse and regarded as connected with the individual unconscious as the sea is connected to a lagoon by a submerged channel. The significant feature of the collective unconscious for magicians is that it is not subject to rational laws, and is therefore beyond rational apprehension;[189] it can only be experienced. However, magicians still feel the need to justify their views to sceptics, so clearly do not wish to be seen as wholly irrational. The problem of justifying beliefs to sceptics is also experienced by Christian apologists, and Luhrmann finds magicians' arguments to be very similar.[190] However, if the theoretical constructs employed are very similar, the language used to describe them is somewhat different.

Partridge[191] suggests that the language used to express spirituality is evolving and will continue to evolve; increasingly, he says, 'Westerners are using the language of occulture to articulate significant religious experience and belief'. Such language includes terms like 'universal consciousness', 'life force' and 'reincarnation' rather than traditional, Christian language such as salvation and atonement. Partridge[192] defines occulture as "the spiritual/mythic/paranormal background knowledge that informs the plausibility structures of Westerners" and says that it "tends to be antagonistic to scientism, secularism and views that dismiss the significance of the sacred".

Indeed, although Pagans are very positive about sciences such as astronomy and physics and biology, they are often critical of science, technology, engineering, and medicine for despoiling the natural world, and using allopathic techniques to fight disease.

Starhawk, in her widely-read book *The Spiral Dance*, whilst acknowledging the inspirational possibilities of science and wanting Paganism to be grounded in science, says that

> "Spirituality leaps where science cannot yet follow, because science must always test and measure, and much of reality and human experience is immeasurable. Without discarding science, we can recognise its limitations. There are many modes of consciousness which have not been validated by Western scientific rationalism, in particular what I call "starlight awareness", the holistic, intuitive mode of perception of the right hemisphere of our brains. As a culture, we are experiencing a turn toward the intuitive, the psychic, which have

---

[188] Luhrmann, T. (1989) *Persuasions of the Witch's Craft: Ritual Magic in Contemporary England.* Cambridge, MA: Harvard University Press. Page 279

[189] Ibid

[190] Ibid, pp 297-300

[191] Partridge, C. (2004) *The Re-enchantment of the West, Volume 1: Alternative Spiritualities, Sacralization, Popular Culture and Occulture.* London and New York: T & T Clarkpage 186

[192] Ibid, page 187

been denied for so long."

Starhawk is here espousing the position that if scientists would embrace more holistic methods, they could discover the imaginal realms of which Pagans speak. Some scientists seem to be cautiously exploring less materialist approaches, so that it is even possible to speak of the *'re-enchantment of science'*.[193]

Postmodern perspectives also undermine the hegemony of scientific rationalism; the changes during the twentieth century in quantum mechanics, ecology, anthropology and other sciences mean that the scientist is now an involved participant rather than an external observer.[194] Pickstone[195] explores the decline in the dominance and confidence of science, technology and medicine during the twentieth century. He points out that feminist, minority ethnic, ecological and other counter-cultural critiques have dislodged science from its position of authority. As the impact of Einstein's General Theory of Relativity became apparent, the confidence in science expressed at the beginning of the twentieth century began to crumble, and it was realised that the notion of rational *a priori* knowledge as fixed for all time would have to be dropped.[196] Kuhn also identifies Einstein's theory as a paradigm shift which changed the rules implicit in scientific discourse about what constituted a valid or correct solution to a given scientific problem.[197] This relativised view gave rise to 'problems and questions concerning the ultimate rationality of the scientific enterprise' and demonstrated that a particular piece of knowledge might be viewed entirely differently in one paradigm than another.[198] This shows that knowledge was discursively and socially constructed, which arguably makes it possible for alternative and relativised interpretations of science to gain credence.

The objectivity or otherwise of scientific knowledge has been hotly contested among scientists in the debate between realists and antirealists.[199] There are a number of realist positions, including viewing reality as objectively knowable, regarding the terms of scientific theories as mapping onto some objective referent in the phenomenon they describe, and complementarity, which 'holds that different exclusive experimental arrangements produce phenomena which are interpreted as providing "complementary information" about "the same

---

[193] Whitehead, C. (1998) 'The Re-enchantment of Science'. *Anthropology Today*, 14(5), pp 20-21. [online] Available from JSTOR

[194] Toulmin, S. (1982) 'The Construal of Reality: Criticism in Modern and Postmodern Science'. *Critical Inquiry*, 9 (1), The Politics of Interpretation, pp. 93-111 [online] Available from: http://www.jstor.org/stable/1343275   page 97

[195] Pickstone, J. V. (2000) *Ways of knowing: A new history of science, technology and medicine.* Manchester: Manchester University Press.pp 52-53

[196] Friedman, M (2002) 'Kant, Kuhn, and the Rationality of Science.' Philosophy of Science, 69(2), pp. 171-190 [online] Available from: http://www.jstor.org/stable/3080974 page 174

[197] Ibid, page 181

[198] Ibid, page 182

[199] Muller, A. and Livingston, P. (1995) 'Realism/Anti-Realism: A Debate'. *Cultural Critique*, No. 30, *The Politics of Systems and Environments*, Part I, pp. 15-32 [online] Available from: http://www.jstor.org/stable/1354431 page 16

object'".[200] This implies that the object cannot necessarily be directly apprehended, but the same object persists from one experiment to the next, allowing the experimenter to discover ore about it. The idea of complementarity, dealing with different perspectives on phenomena, may have influenced Pagan discursive constructions. Toulmin writes:

> "[N]o biological event can ever be viewed as a phenomenon of one and only one kind. On the contrary, every such event has at least four distinct aspects, and biologists ask at least four kinds of questions about it. ... No one of the resulting accounts of the event will be biologically exhaustive. But, taken together, biochemical, physiological, developmental, and evolutionary accounts give us complementary interpretations which between them show us what biology has to teach us about the event in question."[201]

In *The Spiral Dance*, Starhawk describes metaphors as 'separate lights beaming at the same spot' – a clear parallel to the idea of complementarity.

There are also multiple antirealist positions, including empiricist and constructivist.[202] Empiricist antirealists hold that only what is observable is knowable;[203] constructivist antirealists hold that knowledge is socially constructed.[204] It is also essential to distinguish between 'epistemological anti-realism about scientific theories' (the view that scientific knowledge is socially constructed) and 'ontological anti-realism about scientific entities' (the view that reality itself is a construct)[205]. Indeed, both feminists and social constructionists have pointed out that science is knowledge that is culturally situated and neither value-free nor objective;[206] some contemporary Pagans seem to have absorbed this critique and used it to justify their worldview.[207] However, this does not completely

[200] Folse, H.J. (1986) 'Niels Bohr, Complementarity, and Realism'. Proceedings of the Biennial Meeting of the Philosophy of Science Association, 1, pp. 96-104 [online] Available from:
http://www.jstor.org/stable/193111 page 96
[201] Toulmin, S. (1982) 'The Construal of Reality: Criticism in Modern and Postmodern Science'. *Critical Inquiry*, 9 (1), *The Politics of Interpretation*, pp. 93-111 [online] Available from: http://www.jstor.org/stable/1343275   page 98
[202] Godfrey-Smith, P. (2002) 'Dewey on Naturalism, Realism and Science.' *Philosophy of Science*, 69 (3), Supplement: Proceedings of the 2000 Biennial Meeting of the Philosophy of Science Association. Part II: Symposia Papers, pp. S25 -S35 [online] Available from: http://www.jstor.org/stable/3081079
[203] Alspector-Kelly, M. (2001) 'Should the Empiricist Be a Constructive Empiricist?' *Philosophy of Science*, 68 (4), pp. 413-431 [online] Available from:
http://www.jstor.org/stable/3081045   page 414
[204] Demeritt, D. (1996) 'Social Theory and the Reconstruction of Science and Geography' *Transactions of the Institute of British Geographers*, New Series, 21 (3), pp. 484-503 [online] Available from: http://www.jstor.org/stable/622593   page 485
[205] Ibid, page 486
[206] Haraway, D. (1988) 'Situated Knowledges: The Science Question in Feminism and the Privilege of Partial Perspective.' *Feminist Studies*, 14(3), pp. 575-599 [online] Available from: http://www.jstor.org/stable/3178066   page 578
[207] Blain, Jenny and Wallis, Robert (2006), 'A Live Issue: Ancestors, Archaeologists and the

relativise all truth-claims in the manner hoped for by some Pagans, or claimed by some rationalists as a critique of post-modernism.[208]

The process has come full circle; science disenchanted nature, but claimed to have objective truth; but recent thought has concluded that there is no objectivity in science, so now even science is disenchanted.[209] Although scientists might protest that the conclusions of science are at least arrived at by a process of experimentation and peer review, and that they are prepared to change their minds if compelling evidence to the contrary is presented,[210] this would be something of an over-simplification of the post-modernist case, which is that scientific discourses construct reality just as much as other discourses,[211] and that there are numerous discourse positions within science.

The Pagan revival, situated as it is in the context of secularisation and re-enchantment,[212] capitalism and consumerism,[213] and post-modernism,[214] has had to come to terms with competing worldviews, including scientific rationalism, either by relativising them, or including them in its worldview. It may be the emerging new paradigm; or it may form only a small part of a broader tapestry of 'occulture'.

Science itself is not immune to borrowing its terminology, and perhaps its conceptual framework, from theistic discourse. It speaks of laws governing the cosmos, and the very notion of laws seems to presuppose the existence of an external cosmic lawgiver;[215] scientists sometimes write as if natural selection were an external agent acting to cause evolution, yet it is a product of the complex system of nature.[216] Discourse analysis of science is only now beginning to unravel

---

"Reburial Issue" in Britain.' Association of Polytheist Traditions [online] available from: http://www.manygods.org.uk/articles/essays/reburial.html

[208] Fish, S. (2008) 'French Theory in America.' *New York Times*, April 6, 2008. [online] available from: http://fish.blogs.nytimes.com/2008/04/06/french-theory-in-america/

[209] Griffin, D. R. (1988) *The Reenchantment of Science: Postmodern Proposals*. Albany: SUNY Press

[210] Dawkins, R. (2006) *The God Delusion*. London: Bantam Press.page 283

[211] Pickstone, J. V. (2000) *Ways of knowing: A new history of science, technology and medicine*. Manchester: Manchester University Press.page 58

[212] Partridge, C. (2004) *The Re-enchantment of the West, Volume 1: Alternative Spiritualities, Sacralization, Popular Culture and Occulture*. London and New York: T & T Clarkpp 9-59

[213] Coco, A., and Woodward, I. (2007) 'Discourses of Authenticity Within a Pagan Community: The Emergence of the "Fluffy Bunny" Sanction.' *Journal of Contemporary Ethnography*, Vol. 36(5), pp. 479-504 [online] Available from: SAGE Publications http://jce.sagepub.com/cgi/content/refs/36/5/479 DOI: 10.1177/0891241606293160 page 479

[214] Connelly, P. (1994) 'Towards a Postmodern Paganism.' [online] Available from: http://www.darc.org/connelly/pagan1.html

[215] Haila, Y., and Dyke, C. (2006) *How Nature Speaks: The Dynamics of the Human Ecological Condition*. Durham, NC: Duke University Press. [online] Available from: http://books.google.co.uk/books?id=MgUGA5T2ADQC   page 72

[216] Rayner, A. D. M. (2003) 'Inclusional Science - From Artefact to Natural Creativity' [online] Available from http://people.bath.ac.uk/bssadmr/inclusionality/inclusionalscience.htm

these underlying questions and concepts. Science is now less widely regarded as a panacea for the ills of humanity, and no longer enjoys absolute authority. However, many people find scientific discoveries and insights inspiring; accordingly, some Pagan authors have advocated using science as a source of spirituality.

Pagans are ambivalent about belief, and there is a complex interplay between concepts and experiences, theory and practice. Pagans are non-dogmatic and empirical; we are more concerned with *whether* a ritual or spell works than *how* it works, and we tend to be ambivalent about the practice of magic, justifying it sometimes as a psychologically beneficial but metaphorical practice, and sometimes as possibly being effective in the sense of getting results.[217]

It could also be said that Pagans have much for which to be grateful to science; as part of the process of secularisation that weakened the hegemony of Christianity in the West, the rise of science was one of the processes that made it possible to hold pagan and other heterodox views without suffering the fate of Giordano Bruno, the pantheistic scientist who was burnt at the stake in 1600 for his heretical views.

Science does not only come into conflict with traditional and conservative religious views; it sometimes also comes into conflict with politics, the wider culture, and popular 'common sense' worldviews;[218] indeed the promotion of the 'public understanding of science' has been with us since the 1980s,[219] implying that there is a need for science to be promoted and defended, not just from religion, but from general disinterest and misunderstanding. The idea of 'two cultures' was first formulated in the 1950s by C. P. Snow, who pointed out that there was mutual incomprehension between the arts and science, creating a cultural rift.[220] This situation still persists, and many people see art and science as incompatible, because art is believed to be based on the imagination, which is held to be irrational, and science is believed to be based on cognition, which is held to be rational. In reality, neither of these assumptions is necessarily true; and similar assumptions abound in popular discourse about the relationship between science and religion, for example the idea that 'science is the how, religion is the why'.[221] Another problem is that scientific accounts tend to express things cautiously, with many caveats and hesitancies, which is often taken as a sign of lack of authority.[222]

---

[217] Luhrmann, T. (1989) *Persuasions of the Witch's Craft: Ritual Magic in Contemporary England.* Cambridge, MA: Harvard University Press.page 335

[218] Cooper, Q. (2008) 'Material World: Hay-on-Wye Special'. *Radio 4.* 29.05.2008 [online] Available from:
http://downloads.bbc.co.uk/podcasts/radio4/material/material_20080529-1800.mp3

[219] Pickstone, J. V. (2000) *Ways of knowing: A new history of science, technology and medicine.* Manchester: Manchester University Press.page 195

[220] Ibid, page 193

[221] Starhawk (2007) 'Pagans embrace science.' [online] Available from: *On Faith,* http://newsweek.washingtonpost.com/onfaith/starhawk/2007/10/pagans_embrace_scien ce.html

[222] Cooper, Q. (2008) 'Material World: Hay-on-Wye Special'. *Radio 4.* 29.05.2008 [online] Available from:

This is not in conflict with the empiricist attitudes at the heart of Paganism, which values experience over ideas, even if its methods are not as rigorous as those of science.

Pagans generally do see our beliefs as compatible with science, and playfully create a personal bricolage of meaning, allowing them to view the world as enchanted without ceding authority to either science or religion, and retaining a certain amount of scepticism. Most Pagans combine the 'secular' values of tolerance and inclusivity with a view of Nature (including ourselves) as sacred. Pagan discourse is generally oriented towards co-operation with science, as most Pagans want to present ourselves as reasonable and tolerant. Paganism seems potentially to be Carl Sagan's hypothetical religion,[223] stressing 'the magnificence of the Universe as revealed by modern science'. Most Pagans regard cosmology as metaphor,[224] using it as a poetic way of relating to the natural world.[225]

Practical: science quarters

Instead of calling the quarters with the usual classical elements, try it with the three states of matter plus energy and space-time. It is a very different feeling.

> Beings of the North, Powers of Solids,
> Drawing all things to yourself by the power of gravity,
> Bending space-time with your powerful mass
> You are solid, dependable, a place that we can rest against.
> With momentum you are unstoppable,
> With inertia you are unmovable,
> O crystal lattices locked in abstract patterns
> We cannot detect your subtle vibrations
> Or the space that you hold within you.
>
> Beings of the East, Powers of Gas
> You who create vast reservoirs of gas
> Beneath the frozen Siberian earth,
> From ancient forests pressed down
> Through aeons unimaginable.
> O Air that we breathe,
> Oxygen released by burning;
> Laughing gas, trickster miasma
> Gases that burn bright colours
> Helium that bestows high pitched tones

http://downloads.bbc.co.uk/podcasts/radio4/material/material_20080529-1800.mp3
[223] Sagan, C. (1994) *Pale Blue Dot: A Vision of the Human Future in Space*. Ballantine Books.
[224] Gallagher, E.V. (1994) 'A Religion without Converts? Becoming a Neo-Pagan'. *Journal of the American Academy of Religion*, 62(3), pp. 851-867. [online] Available from JSTOR. page 863
[225] Harvey, G. (1997) *Contemporary Paganism: Listening People, Speaking Earth*. New York: New York University Press.

The Five Noble Gases dancing in the void

Beings of the South, Powers of Energy
Bringers of flux, transformation and exchange
The whole spectrum of radiation:
X-rays, ultraviolet, visible light, infrared, microwaves, radio waves
The wild energy of lightning,
Only partly tamed as electricity
The curving embrace of the electromagnetic field
Catching the solar wind to make the aurora borealis
The fusion of hydrogen in the heart of the sun
The source of all fire, all light
For you we sing the body electric!

Beings of the West, Powers of Liquid,
Life-giving water, that forms so much of our bodies
All things may flow:
Rock flows as molten lava;
Molten metal fills the crucible
Liquid Nitrogen dances when scattered;
Mercury, quicksilver, dances
The blood flows around our bodies pumped by the heart
Flow is change and change is flow

Beings of the Centre, Powers of space-time
Curved mirror of darkness
Forming gravity wells,
Lenses that bend starlight
Your mysterious dark energy,
And dark matter, the prima material
Speak to us of the unknown.
The elegance of your geometry and the magic numbers
Call forth our sense of wonder
And the music of the spheres
Rings out through the numinous void.
Hail to thee, mysterious powers.

Visualisation – descent to the quantum realm

Bring to your mind's eye the texture of your skin, then cells, then molecules, then atoms, then electrons and neutrons and protons, then photons, then quarks, strangeness, charm, leptons, bosons. Imagine you are in the quantum realm.

Return via the same route in reverse, gradually returning to the scale of the everyday, starting in the quantum realm, then at the scale of photons, then electrons, neutrons and protons, then atoms, then molecules, then cells, then back to looking at the surface of your skin.

Meditation: experimentation

Close your eyes, and think of a time that you tried something new. Maybe the first time you rode a bike, or your first kiss, or the first time you tried a type of food that you were convinced you didn't like. Maybe it was the first time you tried a new spiritual practice: meditation, or visualisation, or a new ritual. Maybe it was when you did something scary, like capsizing a canoe or doing a parachute jump.

Try to remember how it felt before you did it. Were you scared, resisting, apprehensive, hesitant? Was there someone there to help you get over your fear? What did they do? Were they supportive and kind, or did they push you into it – being "cruel to be kind"?

Try to remember how it felt while you were doing it. When did fear change to pleasure? If it did… What kind of pleasure was it? Quiet satisfaction or wild exhilaration?

Now try to remember how it felt afterwards. Did you want to do it again? Did it make you more willing to try new things? Did it change how you felt about yourself? [pause]

Hold the memory of these feelings in your mind. When you are ready, open your eyes and return to the present and your companions.

Chapter Twelve

What is magic?

The art of causing change in consciousness in accordance with will

Most modern magical writers from Aleister Crowley onwards have affirmed that the primary purpose of magic is to change the practitioner, rather than the external world. It's also possible that having worked on the inner self, change will also be effected in the surrounding reality, either directly, or as a result of the change in consciousness of the practitioner, who is now empowered to go out and make the world a better place.

Will is a tricky concept — it can mean the individual will, or the divine will, or aligning the individual will with the divine will, depending on the perspective of the practitioner, and whether they are more left hand path or right-hand path.

The right-hand path has been defined as becoming one with the Divine (dissolving the ego), whereas the left-hand path has been defined as turning oneself into a deity (achieving apotheosis). I like these two definitions, as they go a long way to explaining what makes Paganism different from other religions.

Magic and ritual certainly work to transform the psyche of the practitioner; tried and tested techniques of initiation, meditation, visualisation, and working with archetypes do seem to have a beneficial effect.

Does magic have an effect on the external world?

Everybody has an anecdote where they did a healing and the recipient felt better; or they did a working for a job and got the job; but these are anecdotal evidence, and there's no way to prove that the ill person wouldn't have got better anyway, or the job seeker wouldn't have got the job anyway. However, even if these workings have no effect on external events, they make the participants in the healing or the spell feel better because they have done something to help. Incidentally, an ethical job spell should always include the proviso that if someone else needs the job even more, they should get it.

I went to a workshop on talismans once where the workshop leader pointed out that magic always follows the path of least resistance. So if you make a talisman for pregnancy but you're not actually having sex, then don't be too surprised if someone close to you gets pregnant instead. This suggests that caution is necessary in the preparation of talismans, in order to avoid "leakage" into someone else's life.

I have had many experiences which suggest that magic does have an effect on the external world, especially healing, but this is very much a subjective perception.

The gods help those who help themselves

In order for magic to work, you also need to be putting in effort on the mundane level. If you do a job spell but don't actually apply for any jobs, you probably won't get a job, no matter how good the spell was. Maybe the spell only works to give you extra confidence at the interview, but that is a good thing in itself. There's a Jewish story about a man who prays every day to God that he might win the lottery. Eventually an exasperated voice booms out from on high, "Meet me half-way already — buy a lottery ticket!"

Another important aspect of magic is not refusing to acknowledge results because they don't look quite like what you were expecting. I have seen people do spells and then turn down the results because they weren't *quite* right — even though they were better than their existing circumstances. There's a story about a man in the middle of a flood, who prays to God to save him. A boat comes by and offers him a lift, but he turns it down, saying, "No, God will put forth His hand to save me." Then two more boats come by, and he says the same. Finally a helicopter hovers overhead, but again he refuses help. Eventually he drowns. When he gets to heaven, he asks God, "Why didn't you save me?" And God replies, "I sent you three boats and a helicopter – what more did you want?"

How does magic work?

So if magic does effect change in external reality, how does it do that? This is usually the point at which people get a bit hand-wavy and start talking about quantum mechanics and "energies".

We exist within the Earth's electromagnetic field. Some people and animals are sensitive to fluctuations in this field. So it can affect us; and maybe we can affect it, or interact with it. Magical energy is presumably transmitted either via some hitherto unknown interaction between consciousness and the Earth's magnetic field; or via one of the seven dimensions that are enfolded within the usual four of space-time. Either way, science has so far mostly failed to verify extra-sensory perception and other psychic powers, so maybe there are no external effects when we do magic.

I was discussing this with a friend, and he said that the problem is, the more people try to use science to justify their belief in faeries and energies and the like, the more ridiculous it sounds. Most of the time, it's just a misuse of the scientific terms (especially if it involves the word quantum). As my friend said, it's one thing to say you saw a faery at the bottom of the garden, and quite another to claim that you have built a device for detecting faeries.

If magic works at all, it should be verifiable by science (though not necessarily by contemporary science, which focuses almost exclusively on the material aspects of reality). However, there are so many variables at play that it would be difficult to envisage a sufficiently objective experiment. Investigations into whether petitionary prayer (asking for stuff) works have pretty much concluded that it doesn't, so I don't hold out much hope for scientific confirmation of results magic.

However, whether or not magic affects external reality, magic, meditation, and prayer can work to transform the psyche, and are therefore still worthwhile practices to engage in. Other scientific experiments have shown that engaging in meditation and contemplative prayer changes the brainwave patterns of the practitioner and makes them calmer.

Energy

I think most Pagans are agreed that the divine and/or deities are immanent in the universe (the ones who don't think that are mostly atheists). I know this because I did a survey for my MA dissertation, and the vast majority of respondents agreed that the divine and/or deities are immanent in the universe; the rest didn't believe in deities at all. So whatever these energies are, they are inside the universe.

Many of my survey respondents also agreed that science will one day be able to describe all the phenomena experienced by Pagans and others. In my view, science describes the material aspect of the universe very well, but rather falls down when it comes to describing consciousness. Arthur C. Clarke once wrote that "Any sufficiently advanced technology looks like magic" (because we don't know how it works); Doctor Who (in his incarnation as Sylvester McCoy) once said that "Any sufficiently advanced magic looks like technology".

People often have experiences which suggest that some kind of spiritual phenomenon has occurred (though Pagans usually draw a distinction between unsubstantiated personal gnosis, and confirmed gnosis). They certainly wouldn't try to draw any broader conclusions about the world from their experience. They would come up with one or more hypotheses to explain the experience, but not insist on the truth of that interpretation of events. For instance, if I had a vision of a deity, it could be a projection from my unconscious mind; it could be a hallucination; or it could be the manifestation of an actual entity. I can choose any of those interpretations, but there's no need to try to convince others of its truth, or to found a religion based on my vision. If the vision instructed me to act contrary to my conscience, then I wouldn't obey it just because it claims to be a deity.

If there is any objective external reality to these manifestations, then how might it work? There is an electromagnetic field around the Earth, and around anything through which electric current flows, including anything that is alive. If the energy that many Pagans talk about is anything, then perhaps it is something to do with electromagnetism.

Scientists tell us that consciousness is an emergent property of complex systems. Humans are one such complex system. What if the Earth and its ecosystem was another such system? That would explain spirits of place. It has also been suggested that the universe itself is complex enough to give rise to mind.

Of course, all this is highly speculative and subjective. Scientists who are studying consciousness and complex systems have not reached any firm conclusions, it seems, but it is a very interesting area.

The trouble with a lot of Western thinking is that (since Descartes) we divide everything between spirit and matter. In Eastern thought, there is no such distinction. Spirit is a subtler form of matter; matter is a denser form of spirit. Eastern philosophy affirms that matter is illusory – and once you get into subatomic physics, this insight is confirmed, as what seems solid actually contains a great deal of space.

The deities (if they exist as objective phenomena) might be made of energy, or of consciousness. Even if they do not exist as objective phenomena, they certainly exist as subjective phenomena, as experiences or as archetypes. If I invoke a particular deity, I will get a similar experience each time, which suggests that there is at least a symbol-complex or thought-form that answers to the name of that deity, even if it is not a conscious entity.

Ethics of magic

There are ethical considerations when using magic, as with physical means of producing change. These are mainly around consent and minimising harm to others.

If you are sending healing to someone, it is a very good idea to get their consent first, and also to send energy in such a way that their body can decide where best to use it, rather than being too specific about what the energy is meant to do when it arrives.

If you do not have their consent, are doing a working with your group, and cannot contact them, one possible way round it is to 'park' the energy in orbit around them, and let them know it is available for their use if they wish it.

If you are working magic for some benefit to yourself, such as a new job or relationship, make sure that you are not violating another person's free will. It is best not to work for a specific job, or a relationship with a specific person, but to work for those things in general. As I remarked earlier, you also need to work for the desired outcome in the physical realm; only using magic is disrespectful to the powers.

Ethics versus morality

I have always felt that ethics are a bottom-up approach to behaviour, where your ethical choices spring from your ethos, whereas morality was a top-down approach, where morals were arbitrarily imposed from above by a deity. (The dictionary definition of morals and ethics does not bear out this distinction, but I still find it useful.)

Some traditions may derive their ethics from the traditional body of lore of a particular culture. This wisdom from the past, embedded as it was in experience and an ethic of responsibility towards other beings, is an excellent source of ethical guidance. For example, the Welsh and Irish triads and Scottish proverbs are full of wisdom.

My criterion for deciding whether anything is right or not is, "does it harm anyone?" Of course it is impossible to completely avoid harm, but we can and should reduce the harm caused by our actions. I also draw on the Eight Wiccan Virtues as a guide to how to act.

Magical tools

The use of magical tools for directing energy is common to many magical traditions. In Wicca, there are eight main tools: **the athame or black-handled knife**, used for directing energy, and representing the will of the individual witch; **the burin or white-handled knife**, which is used for working on other tools, or creating talismans; **the wand**, which is used for communicating with faeries and nature spirits; **the sword**, which represents the will of the coven; **the censer**, which is used to purify the working space and create a welcoming atmosphere for the powers; **the pentacle**, which is used to ground and contain energy; **the cords**, which are used for binding; and **the scourge**, which is used for purification.

I shall not go into great detail about the uses and symbolism of the tools, as it is an excellent exercise for candidates for second degree initiation to prepare for it by researching the uses and symbolism of each tool.

Many magicians have wondered why we use tools instead of just using hands, or even just the mind, to focus and direct energy. The tools are symbols, and the subconscious, which is the part of the mind that is most able to connect with the magical realms and powers, operates primarily through symbol, metaphor, and story. Of course, it is a very good thing to be able to dispense with tools and direct energy with your mind alone, but the tools add an extra aspect to the magical work which helps to connect it to the physical world. We are, after all, embodied, and magic uses the whole body, not just the mind.

I have found that it matters what the tool is made of, as different substances transmit energy differently. In wood, it is transmitted along the grain; in metal, it flows faster; in horn and bone, it does not flow at all, but builds up like electricity in a capacitor. Other people may experience these materials differently. I would recommend experimenting with different materials to find out what works for you.

Types of magic

There are two main types of magic: **imitative magic**, which is where the magician performs an action that is like the effect she or he wishes to bring about, or uses correspondences between the object he or she desires to affect, and the magical object which stands in for it; and **contagious magic**, where the magician brings a magical object in contact with the thing or person she or he wants to affect, or uses an object that has been part of a person or thing to affect that person or thing at a distance.

Spell work

Knotty spell – binding the desired thing; this is a traditional means of fixing a desired outcome.

Fith-fath (poppets) – a form of sympathetic magic where a representation of a person is made and then worked on, usually for healing.

Talismans, charms and amulets – these are three distinct types of magical devices. A talisman is a charged magical object, sometimes engraved with sigils; an amulet is a natural object possessing protective qualities, such as a crystal; and a charm is a small object believed to bring luck to the wearer, often possessing some religious significance.

Spoken charms – there are many traditional rhymes and charms for healing; see *Earth, Air, Fire and Water: Pre-Christian and Pagan Elements in British Songs Rhymes and Ballads* by Robin Skelton & Margaret Blackwood (Arkana, 1990); *Carmina Gadelica*, Alexander Carmichael (Florian Press); any book of Anglo-Saxon poetry.

Distracting the spirits – witch-bottles and spirit traps are traditional folk charms used to distract spirits, the idea being that you fill them with thread or other substances, which distract the spirits and make them stay away from the things you want to protect.

Raising power – the cone of power is a traditional idea where the power gathers in a cone, and can be directed for magical results. The mill of magic is a traditional way to create a cone of power by imagining a mill driven by the four elements. You can also wind energy like a skein of thread onto an imaginary spindle, and then send it out.

There are four stages to a spell (like a 4-stroke engine or the four stages of creation in the Kabbalah):

- Suck – Emanation (Atziluth)
- Squeeze – Creation (Beriah)
- Bang – Formation (Yetzirah)
- Blow – Action (Asiyyah)

(from *Kabbalah and the Art of Motorcycle Maintenance* by David Wadsworth)

The first stage is the gathering of the energy (suck); the second is concentrating it (squeeze); the third is manifesting it (bang); and the fourth is sending it (blow).

For each stage we need to consider the best metaphor for gathering, concentrating, storing, and sending the energy.

For example, imagine it is Autumn Equinox and we want to help someone recover their creativity. Autumn Equinox is associated with the cider harvest, and the person likes cider. So we decide to create a spell by visualising the apple harvest and a cider press, concentrating their creativity into a usable form. As the cider runs out into the pan, their creative juices start flowing.

- Suck – picking the apples
- Squeeze – crushing them in the cider press
- Bang – turning the handle of the press to crush the apples
- Blow – juices begin to flow

Visualisation, meditation, and pathworking

Often people use the terms visualisation, meditation and pathworking interchangeably, but they are different techniques, with different purposes and histories of development.

A meditation invites you to focus on your breathing, your body, or your feelings; it does not usually involve visualising. It is designed to increase awareness of your body. Typically, meditation techniques are drawn from Taoism or Buddhism.

Another related technique is **contemplation**, where the practitioner focuses on a deity, virtue, or quality (such as love). The technique is used in both Christianity and Islam, but was also advocated by Plato. Examples of contemplation include contemplative prayer, centring prayer, and *lectio divina*. Some people contemplate Nature as a spiritual practice.

A **visualisation** invites you to focus on specific images; sometimes it tells a story or involves travelling through a landscape (real or imaginary); sometimes it is intended to bring about a specific result – this is known as creative visualisation. Visualisation is popular with both Pagans and New Agers.

A **pathworking** takes you on a journey through an inner landscape. Pathworking as a technique is derived from magical uses of the Kabbalistic Tree of Life. In that system, a pathworking is a journey along one of the 22 paths of the Tree of Life, each of which has a specific set of landscape and symbolism associated with it (and corresponds to one of the twenty-two cards of the Major Arcana of the Tarot).

I would say that guided meditations were suitable for large groups; guided visualisations and pathworkings should probably be used in smaller groups where the person leading can be more aware of participants' emotional responses.

Some visualisations are not safe (e.g. ones that invite you to visualise going out of your body) and should not be attempted by the inexperienced. People often think that it's all happening in your head and therefore you can visualise whatever you like with no consequences, but that is not necessarily the case. Magic (defined here as "the art of changing consciousness in accordance with will") does have real effects, even if they're only psychological effects.

I never pre-record either visualisations or meditations – I prefer to do them live and feel the mood of the participants, going slower or faster depending on how well I feel the participants are following, and adding bits for the specific audience. Also, I would always try out a visualisation myself before leading others in it.

I have come across a lot of people who cannot visualise at all. For small group work, I always ask if there are people who can't visualise, and adapt by talking about feelings and spatial cues as well as visual imagery.

You can test whether someone can visualise by getting them to think of an orange – most people can manage to see an orange sphere in their mind's eye, and if they can't, the chances are that they are one of those people who cannot see with their mind's eye. I, and several other people that I know, can taste on my mind's tongue (and smell on my mind's nose) but many people can't do this.

You can check whether people can experience all five senses with the orange visualisation – imagine touching the pitted surface, prising the fruit open with your fingers, hearing the noise of the tearing peel, smelling the orange oil from the skin and the juice inside, then tasting the fruit, and feeling the juice on your tongue. For people who can't visualise in any sense modality, get them to remember the emotional feeling they get when they eat an orange; you can then use the same approach for other visualisations.

Healing techniques

The key point with all healing techniques is not to get drained of your own energy. Draw the energies from the universal source; make a connection with the source, and imagine the energy flowing through you. Take your time to establish the connection, and maintain it throughout the healing session.

Chakra balancing

This is a technique where you carefully feel the person's chakras, which according to some schools of thought, should protrude equally from the front and back of the body. If they do not, you can gently push them back into place.

Crystal healing

Different crystals have different molecular structure, and therefore energy sent through them is believed to have different qualities. Amethyst is used for healing, rose quartz for love, and so on. If you use crystals, please check that they have not been produced by strip-mining, which is very damaging to the environment.

Distant healing

This is a means of sending energy to people who are not present at the time of the magical working. You can raise energy by dancing and chanting; or you can make 'energy balls' by drawing energy from the universe, and forming it into balls. If you are working in a group, you can then merge everyone's energy balls together and send them to the person requiring the healing. You can make the energy different colours depending on the object of the working. (This technique can be used for other magical workings too.)

Hands-on healing

This is a technique where you transmit energy directly to the recipient. Again, draw upon the universe rather than depleting your own stores of energy. You don't necessarily need to touch the recipient; you can transmit the energy via their aura. The healing is usually applied directly to the affected area of the body.

Aura brushing

Sometimes the aura can develop thin areas. You can feel these by running your hands over someone's body, about three or four inches away from their skin, and feeling for cold spots. When you find a cold spot, apply a bit of extra energy, or smooth the rest of the aura into the depleted area.

Element balancing

Most people are more in touch with one of the four elements than with the other three, and they are usually out of touch with one in particular. For example, I am very in touch with the element of Water, out of touch with the element of Air, and average with Earth and Fire. You can help people to access the elements they are out of touch with by getting them to dance the movements associated with the elements, or meditate on that element (see chapter 2 – The Wiccan circle).

Wart charming

This is a traditional technique where you buy someone's wart from them, and then bury the money in the earth. As the persistence of warts is often a psychosomatic thing, this can be very effective, as long as the person believes that you have the power to charm their wart away.

Divination

It is traditional at Samhain or Hallowe'en to attempt divination, as it is believed to be a time when the Otherworld moves closer to our own. This has involved such traditional pastimes as throwing apple peel over the shoulder to see how it falls, or cutting an apple in half horizontally and counting the pips.

Divination is the process of seeing beneath or beyond everyday reality, the ability to perceive underlying patterns. These patterns of events are sometimes known as the Web of Wyrd, the web of causality which connects everything together. The concept of Wyrd is the ancient Anglo-Saxon concept of fate as a fluid thing, changing from moment to moment depending on the actions and decisions we take. When we perform a divination, therefore, we can ask what will happen if we take a particular decision, but not what will happen in general, because the future is not fixed.

> "It is a mistake to assume that events far apart in time are thereby separate. All things are connected as in the finest web of a spider. The slightest movement on any thread can be discerned from all points in the web...
>
> Imagine you were to witness a raven swooping from the sky to peck out the eye of a warrior... You would say that the flight of the bird was

connected directly with the wound. But if you had observed the flight of the same raven half a day before the attack, you would see no connection with the warrior's injury. Nevertheless the pattern of a raven's flight at noon is bound to the pattern of its flight at dusk, just as surely as the progression of day and night. One can read the pattern and see what the future has in store...

Omens frighten the ordinary person because they believe them to be predictions of events that are bound to happen: warnings from the realms of destiny. But this is to mistake the true nature of omens. A sorcerer can read omens as pattern-pointers, from which the weaving of wyrd can be admired, and from which connections between different parts of patterns can be assumed...

The pattern of wyrd is like the grain in wood, or the flow of a stream; it is never repeated in exactly the same way. But the threads of wyrd pass through all things and we can open ourselves to its pattern by observing the ripples as it passes by. When you see ripples in a pool, you know that something has dropped into the water."

~ from *The Way of Wyrd* by Brian Bates

The word divination is not derived from the Latin for guessing, but from the word 'divine' - hence it means to consult the deities. A deity's perception is non-linear and non-temporal, and if we can partake of this consciousness ourselves, it is possible to step out of time, and perceive the underlying patterns of reality.

The symbols used in any divinatory system (Runes, Tarot, etc.) allow us access to this state of mind. The right hemisphere of the brain, which is associated with the perception of pattern and rhythm, is stimulated by symbolic input. The symbols used in divination derive from the collective unconscious, that part of the mind which responds to our common cultural heritage. It is in the collective unconscious that we find archetypes such as the World Tree and the World Mountain. The concepts in the Tarot and the Runes relate to archetypes.

Other forms of divination, such as scrying, involve distracting the left brain (which is associated with linear, logical functions) in order to free the right brain to become aware of the realm of archetypes.

Divination can be used to gain understanding of psychological and emotional situations.

Simple divinatory exercises

- Use a set of stones or crystals of various colours to correspond to the astrological planets, and cast them on a cloth (having meditated on the question being asked). Interpret according to their proximity to each other.

- Scrying: use a bowl of water darkened with black ink, and gaze at it until pictures begin to form in your mind. Alternatively, use a scrying mirror (a piece of convex glass with the back painted black).

Protection magic

Protection magic is the use of energy, talismans, or sigils to protect yourself or your home from psychic and physical attack.

How to strengthen your aura

Ground and centre (see chapter 1), draw energy from earth and sky, blend the two together in a spiral in your solar plexus, feel the energy spreading and filling your whole body and aura.

The thirteen openings of the body

There are thirteen orifices of the human body, which some see as vulnerable to psychic attack. The thirteen openings are the eyes, the ears, the nostrils, the mouth, the nipples, the belly button, the vagina in a woman, the penis in a man, the urethra, and the anus. Visualise white light sealing the thirteen openings of the body – touch each one if it helps, or seal it with consecrated water.

Skein of white light

Visualise a white thread of light winding around you like thread on a spindle, until you are completely cocooned in white light.

Setting wards and threshold guardians

You can ask elemental spirits to guard your space – rather like calling the quarters, but creating an impermeable sphere of light around you. You can also create threshold guardians. Find a picture of a warrior, and charge it up with power; place it near the entrance to your home. Any strong protective image will do.

Sealing the openings of the house

Draw pentagrams on each door, window, and mirror, and really focus on sealing them with light so that no harmful thing may enter.

Sphere of light

Create a sphere of light around yourself or your house. Relax and breathe deeply for a few moments; imagine a glow of bright white light deep in your heart chakra; as you breathe the shimmering white bubble grows and grows, until it surrounds you entirely; your body and your aura are now completely cocooned within this glimmering bubble. (You can expand this out to protect the house, but remember to draw energy from your surroundings to augment your own energy.) You can now turn the bubble any colour you like. You can call on any sacred guardian to protect you. This will anchor and strengthen the sphere.

Traditional techniques for protection

Sprite flails (made of bramble), red thread around the wrist, sprigs of rowan carried in the pocket or over the door, witch bottles (a bottle full of pins or coloured threads), spirit traps, shoes in the wall, an egg buried at the threshold, runes and bind-runes, patterns to distract the spirit, amulets and charms, protective sachets of herbs (see *Practical Magic in the Northern Tradition* by Nigel Pennick).

Chapter Thirteen

Initiation

In my view, there are six separate aspects to initiation. There is the inner process of transformation; the initiation by the gods and goddesses (making contact with the numinous); experiencing the Mysteries (that which cannot be spoken, or *Arrheton*); being given the secrets of the coven (that which must not be spoken, or *Aporrheton*); joining the group mind of the coven; and the joining of the lineage or tradition of which the coven is part. Some of these aspects can be conferred by self-initiation – but the coven and lineage-related aspects cannot, and that is the main difference between self-initiation and coven initiation. It is not that a self-initiation cannot confer genuine contact with the deities and genuine inner transformation; it is that the coven and lineage-related aspects can't be part of self-initiation by its very definition. Similarly, if the group into which someone is initiated is not part of a lineage or tradition, then the initiation cannot confer membership of a lineage. (I would like to thank James Butler for pointing out the *Arrheton* and *Aporrheton* distinction.)

It might be helpful to lay out the aspects of initiation in a table:

Aspect	Self-initiation	Group initiation (no lineage)	Coven initiation with lineage
Inner process of transformation	Yes	Yes	Yes
Initiation by the gods and goddesses	Yes	Yes	Yes
Experiencing the mysteries - *Arrheton*	Yes	Yes	Yes
Being given secrets - *Aporrheton*	No	Yes	Yes
Joining the group mind of the coven	No	Yes	Yes
Joining the lineage or tradition	No	No	Yes

In the Eleusinian mysteries, *Arrheton* was that which could not be spoken of, and *Aporrheton* was that which must not be spoken of by the initiates.

All six aspects of initiation might not happen at the same time – the timing of the initiation by the gods and goddesses is up to them, and the inner process of transformation is an ongoing process, both leading up to the initiation ritual and continuing after it. After all, to initiate means to begin something.

Let's now look at each of the six aspects in more detail.

Inner process of transformation

"Know thyself" said the inscription at Delphi, and initiation is a significant step – sometimes the first step – on a journey of self-knowledge: understanding one's inner processes; finding out what archetypes one identifies with, but then rounding them off into real personality traits by bringing them into conflict with other archetypes. This last idea comes from an excellent book called *45 Master Characters* by Victoria Lynn Schmidt; it's actually a book about using archetypes to write better fictional characters, but it's also useful from a self-development point of view.

We also need to be aware of the contents of our shadow and golden shadow, bringing them into conscious awareness.

The golden shadow is the characteristics of people you admire, but which you do not recognise in yourself. For example, if you admire someone who is brave, then you probably are brave as well, though you might not realise it.

The shadow is all the aspects of people you dislike, but which you do not recognise in yourself. For example, you might dislike someone because they are lazy, but in fact this might be because you are projecting your own laziness onto them.

Initiation of the gods and goddesses

The deities are both real and a metaphor – an expression of our relationship with the world of archetypes, the land and the collective unconscious. According to many Hindu schools of thought, the deities are just forms and faces of the Infinite – Brahman at play in the universe.

When we encounter the divine in an initiatory experience, it can be as a result of an initiation ritual, or it can happen when the deities decide it will happen – it's not really under our conscious control. But the experience is one of great power and energy, of connectedness to all that is – perhaps a vision in which it's suddenly clear how everything fits together, or maybe a sense that everything is full of gods and illuminated from within.

Experiencing the mysteries (Arrheton)

The awareness of the ineffable nature of the divine – that which underlies what is manifest – cannot be communicated in words. It may be experienced as a result of an initiation ritual, or as a result of some other experience or inner process.

Being given secrets (Aporrheton)

The secrets of a group or lineage are by definition only available from people who already know them. The reasons given for why they must not be spoken vary. Carl Gustav Jung said that people need secrets to create a sense of group identity. My own view is that it is because they are private and can only be understood in the context of the whole of Wiccan culture and symbolism. Wiccan symbolism is highly erotic and this is not the norm in mainstream ideas about spirituality. Because we are so steeped in the idea that *eros* and spirituality are intertwined, it's easy to forget that other people just don't get it, so perhaps we need the injunction to secrecy to remind us. There is also the argument that the mysteries are revealed in a certain order because they make more sense that way, and people can't have the secrets till they have reached the right level of initiation. However, we must be careful not to act as if being given access to the secrets was the whole purpose of initiation – it is not.

Joining the group mind of the coven

Most covens seem to have had experiences of the group mind – knowing what is coming in a visualisation before the person leading it has said it; being able to sense where your coveners are in a visualisation; all turning up with the right food to make a feast; and so on.

Joining the group mind is obviously not available through self-initiation, because that is a solitary experience. The sense of a group mind develops gradually through working together, but if a new person joins, perhaps the jolt administered by the initiation ritual, and the shared experience of it, may be what inducts them into the group mind.

Joining the lineage or tradition

The idea of a lineage is that you inherit and have transmitted to you a particular current of energy that is special to your particular lineage, presumably because it has been modified by the people it has passed through, giving it a particular flavour.

There is also the possibility that you become part of the Wiccan egregore or group mind when you have been initiated. This is much more nebulous than the group mind of the coven.

The idea of a lineage may be related to the Christian idea of apostolic succession – but maybe it is older than that. The title of *Pontifex Maximus* used by the Pope originally belonged to the Roman emperors, as chief priests of the cult of the deities of Rome. Also, many ancient pagan priests became Christian priests, so the apostolic succession of the Christian church also contains lineages from pre-Christian traditions (both Jewish and pagan). More detail on this subject can be found online in an excellent article by Tau Apiryon (1997), *The role and function of Thelemic Clergy in the Ecclesia Gnostica Catholica.*

Again, joining the lineage, tradition or egregore is obviously not possible through self-initiation, because it is a solitary act.

When initiation goes wrong

Sometimes, despite the best efforts of all concerned, an initiation just doesn't "take". It appears to have had no effect. Perhaps the ritual was performed badly, or perhaps the candidate was not ready, psychologically or spiritually, for the experience. Or perhaps there were warning signs during the preparation for the ritual that were ignored.

One of the key things about the initiation is that it is an ordeal, with experiences included in it that are difficult. The candidate must trust their initiators, and submit to the ordeal. In return, the initiators ensure that the experience is the same as that undergone by all other Wiccan initiates, or as similar as possible, and that it is not over-the-top, and it is done with reverence and care. One of the things that connects all Wiccan initiates together is that we have all undergone the same initiation.

If the candidate refuses an aspect of the preparation, or an aspect of the ordeal, then the initiation cannot continue. If the candidate wants exemptions for things that are not a disability or an intrinsic aspect of their nature, it may be a warning sign that they are not ready. If you pick up on these warning signs and call off the initiation, you will save yourself a great deal of hassle further down the line.

Criteria for initiation

These vary from one lineage and coven to the next, but these are the criteria that I use. I take people through a process of pre-initiation training, and although this does not automatically lead to initiation, it is an excellent preparation for it.

How do you know when someone is ready for the first degree?

- they want to be a priestess or priest, and develop their magical skills
- they can direct energy, and perhaps feel it as well
- they can explain what they believe (though it may change over time)
- they feel drawn to the gods and goddesses

What do you expect of a first degree witch?

- they develop their all-round magical skills, i.e. circle casting, quarter calling, healing, visualisation, chakras, moving energy around, etc.
- they start learning to write a ritual and run it themselves
- they begin to learn invocation
- they will learn to use all the tools of the Craft

- they begin to develop an in-depth knowledge of mythology and symbolism
- towards the end of first degree, they begin to develop community involvement or healing practice

How do you know when someone is ready for the second degree?

- they have had an encounter with death, dissolution, transition, or surrender of control, or whatever their particular issue happens to be.
- they are starting to see themselves as a "community witch" and practising their priesthood for the benefit of others
- they can write a ritual and run it themselves
- they can do a successful invocation (both receiving and transmitting)
- they can use all the tools
- reasonable knowledge of mythology

What do you expect of a second degree witch?

- they further develop their community involvement
- they develop a particular skill, e.g. healing, divination, counselling
- they can write a ritual and run it themselves
- they can do a successful invocation (both receiving and transmitting)
- they can use all the tools
- in-depth knowledge of mythology and symbolism

Preparing for initiation

Many covens have the candidate choose a pre-initiation ordeal such as spending a night in a cave, climbing a hill at night, or overcoming a fear that they have.

Conclusion

Initiation is a multi-faceted experience and part of a process of transformation. It is not just about the ritual itself, but the experiences leading up to it, and the ongoing processes following it. Some of the transformation is internal and personal, and some of it is bestowed by the deities.

Chapter Fourteen

The hidden children of the Goddess

Wicca is a religion, but it is also a craft. It could be argued that it is a form of shamanism, in that witches are the magical technicians for our local community. We are not mediators with the deities – anyone can approach the deities – but rather the technicians of the sacred: healers, diviners, finders of lost things, creators of ritual.

Witches are sometimes called "the hidden children of the Goddess", and this is really important. If people know you are a priestess or priest, they see you as somehow set apart, taboo, sacred. If they don't know for definite, they may sense that you can help them, but not know why. You are not wearing a special hat, or a special outfit, so that makes you more approachable. I had a discussion with some Unitarian ministers about the wearing of dog collars, and someone said that it helped because people knew he was a religious functionary and that they could approach him for help. I said that people instinctively approach me for help; they don't need to know that I am a witch, unless they are looking for magical assistance; if they are looking for a friendly ear or a shoulder to cry on, that is not a specific role of a witch, though a witch might bring other experience and abilities to the role of listener.

The problem with having a public persona as a priestess or priest is that people project their inner archetypes onto you, and this can adversely affect your priestessly function. Witches are seen as a bit sexy and glamorous (when we are not being viewed as old hags with warty noses), a bit edgy and dangerous. Ministers are constantly assumed not to have a sex life, and not to be allowed to drink, swear, or even talk about sex. The archetype of a priest is overlaid with ideas about celibacy – something that has no place in Paganism, a religion that regards all acts of love and pleasure as sacred rituals of the Goddess. In Paganism, and especially in Wicca, sexuality and spirituality are intertwined. Sexual union can lead to feelings of oceanic bliss, very much akin to experiences of encounter with deities; and encounters with deities can lead to feelings of sexual arousal. The medieval mystics knew this very well, and their poetic outpourings are filled with sexual imagery, such as "O that he would kiss me with the kisses of his mouth" (a reference to *The*

Song of Solomon in the *Tanakh*).[226]

The function of a priestess or priest is to facilitate ritual, and to serve the tribe or community by so doing. A priestess or priest conducts rites of passage, instructs the young, and acts as a guide. He or she or ze[227] is a skilled intermediary between the realm of the deities and the realm of humans.

It has also been suggested that the role of a priestess or priest is to serve the deities. My personal view on this is that, as a magical practitioner as well as a priestess, deities are my allies; I do not serve them, and they do not serve me. As my friend John Macintyre once pointed out, humans inhabit a finite and local position in time and space; deities are infinite and non-local. Humans need to access the divine perspective from time to time; but deities need to access the human perspective sometimes. Therefore, they have a perspective that we want, and we have a perspective that they want. Our respective powers are different in our different realms.

It has been argued that lesbian, gay, bisexual, transgender (LGBT), genderqueer, and queer people are particularly suited to being priestesses and priests because of our intermediate status. In his book *Coming Out Spiritually: The Next Step*, Christian de la Huerta identified ten queer spiritual roles. These are not necessarily essential characteristics of LGBT people; they may be the result of having been marginalised.

- *Catalytic transformers.* We are very aware of the stress points in society, and what needs to be changed, and therefore participate in movements for social justice.

- *Outsiders: Mirrors of Society.* We are the ones who challenge 'traditional' boundaries, so we compel others to look at aspects of life that get brushed under the carpet.

- *Consciousness scouts: Going First and Taking Risks.* Shamans often have gender-bending practices (consider the Norse practice of seiðr, which involved gender-bending); LGBT people have been pioneers in the arts and music, as well as in spirituality.

- *Sacred clowns and eternal youth.* According to James Broughton, "We are the Peter Pans of the world, the irrepressible ones who believe in magic, folly, and romance....That's part of what being gay signifies: innocence of spirit, a perennial youthfulness of soul." The edgy trickster energy characteristic of camp is part of this archetypal role.

- *Keepers of Beauty.* LGBT people are frequently associated with the creation of beautiful things – music, art, theatre, interior décor, and so on.

---

[226] The *Tanakh* (short for *Torah, Nevi'im, Ketuvim*) is the Jewish name for what Christians refer to as *The Old Testament*, a term that is intended to imply the obsolescence of the *Tanakh*, which is why I prefer the Jewish term.

[227] Many genderqueer people prefer the pronoun ze. As we shall discuss the special aptitude of LGBT people for priestessly functions later in the chapter, it seemed especially appropriate to include the use of a genderqueer pronoun here.

- *Caregivers.* LGBT people are often found in the caring professions. In nature, gay, lesbian, and bisexual animals seem to have evolved to help take care of other animals' young.

- *Mediators: the In-Between People.* In many cultures, LGBT people are seen as "the in-between people", because we express characteristics of both genders. We have been valued as mediators between men and women, and also between the physical and the spiritual worlds.

- *Shamans and Priests: Sacred Functionaries.* In many different cultures and times (Africa, Mesopotamia, ancient Greece and Rome, China, India, ancient Russia, and among the Native American, Celtic and Polynesian peoples, LGBTQ people have been shamanic practitioners.

- *The Divine Androgyne.* Several authors, including Edward Carpenter and Carl Gustav Jung, have suggested that the archetype of the Divine Androgyne, has both masculine and feminine characteristics, is the desired outcome of the magical and spiritual journey.

- *Gatekeepers.* In several African tribes, including the Dagar tribe, LGBT people are believed to be particularly adept at contacting the spiritual realms. They believe that our function is to keep the gates open to the Otherworld. The way that many LGBT people are prevented from fulfilling this function in Europe, they say, is one of the causes of the spiritual malaise of Europeans.

The experience of coming out of the closet as a LGBT person is similar in many ways to the Pagan experience of coming out of the broom closet – revealing oneself to be a Pagan or a witch. The term 'coming out of the broom closet' was intended to reference the LGBT experience.

Left-hand path or right-hand path?

The priest or priestess is in the community, but not of it. By virtue of their office, they are distinct and set apart. That is why they wear special clothing. The same has often applied to magical practitioners in the past. The shaman wore special clothing for magical purposes (sometimes to distract hostile spirits), and it is possible that some priestly garb is derived from this apotropaic function of turning away harm. However, a priest serves a community; a shaman tends to be more associated with a tribe.

Communities are often seen as monolithic groupings with a common purpose, common beliefs, and common values; a priest traditionally served a community, and was seen as the spokesperson for that community. According to the *Online Etymology Dictionary*, the word 'community' is derived from Proto-Indo-European **ko-moin-i-* meaning 'held in common', a compound adjective formed from **ko-* 'together' + **moi-n-*, suffixed form of root **mei-* 'change or exchange', hence literally 'shared by all'. An Old English word for 'community' was *gemænscipe* meaning 'community, fellowship, union, common ownership', and is related to the German word *Gemeinschaft* (a social relationship based on affection or kinship). Communities can consist of people who are often seen as being all the same and having common interests (a community of metalworkers, the gay community, the Muslim community, and so on). This can be disadvantageous if you are in a minority within your own community and want to express a different view, as governments often assume that because they have heard from the spokesperson of a particular community, they have heard from the whole of that community. This is actually rather anti-democratic.

In many spiritual communities (such as some monasteries), individual friendships were discouraged as distracting from the communal spirit. Tribal societies, on the other hand, have strong friendship links and rituals for formalising friendships into blood-brotherhood. One such ritual, *adelphopoiesis*, found in Albania, may also be an early form of same-sex marriage.

A tribe, on the other hand, is necessarily diverse because it must include people who specialise in many different tasks (metalworking, flint-knapping, weaving, gathering, hunting, magic, and so on). Tribal societies were often friendly towards gender-variance and same-sex relationships, and had special rituals and roles for gender-variant people.

I see Wicca as a tribe or a clan, rather than a community. Each coven has autonomy within the Craft. There is no hierarchy beyond the coven group, though there are many people who are informally respected as elders. A high priestess (the leader of a coven) is first among equals; she generally has more experience than the other members, but she is a facilitator rather than a dictator.

Left-hand path magical traditions tend to involve spiritual rebellion against the world and its organised systems. They are less about compassion, and more about passion for life; a Nietzschean will to power.

Right-hand path traditions (which can be esoteric or exoteric) tend to emphasise the community over the individual, and to value compassion for the weak. However, there is a risk that this will become pandering to the lowest common denominator, diluting the power of the tradition, and allowing the weak to drag down the strong.

In practice, most spiritual and religious systems contain both right-hand and left-hand path elements. But the ultimate goal of the right-hand path practitioner is to become one with the Godhead. The ultimate goal of the left-hand path practitioner is to become divine.

A much better system would be a compromise between the best features of the left-hand and right-hand paths. In a tribe, the strong raise up the weak; individuality is praised and valued; the needs of the group and the needs of the individual are in balance; and friendships are valued.

In left-hand path traditions, practitioners demand service from spirits; in right-hand-path traditions, people serve deities; in a balanced system, deities, spirits, and humans would form alliances.

Wicca is a compromise between the left-hand path and the right-hand path. Every initiate of the Craft is a witch and priest(ess). This means that we are both magical technicians and specialists in ritual for the community. We work with deities and spirits as allies, and we work magic for healing, divination, and other beneficial outcomes. However, traditionally the witch's house was the last house in the village; witches are set apart, by virtue of our dealings with the uncanny, our knowledge, and the taboos surrounding the role of priestess or priest.

So how does one become a priestess or priest in Wicca? Wicca has three degrees of initiation. At the first degree, each witch is a priestess or priest unto themselves. At the second degree, the initiate gains the title of high priest(ess). Second degree witches are able to act as priest or priestess for other people. At third degree, the initiate becomes a priest or priestess for the whole community.

The functions of a priestess or priest are to conduct rites of passage (naming, initiations, weddings, funerals); to offer guidance and support on spiritual matters to the tribe or the community; to create meaningful rituals (to celebrate the seasons and the phases of the Moon); to preserve, develop, and pass on the traditions, stories, and wisdom of the tribe.

These overlap significantly with the function of witches and shamans, who also create meaningful ritual, tell stories, and perform rites of passage. However, the shaman and the witch are also practitioners of magic and herbal medicine, performing healing, divination, abortion, soul retrieval, and helping people deal with the more traumatic aspects of life.

It is possible that the split between the idea of a priestess and the idea of a witch first came about when an older cult was pushed underground, because of being deemed too wild and unacceptable. Both ancient and modern Pagan traditions are relaxed about sexual orientation, gender roles, and the use of magic. With the arrival of the Axial Age (the age that gave rise to individual prophets such as Zoroaster, Socrates, Buddha, Jesus, and Mohammed), the wilder and more Dionysiac aspects of religion, such as magic, sexuality, and the worship of Goddesses, were driven underground and relegated to the realm of sorcery. In order to create a fully-functioning religion, these separated functions need to be reunited, and that is why the witch is both priest(ess) and magical practitioner.

Wicca is primarily a lunar religion. Its rituals are conducted at night; it celebrates the phases of the Moon (new, waxing, full, waning, and dark); it seeks to develop the mental and spiritual powers traditionally associated with the Moon, such as divination, meditation, and imagination. In ancient times, the witches of Thessaly were associated with the Moon and the goddess Hekate.

The reason for Wicca's emphasis on the Moon, the night, and the sacred feminine is that these aspects of spirituality have been lost, suppressed, and denigrated, and need to be recovered.

Druidry, by contrast, focuses much more on the Sun, and consequently the solar festivals (the solstices and equinoxes) are much more emphasised in Druidry. Interestingly, Philip Carr-Gomm has created a blend of Druidry and Wicca called Druidcraft, which presumably honours Moon and Sun equally. He writes:

> "In the end it all boils down to this. There is you and the ocean. You and the sky. You and the land. Now and here. The old lore is not meant to remain preserved in a glass case. It is meant to be used, changed, added to and improved. It only stays alive if each of us takes it, and uses it in our own way, with our own creative additions and insights, to help us live a life of depth and meaning, beauty and celebration, here and now - upon this earth, beneath this sky, beside this sea."

The land and sacred places in Nature are very important in Wicca, as well as in other Pagan traditions. It is believed that in ancient Pagan traditions, the king married the land, which was personified as a woman. Before that, in matriarchal societies, the queen was seen as the embodiment of the land, and the power of the king was derived from her. The monarch also performed priestly or priestessly functions. In ancient Rome, the priests and priestesses (*flamines*) were hedged about with various taboos, because it was their responsibility to maintain a magical connection with the deity to whom they were devoted. Similar magical beliefs have surrounded monarchs – one notable one being the belief that the British monarch can cure scrofula by touching its victims (this was known as "Touching for the King's Evil"). The last reigning monarch to practice this was Queen Anne in 1712; though the Jacobite claimants to the throne continued it until 1780. These taboos and powers represented the monarch's or priestess's special relationship with the divine powers and with the land. It could have been a similar taboo that gave rise to the idea that witches and wizards cannot cross running water (this is pure speculation on my part, but an interesting idea nonetheless).

Conclusion

Wicca is a mystery religion, and as such, all of its initiates are priests and priestesses, and expected to develop at least a basic understanding of priestcraft. However, just as in other religions, some will feel more drawn to contemplation and solitary ritual; others will feel drawn to serve a community; others will feel drawn to healing and herbs; and so on. There is plenty of room for people to specialise in a particular aspect of priestcraft, and not feel that they have to be "all things to all men".

There are several aspects to being a priest or priestess and a witch:

- Consecrating magical tools
- Performing sacraments (cakes and wine, invocation, creating sacred space)
- Conducting rites of passage (naming, weddings, funerals)
- Communicating with the deities and spirits
- Creating rituals to celebrate the seasons and cycles of the year
- Healing using magic, listening, herbs, counselling, therapy (the last three on this list should only be attempted by qualified practitioners)
- Contemplation, meditation, prayer, magic
- Researching new magical techniques
- Initiating others (in Wicca, only second and third degree initiates can initiate people to first or second degree; and only third degree initiates can initiate people to third degree)

I am not saying that any of the items on the above list should only be done by Wiccan initiates; nor that all Wiccans can or should reach the same level of expertise in all of these areas. Nor is it necessarily a complete list.

Practical

- Meditate on what being a witch means to you. What other archetypes do you associate it with? What is your inner image of a witch? What do you see as a witch's relationship to deities?

- Meditate on what being a priestess or priest means to you. What other archetypes do you associate it with? What is your inner image of a priestess or priest? What do you see as a priest's or priestess's relationship to deities?

- Discuss these topics with your coven

- Ask your non-Wiccan friends for their archetypes and stereotypes around the words priest, priestess, minister, vicar, and witch.

Chapter Fifteen

Secrecy and confidentiality

Much of this chapter was jointly written with Fred Lamond in 2004.

Why secrecy?

Knowing when to speak and when not to speak is a normal part of human social intercourse, e.g. when someone asks you if you like their new dress, and the truth is that you hate it, it's best to say something non-committal rather than going into explicit detail about how and why you don't like it. Not long after children learn to speak, they learn when not to speak and develop the important bonding and survival mechanism of sharing or keeping secrets.

It's actually impossible to communicate the Mysteries verbally anyway, as they are a feeling you experience rather than something you can describe; but trying to describe it often makes the feeling less real because you have distanced yourself from it by describing it.

The other issue is that the Mysteries have always been revealed sequentially. You get the experiences you can handle; these enable you to handle more, which are subsequently revealed at the right time, and so on.

Many people have wondered, since there is so much Wiccan material that has already been published, whether there is anything left to keep secret. In fact, there is a lot of unpublished material. And, more importantly, there are two types of secret: There is *Arrheton* - that which **must not** be spoken about (because it is oathbound); and there is *Aporrheton* - that which **cannot** be spoken about, because it is ineffable and incommunicable with words, and can only be **experienced**.

The reason things are oathbound is to create a fence around the Mysteries (the *Aporrheton*) to create the conditions in which the Mysteries may be encountered. If we did not keep secret the means of creating the conditions for encountering the Mysteries, then it would be harder to create those conditions, because people would take them for granted, and perform the rituals without the necessary initiation having been done first, which brings about a transformation in the psyche.

What should remain secret (only being revealed to fellow Wiccans)

The following are my personal views, which have remained consistent over a number of years and are based on experience.

A lot of the Mysteries cannot be transmitted by word of mouth, they are ineffable, and can only be experienced in a circle at a certain level of experience, having been opened by the initiatory experience and the spiritual journey.

Invocation, evocation, the Great Rite, sky-clad workings, the deeper mysteries, and any material from Books of Shadows that remain unpublished should be initiates-only.

Information that people reveal about themselves in the intimacy of the coven should be confidential. If the coven is not competent to deal with someone's trauma, however, extended confidentiality (telling it to a competent professional) might come into play.

Details of magical workings performed should be kept secret until well after their intended aim has been achieved. Talking about magical working – be it remote healing, helping a friend find a job, etc – after it has been done dissipates its power and diminishes the chances of it successfully achieving its object. This applies even to a discussion within the drawn circle, but much more so to discussions outside it and to fellow Pagans who do not belong to the coven. Only when a working's intended effect has been achieved does it become safe to talk or write about it.

As for to whom you then talk about it, the main thing here is the principle of "cast not your pearls before swine" - if you make something explicit that was implicit and subtle, it somehow cheapens it or sullies it. As non-Pagans do not understand our world-view, they inevitably read entirely the wrong thing into Craft-related matter.

I also feel that a large number of aspects of my Craft life are private. These include my working tools, various experiences that I have had, and so on.

What is okay to reveal to other Pagans

Calling the quarters, casting the circle, the meanings of the festivals, offering praise to the gods and goddesses, names and attributes of gods and goddesses, stuff that has already been published, general healing, etc. should all be generally available. It is also alright to mention what you did to celebrate a festival.

When it is necessary to speak out

If ever you find yourself in an abusive situation, then tell someone else, get help. If the person concerned is doing something illegal, then tell the police. Don't be swayed by the argument that revealing what they are up to would bring the Craft into disrepute – nefarious activities have a way of being discovered, and then it would be much worse if other Craft members were covering up for the miscreant.

Practical

Draw a mind-map of all the concepts you associate with secrecy, and get other members of your coven to do this as well.

Chapter Sixteen

Invocation

Invocation is the practice of inviting a deity to enter the body of a priestess or priest. In some traditions, the invokee is said to go elsewhere while the deity is occupying their body; in Wicca, the deity is usually regarded as co-inhabiting their body.

Why do we do invocation? Who benefits from it? I would argue that both the deity and the practitioner benefit (and hopefully so do the other coveners). Human awareness is finite and local to one particular area of space-time, that is to say, here and now. Divine consciousness seems to be both spatially and temporally unfocussed, and potentially infinite. So deities can benefit by accessing our local, temporal and focussed consciousness, and we can benefit by accessing their atemporal, non-local and multiple perspective consciousness.

Another benefit is that by practicing theurgy, some of the virtues of deities might rub off on us. In Eastern Orthodox Christianity, the divine presence is invoked into the Eucharist before it is distributed to the communicants, who then ingest their deity. This is said to brings about the process of *theosis*, which means becoming divine. Indeed, Jesus actually said, "I have said, ye are gods." (The trick is becoming aware that we are gods.) A similar practice occurs in Tibetan Buddhism, where special consecrated pills are distributed to the people. Indeed, our own Wiccan cakes and wine contains echoes of this idea, as we consecrate the sacral meal by infusing it with spirit. But invocation should, at least in theory, be a shortcut to theosis, because instead of eating food that has had a deity invoked into it, the deity is directly invoked into the practitioner. One possible pitfall here would be if you always did invocations with the same type of deity, for example, always "dark" goddesses like Kali, the Morrigan, and so on. I also do not see why we cannot invoke goddesses onto men and gods onto women. So I think we should take care not to get typecast. If you always go for a particular type of deity, you might want to consider why this is, and try balancing it with a different type. Later in this chapter, I will be telling you about a Tantric Buddhist practice which has great potential for overcoming this problem. Another possible pitfall is that you might get so into the power and glamour of the whole experience that you become convinced that you're the most magical being since Aleister Crowley –

though this might just be a pitfall of the magical path in general.

When discussing invocation, the role of the invoker is often overlooked. But it is very important; otherwise the invokee either has to say that they are not invoked (my coven has a convention that we will use the gesture of crossing the arms in the God position for this, though we have never had to use it). Or they have to fake being invoked (which is a bit like faking an orgasm in my opinion). Or they have to use a previously prepared charge. Or they have to quickly invoke themselves (which is a bit like self-initiation – very difficult, but not impossible). So the invoker is very important. In classical Indian music, they identify three movements of the *raga*, which is a piece of music that calls to a deity. The first movement is the expression of the performer's yearning for the deity; the second is the actual call to the deity; and the third is the celebration of their arrival. The Wiccan invocation – in both its verbal and non-verbal aspects – is rather like this. The invoker must want the deity to appear. Then they must call them; and then they must be pleased to see them. A successful invocation requires these emotional states to be present in the invoker, and preferably also verbally expressed in the text of the invocation, to get the coveners in the mood and participating in the act of invocation.

Similarly, in *Magick in Theory and Practice*, Aleister Crowley identifies the process of invocation with the four elements, or the Tetragrammaton:

- Fire is the eager prayer of the magician to the deity;
- Water is the magician listening to, or catching the reflection of, the deity
- Air is the marriage of fire and water, when human and deity have become one
- and Earth is the condensation or materialisation of the three higher principles

In David Wadsworth's classic talk, *Kabbalah and the Art of Motorcycle Maintenance*, he likened the four worlds of the Kabbalah and the four stages of an invocation to the phases of a four-stroke engine: suck, squeeze, bang, blow. I quote from the maestro himself:

1. **Suck:** Initially the piston is at the top and both valves are closed. As the crank shaft turns, the inlet valve opens, the con rod pulls the piston down which draws air and fuel in. At this point in an invocation, the invoker is opening his chakras and drawing the cosmic energy which surrounds us into his body.

2. **Squeeze:** The crank shaft continues around, the inlet valve shuts, and the piston is pushed up, squeezing the gases together. This is when the invoker says the invocation and passes the power to the invokee.

3. **Bang:** The fuel/air mixture ignites and pushes the piston down. The priest/ess takes on the aspect of God/dess being invoked.

4. **Blow:** The exhaust valve opens and the piston pushes the charge into the exhaust pipe. The God/dess charges and shares his/her power with those assembled.

Also, the invokee must be in a suitably receptive state to receive the deity, and not be afraid of being possessed or the like; so they must have confidence in the invoker and in themselves and know that they will be able to de-invoke the deity at the end of the process. I was taught that learning to be invoked upon is a gradual process; the first few times, the deity only descends into the top three chakras or so, and it takes time for them to descend further into the body.

Personally, I have always objected to the practice of delivering a Charge and then not allowing the deity to speak through you. There is nothing wrong with delivering a Charge to get you in the flow, and then allowing the deity to speak through you, but if you just do a Charge and then stop, it's hardly worth the deity bothering to turn up.

The way I see it, there are five levels of invocation in Wicca.

The first level is the light glamour that occurs when doing cakes and wine. As the priest kneels before the priestess, he may lightly invoke the Goddess such that the priestess has an overlay of Goddess energy; or the Goddess energy may well up from within her. She is then empowered to bless the cakes and wine. However, there is usually no intention of fully invoking the Goddess here, or channelling the Goddess's utterances. Similarly, the God may be lightly invoked on the priest in the blessing of the cakes and wine.

The second level occurs in the rite of Drawing Down the Moon. Here the Goddess energy is much stronger than in the blessing of cakes and wine, and it is specifically the Moon Goddess being invoked, but again, we are just conveying Goddess energy to the other participants in the ritual, rather than channelling the Goddess's utterances. (Similarly for the newer ritual of Drawing Down the Sun.) As an aside, some mythologies have Sun Goddesses and Moon Gods, so there is no need to restrict Drawing Down the Moon to priestesses, or Drawing Down the Sun to priests.

The third level doesn't have a name, but it feels as if the invoked deity is standing just behind you and whispering in your ear, and you are translating what they are saying for the benefit of the rest of the coven. You (the invokee) and the deity are both standing in the realm of the gods, but they are not fully in you.

Sometimes the third level happens very briefly as a preparatory phase just before the fourth level.

The fourth level is where the deity is in you but not intermingled with your consciousness; it's more as if they're alongside you inside your body, and have just borrowed your voice to say what they have to say. This level is invocation proper; but it's like one of those executive toys with oil and water in a transparent chamber, where the oil and water can be shaken up but do not mix.

The fifth level is where the consciousness of the deity is intermingled or merged with your consciousness (the oil and water have been shaken up and formed an emulsion). In this level of invocation, it is difficult to know where the deity ends and you begin. It feels to me as if they have descended into me through the top of my head, and I have opened up to receive them. Other people have told me that it feels as if they have stepped in through their back (I have also experienced this feeling).

There are further levels of invocation, but they do not seem to be generally practiced in Wicca.

The sixth level is where your consciousness is entirely displaced, so that the deity has completely taken over and you don't remember anything about what happened during the period while the deity was present. I do not think this is a beneficial practice. This is apparently what happens during a Voudun possession, and in certain shamanic traditions. In his classic travelogue about the Caribbean, *The Travellers' Tree*, Patrick Leigh Fermor says that possessed practitioners retained an awareness of themselves, albeit dimmed; but more recent accounts by anthropologists and by practitioners themselves have stated that they did not recall anything that happened during the possession. Interestingly, practitioners are always "ridden" by the same *lwa* in Voudun, another practice which I do not consider beneficial. The *lwa* are said to enter the human body at the base of the skull.

In October 2008, I attended an academic conference in Heidelberg on the dynamics of ritual. There were five days of talks by anthropologists, theologians, psychologists, scholars of religion, sociologists and so on. Many of them were also practitioners of various paths. I attended a strand entitled *"The Inner Work of Ritual"* chaired by Geoffrey Samuel. One of the papers in this strand was by an anthropologist who had compared shamanic possession with Tantric Buddhist invocation. The shamanic possession was similar to the experience of being ridden by the *lwa* in Voudun – the shaman left his body for the duration of the possession trance.

In Tantric Buddhist practice, however, the practitioner invokes a Buddha or a deity (such as Tara) and "ascends" to the realm of the deities (remember that up and down are just metaphors here). There, the practitioner merges his or her self with that of the deity, and then goes beyond the deity to the nameless divine ocean of bliss. This practice solves two problems: the problem outlined at the beginning of the chapter about getting typecast or acquiring the characteristics of a particular type of deity; and it also means that we can go deeper and merge with the infinite without losing our awareness in the process.

I have not yet succeeded in attaining the Tantric Buddhist level of invocation, but I am working on it. Interestingly, Aleister Crowley appears to have experienced this level, because in *Magick in Theory and Practice*, he writes:

> "This consists of a real identification of the magician and the god. Note that to do this in perfection involves the attainment of a species of Samadhi; and this fact alone suffices to link irrefragably magick with mysticism."

Another question we might ask about invocation is whether it is all happening internally, or whether there is an external consciousness actually entering us. Patrick Leigh Fermor discusses the dynamics of possession by the *lwa*. He suggests that possession works by calling up some unconscious aspect of the self from the depths of the psyche and allowing it to take over from the ego for a while. He is sceptical of any external consciousness being involved. However, the idea of something arising out of the depths of the psyche is a useful one, as according to Jungian psychology, it is our subconscious that is connected to the collective unconscious.

It is also worth comparing the Wiccan practice of invocation with that outlined in Aleister Crowley's *Magick in Theory and Practice*. Crowley identifies three main methods of invoking deities. The first is devotion to the deity; the second is straightforward ceremonial invocation; and the third is to enact a drama of the deity's legend. He says that in invocation, the macrocosm floods the consciousness; whereas with evocation, the magician identifies with the macrocosm and creates a microcosm (the triangle into which the spirit is evoked).

Crowley outlines six phases of invocation, using the method where the magician identifies with the deity: First, the magician studies the symbolic form of the deity and builds up a mental picture, with as much care as the artist would bestow upon a model. The invocation begins with prayer to the deity, commemorating their physical attributes, but mindful of the symbolic meaning of these. Then the magician recites the deity's characteristic utterance, and then asserts the identity of his or her self with the deity. Then the magician invokes the deity again, but this time it is as if it is the deity's will that he or she should manifest in the magician. Finally, the magician becomes passive, and then the deity speaks through the magician.

Preparing for invocation

The first time you try to do an invocation, you may find that it is not very effective. It takes a few attempts before the ritual practitioner can open themselves sufficiently to allow the deity to enter. It is advisable to start by evoking the quarters, then progress to consecrating the cakes and wine at the end of the ritual, which involves only a light overlay of invocation, then proceed to drawing down the Moon, and so on through the different levels, until you reach the deepest level.

Many people find it helpful to start by choosing a specific deity to whom they feel attracted, and reading as much as they can about that deity, their myths, culture, symbols, and attributes. It is especially helpful to read poetry about the deity, and meditate on them. Carrying an object associated with the deity as a talisman may be helpful, or listening to songs about them, or burning incense that is sacred to them. You may also wish to do a solo ritual to get in touch with the deity. Establishing a connection with the deity to be invoked helps to create an atmosphere of trust between you and the deity.

It is a good idea not to get "typecast" and always invoke the same deity, however, as this can lead to obsession and imbalance. Try to choose deities that balance some deficiency or excess in your own psyche – if you are excessively emotional, you might want to invoke Apollo or Athena, both associated with intellect; if you are strongly intellectual, you might want to invoke Venus or Eros, both associated with the emotions. Balance earthy tendencies with airy qualities, and watery tendencies with fiery qualities.

If an invocation doesn't work, you can either recite a piece of poetry that is associated with the deity, or just indicate that the invocation has not worked by crossing your arms and sitting down.

Questions for discussion

- How does invocation feel to you?
- Where/how does the deity enter?
- Has it benefited you?
- Any issues with it?
- Should you deliver a Charge, or allow the deity to speak through you, or both?
- Should you invoke specific deities, or just do a generic invocation and see who comes?
- Should you vary the deities you invoke to avoid getting "typecast" or fixated on a particular deity?

Chapter Seventeen

Mythology for Wiccans

Pagan mythology is key to an understanding of Pagan theology – these stories are part of humanity's heritage, and often sadly neglected. Many Wiccans have been fascinated by Pagan mythology from an early age, and this is one of things that led us to practising Paganism as a religion. Many of the rituals in Gardner's Books of Shadows drew on ancient pagan mythology as source material. Ritual drama enacting the story, or part of the story, or a reinterpretation of the story, can be an effective way of experiencing the mythology directly. I usually encourage coveners to read the story in advance, especially if they are unfamiliar with it.

The story of Demeter and Persephone

This is important for the festival of Samhain, because one aspect of Samhain is the descent of the psyche into the underworld for rest, renewal, and introspection. Other relevant myths on this theme are the story of **Orpheus and Eurydice**, and **Inanna's descent to the Underworld**. Another key aspect of these stories is the relationship of the living and the dead, and the opportunity for individuals to come to terms with our mortality.

Oðinn's quest for the Runes (from the Hávamál)

In the *Hávamál,* it is recounted that Oðinn hung for nine days and nights on the World Tree in order to fathom the mystery of the Runes. He sacrificed himself to himself (giving up his ego in order to attain divine status), and suffered a ritual ordeal in order to gain new knowledge. This story can teach us that it is necessary to suffer to gain wisdom. It can also teach us about Pagan cosmology, namely the idea that all the worlds are interconnected by a vast tree.

Robin Hood and Maid Marian

The archetypal lovers, Robin and Marian were celebrated in May Games throughout the medieval period. People made "Robin Hood's Bower" for the May

King and May Queen, and held games in honour of Robin and Marian. Robin was the lord of the greenwood and the symbol of freedom from oppression.

King Arthur and the Holy Grail

The stories of King Arthur and the Holy Grail are sometimes known as the Matter of Britain. They are the basis for our notions of chivalry and honourable conduct. They explore the mysteries of the relationship between the sexes (especially the stories about Gawain and Lancelot), and the four sacred things (Grail, Lance, Cup, Sword) at the heart of the Arthurian legends correspond to the Four Elements, and some of the working tools and regalia of Wicca. It is also worth reading *Sir Gawain and the Green Knight*, *The Wife of Bath's Tale* (in *The Canterbury Tales*), and *The Wedding of Sir Gawain and Dame Ragnelle* (a later ballad version of the story of Gawain and the Loathly Lady).

The Mabinogion (especially the stories of Pwyll and Rhiannon and Gwydion)

The Mabinogion is a cycle of Welsh tales, some of which relate earlier versions of the stories of King Arthur, and some of which recount other tales from Welsh mythology; there are various references to older Celtic legends, lost fragments of mythology which perhaps derive from the oral tradition which preceded the written text. In one tale, Pwyll, Lord of Arberth, is hunting a stag when he meets Arawn, King of Annwn (the underworld). Pwyll's dogs are set on a stag, but then another pack of hounds appears; these are Arawn's hounds, shining white with red ears. Pwyll claims the quarry for his own, so Arawn and Pwyll meet in anger. But Arawn needs a human hero to fight for him against Hafgan, a rival Otherworld king. There are also enchanted animals in the *Mabinogion*, such as Twrch Trwyth, a magical boar. Before Culhwch can marry Olwen, he has to carry out a series of tasks for her father, the giant Ysbaddaden. These tasks culminate in the hunt for Twrch Trwyth, who is really a king who has been transformed into a boar. The task is to obtain the shears, comb, and razor from between Twrch Trwyth's ears. Culhwch obtains the help of Arthur and Mabon (the divine hunter) in his quest. First, however, they have to find Mabon. The Stag of Rhedynfre (one of the Oldest Animals) helps to find him. The Stag is a magical animal and can communicate with one of Arthur's men, Gwrhyr the Interpreter of Tongues. The idea of someone who can understand the speech of animals is a frequent one in myth and folktale, and often signifies a person in tune with their instinctual nature. The folk tale of *The Three Languages* (retold by the Brothers Grimm) tells of a boy who goes out into the world to obtain an education, and learns the language of animals, much to his father's chagrin. However, the acquisition of the language of frogs, dogs, and birds stands him in good stead on his travels.

Aradia

The legend of Aradia (as recounted in *The Gospel of the Witches* by Charles Godfrey Leland) has become one of the central myths of Wicca. Regardless of whether Leland made up most of *Il Vangelo delle Streghe*, it is still a classic work of late nineteenth century folklore collecting, and provides the basis for *The Charge of the Goddess* (later adapted and expanded by Doreen Valiente). It also recounts some interesting beliefs and practices, possibly sourced from accounts of medieval witchcraft, or perhaps from an actual Italian witch as Leland claimed. Aradia is the daughter of Diana, goddess of the Moon.

Hekate

Hekate is the original goddess of witches. She rules the crossroads, a traditional location for magic, and also holds sway in the underworld, where witches and shamans must traditionally descend in order to retrieve magical powers. She is often represented as having three faces, and is associated with the Moon. In ancient times, the witches of Thessaly were associated with the Moon and the goddess Hekate.[228]

The Moon

Wicca is primarily a lunar religion. Our rituals are conducted at night; we mark the phases of the Moon (new, waxing, full, waning, and dark); we try to develop the mental and spiritual powers traditionally associated with the Moon, such as divination, meditation, and imagination.

The reason for Wicca's emphasis on the Moon, the night, and the sacred feminine is that these aspects of spirituality have been lost, suppressed, and denigrated, and need to be recovered.

The Moon, and the phases of the Moon, were traditionally associated with witchcraft and folk magic. It is believed that magic for increase and growth should be done at the time of the waxing Moon, and magic for decrease and diminution should be done at the time of the waning Moon.

The Moon is particularly associated with the hare in folklore, because of the way in which the craters of the Moon sometimes look like a running hare, particularly when the Moon rises at dusk. The lunar hare and the lunar toad are often three-legged to represent the three phases of the Moon, or past, present, and future. The rabbit is also a lunar creature. Another important aspect of Moon symbolism is the Moon Tree, which is often guarded by animals. In Assyrian and Phoenician depictions of the Moon Tree, it is guarded by lions, unicorns, goats, or winged beasts. In some myths, these attack and kill the Moon God. In other stories, they are there to guard the treasures of the tree from the hero who comes to steal them.

The Wild Hunt

The Wild Hunt is a recurring motif in folklore from all over Europe, where the leader of the Wild Hunt may be Oðinn, Woden, Wild Edric (a Saxon

---

[228] For more on Hekate, see Sorita d'Este (2010), *HEKATE Her Sacred Fires.* Avalonia

nobleman who surrendered to the Normans too soon), Herne the Hunter, Friedrich Barbarossa, Hecate, King Herluin or Herla (possibly the origin of the name Harlequin). When people heard the calling of wild geese, and their wing-beats ringing through the air, they said it was the sound of the Wild Hunt. When thunder rolled through the heavens, it was the sound of the Wild Hunt. In medieval folklore, it was said that the dead who could not go to Heaven but were not bad enough for Hell would be sent to ride with the Wild Hunt. In India, Rudra leads the Maruts, who ride on the wings of the storm. The Wild Hunt often appears in winter.

The Lord of the Animals and the Lady of the Flowers

The Horned God, the tutelary male deity of Wicca, is often represented as the Lord of the Animals; and there are many goddesses who are represented as flowery. These are archetypes found in many cultures.

In India, various deities have been identified with the Lord of the Animals; in the case of some animal species, there is a specific deity for that species. The Lord of the Elephants is Palakapya (or, in Vedic writings, Matangalua). There is possibly also a Lord of Horses, called Salihotra. However, Indra is also referred to as *asvapati*, Lord of the Horses. There may be a Lady of the Animals as well. A possible candidate for the role is Padumavati, one of the Mrgas, who are associated with Rudra. Alternatively, it may be that Aranyani, Lady of the Wood, is also Lady of the Animals. Aranyani has a number of parallels with the Tamil wood goddesses, Katamarcelvi, Katteri, Katukilal, etc. There is also a goddess of the Chenchu (a caste near Hyderabad) called Garelamaisama, who has a special power over the wild animals of the forest, and can grant success (or cause failure) in the hunt. The Chenchus say that in ancient times only male animals were hunted. If female animals were hunted, it would make Garelamaisama very angry. In pre-Vedic times, the Lord of the Animals was Pasupati or Prajapati. A seal found at Mohenjodaro (dating from 2600 to 1900 BCE) has a depiction of an enthroned man sitting in the lotus position, with a huge pair of bison horns on his head. In the middle of the horns is something resembling a bunch of feathers (or possibly a flame, as is often found on depictions of stags in the West). This deity also has three faces, and is depicted as ithyphallic (semi-erect). He has heavy gold chains around his neck, and there are arm-rings on his arms. He is surrounded by four animals: a rhinoceros, a bison, a tiger, and an elephant. The first three are facing the god, whilst the elephant turns its back. It appears that this is a representation of the Lord of the Animals, indeed of wild animals, since there are no domestic animals depicted. In the *Rig Veda*, however, Pasupati is not mentioned anywhere, and Rudra is not described as the Lord of the Animals, but as a dangerous power who kills for pleasure. In pre-Vedic writings, Rudra is clearly identified with Pasupati.

Pashupati seal from Mohenjodaro

In the twelfth century text *Vita Merlini*, Merlin becomes the Lord of the Animals; dressed in antlers, he summons an enormous herd of stags and she-goats as a wedding gift for Guendoloena, who is amazed at his affinity with the animals. The name Gwendolen means 'white circle', and in this story Guendoloena appears to be a type of flower maiden. (In modern Welsh, *gwyn* or *gwen* means white or blessed, and *dolen* means a ring, link, loop, or bow.) It is appropriate that the Lady of the Flowers should be the consort of the Lord of the Animals. She represents the growth and burgeoning of nature; he represents the powers of hunting, culling, and death, which must occur so that the powers of fertility can progress without stagnation. Cernunnos is often identified with the Lord of the Animals, since he (or some other antlered god) is depicted on the Gundestrup cauldron with a stag and other animals, and holding a ram-headed serpent in one hand and a torc in the other.

In the *Mabinogion*, in the story of *The Lady of the Fountain*, the Lord of the Animals is described as "a black man of great stature on top of the mound. He is not smaller in size than two men of this world. He has but one foot, and one eye in the middle of his forehead. And he has a club of iron, and it is certain that there are not two men in this world who would not find their burden in that club. And he is not a comely man, but on the contrary he is exceedingly ill-favoured; and he is the woodward of that wood. And thou wilt see a thousand wild animals grazing all around him."

In European folktales, the Lord of the Animals makes an occasional appearance as an old man. In a Russian folktale, this old man appears as the King of the Forest, who is described thus: "all wrinkled he was and a green beard hung down to his knees. 'Who are you?' asked the peasant. 'I am Och, King of the Forest', said the little man." The King of the Forest lives underground in a green hut with his green wife and green children, in 'that other world under the earth'.

A South American people, the U'wa (Tunebo) of Colombia, have a deity called Ruáhama, the Master or Leader of Animals. At the making of the world, he cleared the thorny plants and bushes, while Thírbita (original Earth Sun) warmed the lake water. Then Ruáhama sowed the essential elements of life around the lakes. Ruáhama and Thírbita are shamanic deities. They are associated with Yagshowa, a tree turkey who can shape-shift, amongst other magical activities. The magic referred to is *kwika*, which signifies the reversal of order, changing of appearance and sexual practices. The first animals to emerge were the deer, hare, and peccary, but Thírbita promptly ate them (thus fulfilling their fate), leaving nothing but the bones. According to U'wa belief, animals change according to altitude, and things become what they eat. The faster animals, such as hare and deer, live in the highlands, whilst slower ones, such as monkeys, live in the lowlands.

This list represents a minimum compendium of myths and legends that Wiccans should know, in my opinion. Knowing about the stories on this list will help when writing and participating in rituals, as then you will get more out of them. You should also be well-versed in the myths of whichever particular pantheon(s) and deities you feel drawn to.

You should also know the myths of your local folk heroes (e.g. Tam Lin and Thomas the Rhymer in Scotland, Owain Glyndwr in Wales, El Cid in Spain, Jeanne d'Arc in France, Tannhäuser and Herman in Germany, Ctirad and Šarka for Czechs, High John the Conqueror for African Americans, etc.) I have included Robin Hood and King Arthur in the main list because ideas relating to them have fed into Wiccan ideas and philosophy.

Folklore and folktales

Folktales are very definitely "of the people". They show that the humble and the poor can triumph by using their wits, even against a seemingly insuperable adversary. Jawaharlal Handoo[229] has shown that animals in folk tales behave differently to animals in the "real world". In the "real world" we expect the larger animals to overpower the smaller. In folktale, the small and weak use their cunning or wisdom to outwit the big and strong; the humble hero, by use of observation and by making alliances with animal helpers, succeeds where the proud warrior has failed. In folk tale, the cunning always have the last laugh over the powerful. Folklore and folktales are wonderful sources for ritual – e.g. Robin brings back fire for the people (Midsummer), John Barleycorn is slain (Lammas), etc.

---

[229] Jawaharlal Handoo, "Cultural attitudes to birds and animals in folklore", in *Signifying Animals*, ed. R G Willis

21 December	Yule	The cutty wren; holly; wassailing
2 February	Candlemas (Imbolc)	Growth, light, increase
21 March	Spring Equinox	The return of the Lady to the land
31 April	May Eve (Beltane)	Maid Marian and Robin Hood
21 June	Midsummer	The robin; the oak; the sun
1 August	Lammas (Lughnasadh)	Mysteries of John Barleycorn
21 September	Autumn Equinox	Fruit harvest
1 November	Samhain	Entering the underworld / bonfires

Any folktale or custom could be enacted at the relevant festival depending on the local traditions (e.g. the Belfire was only customary in Celtic parts of Britain, whereas elsewhere people erected a maypole). A wonderful resource for folk customs and the ritual year is *The Stations of the Sun: the ritual year in Britain* by Ronald Hutton.

In the past, I have devised rituals based on a folktale depending on what I have seen during the day. For instance the idea of the robin for Midsummer came because I saw a robin and remembered the story that the robin fetched fire for humans, and decided that my ritual that year would be an enactment of this myth. In some traditions it was the swallow (because of its russet rump). In the ritual, each person takes the role of a character in the myth, gets into that character, and extemporises around a predetermined story-line. If a new story element arises, it can do so spontaneously from the loose structure of the rite.

At Lammas, a particularly effective motif is the killing of the corn-spirit, where the reapers chase the corn-spirit through the corn and cut down the last stand of corn. All the reapers must be responsible for the 'killing'. It is a good idea to find out your local vegetation-spirit (this can often be found in The Golden Bough by J.G. Frazer). A poem from *The Corn King and the Spring Queen* by Naomi Mitchison is good for Lammas:

> Hard is the grain,
> The sun thaws it,
> Without pain
> The rain draws it.
> The sods rend
> It leaps between:
> At death's end
> The blade is green!

Other folklore-related activities

- Learning **folk songs** to sing during the feasting. Folk songs are a major source of Pagan ideas about love, death, gender, honour, the seasons, and life in general.

- Developing musical skills with a tonal instrument (e.g. penny whistle, recorder, fiddle, etc.)
- **Storytelling** (traditional stories or story-in-the-round). This is a great way to really learn and experience mythology and folk-tales, as well as entertaining others.
- **Mummers' plays** – these have been regarded as survivals of Pagan fertility rituals. Whether they really are or not, they are certainly part of the folk tradition which appear all over Europe, and probably do express ancient archetypes. At New Year or at Yule, medieval mummers wore animal masks, possibly continuing an indigenous Pagan tradition. Animal masks included representations of stags and hares.
- **Morris dancing** – the Puritans were against Morris dancing, regarding it as lewd and suggestive – and anything the Puritans were opposed to is alright by me. It has also been described as a fertility tradition, and is associated with Maypoles and other revelry.
- **Wassailing** your apple tree or local orchard – many apple-growing areas have revived the practice of wassailing, usually celebrated in January. It is great fun and involves drinking cider mulled with stewed apple, singing loudly to wake the trees up, putting toast in the branches for the robins, and sometimes letting off air rifles to wake the trees.

Cultural appropriation

Cultural appropriation is acting as if someone else's mythology or ritual belongs to you, or pretending that you were trained by someone from the culture where the mythology or ritual originated. It's about power, and context, and histories of persecution. The Native Americans had their land and livelihoods taken away, their cultural identity erased and derided, and now people are taking their spiritual practices. Some Christians hold Passover Seder meals immediately before Easter communion; this completely changes the meaning of the Passover Seder; and also there is a long history of Christian persecution of Jews, so this feels inappropriate to me. (I am neither Jewish nor Native American, so it's not my personal fight, but I do want to be a good ally here.) Some may argue differently.

Buddhists are not a persecuted minority in the UK or the USA, so if the rest of us borrow their spiritual practices, there's no colonialist / power issue. The way Buddhism is disseminated involves a blending with local and pre-Buddhist traditions anyway, and some see Buddhism as a philosophy rather than a religion, so arguably Buddhists might be pleased. However, borrowers of Buddhist practices should acknowledge their debt to Buddhism, and make an effort to understand the Buddhist philosophy behind the practice, and learn the safeguards that come with the practice.

There is also an issue of context – many spiritual practices and especially specific rituals have a specific historical and mythological context. For example, Pagans calling the quarters relies on some sort of belief in the elemental spirits of the four quarters (or at least an understanding of the symbolism), so if you lift that and put it in, say, a Unitarian service, it might not work too well, unless you have figured out what this means to Unitarians. Conversely, the Unitarian Flower Communion has its roots in a specific historical moment and expression of Unitarian identity, so if Pagans were to borrow it, it would feel weird, because it is part of Unitarian identity, context and history.

One of the things that Native Americans object to is the way that 'plastic shamans' make up any old nonsense and claim that it is Native American, and also call themselves pseudo-Native-American names to make it sound more genuine and make a lot of money from selling books and workshops, not a penny of which actually goes to help genuine Native Americans. The peddling of inaccurate information about a tradition can also bring that tradition into disrepute, or misrepresent the practices being described as the norm for that tradition.

For instance, there are any number of books on the market purporting to be a definitive description of how Wicca is practised, and I disagree with large swathes of what is written in them – but other people assume that because I am a Wiccan, I must agree with what is written in those books; or even worse, that what is written in those books is the "proper" way to do Wicca, and I must therefore be doing it wrong. One example of this is the widespread misinterpretation of the *"Law of Threefold Return"*. Another example is the fact that genuine Wiccans train aspirants for free, but there are sadly people out there charging £300 for workshops on Wicca. This brings real Wiccans into disrepute.

Cultural appropriation often involves the erasure of the contemporary issues of the people whose culture is being appropriated. For example, in December 2012, when the "Mayan end of the world prophecy" was all over the internet (and many tour companies were making a lot of money out of New Age Mayan-themed holidays), the real Mayans, who still exist, were justifiably angry because their culture was being misappropriated and misinterpreted (and people were making really crass jokes about them too) and people were assuming that the Mayans died out (and if they had actually died out, it would be because of colonialism). In fact, the supposedly Mayan calendar that was shared widely on social media was actually an Aztec artefact. Indeed, New Agers often commit cultural appropriation, as the New Age movement is blissfully unaware of historical context, colonialism, and other gritty realities. However, other liberal religious groups can occasionally do it as well.

A guy called Chris said that he once went to a society for shamanic practitioners conference where they held a ghost dance ritual. The ghost dance was something created by Native Americans in response to increasing oppression from the colonial powers, but there was no acknowledgement of this. When Chris mentioned it to someone, they clearly misunderstood his concerns and said "but you can do it for whatever you want".

Teaching these practices as if they existed outside of the real history of oppression and colonialism does harm the people who invented the practice by ignoring their current existence and current problems. Making money out of someone else's spiritual practice, without acknowledging your debt to them, or giving them any of the money to help their cause, seems unethical to me. A related issue is where pharmaceutical companies go to South America, obtain indigenous knowledge of healing plants, make millions from new drugs derived from those plants, copyright the drugs, and don't give any money to the indigenous communities whose knowledge they have acquired.

I have attempted to come up with a list of what defines cultural appropriation, with additional suggestions arising from discussion:

- taking someone else's practice without permission or proper handing-on of the tradition and making money out of it (especially if the originators of the practice have a tradition of teaching it to people for free)

- taking someone else's practice and doing it in a completely different context where it does not fit

- taking someone else's rituals, practices, or stories and pretending they are your own

- taking someone else's ritual and then excluding them from it

- doing someone else's practice and pretending that you are authorised by the people whose practice it is

- claiming a fake identity as an indigenous practitioner

- doing others' spiritual practices and changing the meaning, and/or failing to build in the appropriate safeguards, and/or failing to acknowledge that you've changed the meaning in the new context

- failing to acknowledge the history of oppression suffered by the people whose practice is being copied

- doing something which has nothing to do with a culture and dressing it up and claiming it as part of that culture, when you aren't a member of that culture.

- all this adds to a culture that misrepresents ('noble savage' discourse for example) and mythologises indigenous peoples and makes their real struggles invisible

- wearing an item of clothing that expresses someone else's identity and sacred traditions as a fashion statement or a joke

There is of course, a problem with seeking permission – one person from a community might give permission for a borrowing, but others in that community might disagree. For example, Western occultists have borrowed Kabbalah for centuries, and the borrowed version often feels very different to the original Jewish version – but that particular cat is well and truly out of the bag, it would seem.

Here is a suggested definition of **cultural bricolage**:

- sensitive borrowing of stories and techniques (but not historically-situated rituals), fully acknowledging their source and original context, and that you might have changed the meaning in the new context (e.g. I do *lectio divina* workshops, which is a Christian technique, but I always acknowledge that that is what it is, explain the context in which it arose, and acknowledge that doing it with non-Biblical texts changes the meaning of the practice)

- thoroughly investigating the context, history and safeguards for the technique you propose to borrow; acknowledging your source and directing people to resources that explain these (e.g. if teaching Metta Bhavana, teach the safeguards that go with it)

- reading from the sacred texts of other traditions, where these are publicly available
- telling a story from another tradition, fully acknowledging that it came from that tradition, and explaining its original context if necessary

The section on cultural appropriation arose from a discussion with my friend Noam. Thanks to him for starting the discussion.

Discussion and activities

- What myths and legends do you find particularly attractive?
- How do you define cultural appropriation? How can we avoid it?
- Find out local folktales and incorporate them into your seasonal rituals
- Hold a storytelling evening

Meditation

Choose a story that you feel drawn to, and meditate on it. Visualise the story, perhaps with yourself as a character in the story. Rewrite the story from the viewpoint of a minor character. Use the story as the basis for *lectio divina*.

Chapter Eighteen

Wiccan rituals

Wiccan rituals are joyful events: celebrations of life, magic, sacred sexuality, and the cycles of nature and the seasons. They aim to deepen our connections with each other, and the landscape, and all beings.

Ritual modes

The structure of ritual in Wicca involves creating the sacred space as a microcosm representing the whole cosmos, then raising power within it, then wielding the power, thanking the divine powers and/or communing with them, and then dismantling the whole structure. This format is essentially derived from the Western magical tradition. If you go to a church service, where the ritual mode is liturgical, there is no wielding of power; rather the approach is to wait for the power to manifest.

Ronald Grimes, theorist of ritual, identifies several different modes of ritual.

	FRAME OF REFERENCE	DOMINANT MOOD	'VOICE'	BASIC ACTIVITY	MOTIVATION	EXAMPLES
RITUALIZATION	Ecological Psychosomatic	Ambivalence	Exclamatory	Embodying	Compelled	Symptoms Mannerisms Gestures
DECORUM	Inter-personal	Politeness	Interrogative	Cooperating	Expected	Greeting Departing Tea Drinking
CEREMONY *"honouring power"*	Political	Contentiousness	Imperative	Competing	Enforced	Inaugurations Rallies Legalities
LITURGY *"waiting upon power"*	Ultimate	Reverence	Interrogative / Declarative	Being	Cosmically necessary	Meditation Invocation Praise
MAGIC *"wielding power"*	Transcendent	Anxiety	Declarative / Imperative	Causing	Desired	Healing Fertility Divination
CELEBRATION *(power unleashed?)*	Expressive	Festive	Subjunctive	Playing	"spontaneous"	Carnivals Birthdays Feasts

Grimes, Ronald L. (1982) *Beginnings in Ritual Studies* Lanham & London : United Press of America

This diagram repays a lot of study and thinking. Most church services are liturgical; most Pagan rituals are magical or celebratory. If you go to a ritual expecting one mode, and it turns out to be in another mode, it can be very jarring, especially if you were expecting a magical or liturgical ritual and it turned out to be celebratory.

Examples of **ritualisation** include your morning routine (get up, have breakfast, have a shower, brush your teeth, go to work – or some variation on that set of actions); your evening routine (come home, kick off your shoes, maybe change your clothes, have a glass of wine); and so on. They are psychosomatic because you don't even think about them; they are automatic. They are embodied because they are physical actions.

Examples of **decorum** include shaking hands, waving goodbye, asking someone how they are. These are polite gestures that smooth your passage through your social milieu.

Ritualisation and decorum are not full-blown rituals; they are mini-rituals. The other categories are performed at greater length.

Typical **ceremonies** would include the crowning of a new monarch, the inauguration of a new President, the state opening of Parliament, and so on. They honour the power that is vested in the status quo.

Liturgy, which means 'the work of the people' is a collective affirmation of what is of ultimate worth, also known as "worship". If you have issues with the word *"worship"* because you think it means self-abasement, I highly recommend reading *An Abraxan Essay on Worship*, available from <www.uua.org/worship/theory/abraxanessay/>. This essay reclaims the word to mean 'honouring whatever we regard as being of ultimate worth', and draws on the theology of Paul Tillich, including the idea of the ground of all being.

Liturgy may involve waiting for power to manifest, but there is a dignity and solemnity in liturgical ritual which can be very enjoyable, and if it is done well, it can bring power through just as much as a magical ritual does. I would like to see more of the liturgical mode in Wiccan rituals.

Magical rituals are intended to cause change and transformation, either in the inner states of the participants, or in the external world. These include rites of passage, whose function is to bridge the divide between one psychological state and another (for example, to manage the transition between childhood and adulthood); and healing rituals, whose function is to transform an ill person into a well person. Even seasonal festival celebrations could be said to be magical rituals, because they manage the transition between one seasonal and the next.

Celebratory rituals can include birthday parties, but also parties to celebrate seasonal festivals. The aim of such a festivity is not to transform anything or manage a transition, but to let off steam. In the ancient world, carnivals inverted the normal social order and allowed everyone to let off steam, and then they returned to the normal social order when the festivities were over.

When writing rituals, you can deliberately make use of these different modes to create a different mood, depending on the purpose of your ritual. Sometimes a ritual can include more than one of these modes.

Rites of passage

A rite of passage is a ritual designed to make sacred a particular life event or transition from one stage of life to another. We might also call these rituals 'sacraments'.

The *Oxford English Dictionary* defines a sacrament as "a thing of mysterious and sacred significance; a religious symbol". The etymology of the word is from Latin *sacramentum* 'solemn oath' (from *sacrare* 'to hallow', from *sacer* 'sacred').

An important element of rites of passage and sacraments is that they have a physical component, often linked to one or more of the classical four elements (earth, air, fire, water). Immersion in water is used in both Judaism and Christianity to signify entering into a new phase, being consecrated (baptism) or re-consecrated (*mikveh*). Fire is used as a purifying medium in the Hindu ritual of *aarti*, which is both an offering and a purificatory ritual. Water is used for the Sikh baptism ceremony called *Amrit Sanskar*. The ancient druids are reported to have used sensory deprivation by requiring candidates for initiation to lie in darkness for several days and then thrusting them into the light, according to OBOD. All these rituals signify some sort of symbolic death and rebirth experience.

Life-rites

Most Pagans presume that everything is already sacred, because deities are immanent in the world. Therefore, rituals of consecration are about creating extra sacredness, or reconnecting us with the deities, the community, or the natural world.

Birth and naming

Pagans do not perceive a need to purify either the mother or the child after birth, considering that people are born innocent. The child will typically be welcomed into the community and given a name, but will not be committed to any particular religious tradition, as most Pagans believe that children should be able to choose their religion when they are old enough. Although the naming ceremony in Wicca is sometimes called a Wiccaning, it does not mean that the child is considered to be a Wiccan as a result of the ceremony.

Coming of age

There is a distinct lack of coming of age rituals in Western culture generally, and this is echoed in Pagan traditions, although some groups do celebrate the onset of menstruation, as long as the young woman in question actually wants this.

Initiation

Wicca has initiation rituals, partly based on the initiation rituals of occult orders such as Freemasonry. Isaac Bonewits identified three types of initiation ritual:

- Initiation as a recognition of a status already gained
- Initiation as an ordeal of transformation
- Initiation as a method for transferring spiritual knowledge and power

I have identified six aspects of initiation, which may be present in a single ritual, or may be a gradual process. There is the inner process of transformation; the initiation by the gods and goddesses (making contact with the numinous); experiencing the Mysteries (that which cannot be spoken, or *Arrheton*); being given the secrets of the initiating group (that which must not be spoken, or *Aporrheton*); joining the group mind of the initiating group; and the joining of the lineage or tradition of which the coven is part.

Handfasting

This is the term for a wedding, mainly in Wicca and eclectic Paganism. The term has been in use since the 1960s, according to Wikipedia. The ceremony generally involves the symbolic crossing of a threshold, such as leaping over a broomstick or a small fire. The use of ribbons to fasten the couple's hands together has been practised since the 2000s, again according to Wikipedia. Rings and vows are usually exchanged.

Croning

A ceremony for a woman who has reached menopause, usually celebrated in Wicca. A croning ceremony usually takes place around the age of fifty, and celebrates the achievement of elder status in the community, and feminine wisdom.

Dying

There is no set ritual for preparing for death, but there are many excellent resources in *The Pagan Book of Living and Dying*, by M Macha Nightmare (formerly of the Reclaiming tradition) and Starhawk.

Preparing sacred space (the circle)

Most Pagan traditions have a preparation for ritual, as rituals are often held in spaces which also have other uses, such as a living room, a garden, or a park. Therefore sacred spaces are temporary and have to be re-consecrated. It is also necessary for the participants in a ritual to be prepared for ritual, in order to help us enter into the right mind-set. Preparation typically includes some form of consecration of both the space and the participants with the four elements (earth, air, fire, and water). Incense, water, salt, and other symbols of the four elements may be used to create sacred space.

Cakes and wine

In Wicca, cakes and wine are consecrated and shared. This happens at every circle.

Libations

These are offerings of mead or wine poured for the deities and spirits of place. The libation is important in Religio Romana, Heathenry, and Wicca.

Effective ritual

There are some key pointers I give to my coven members to help keep the ritual running smoothly:

- Never comment on the ritual during the ritual (so don't comment on how well or how badly something went, just do it) because this breaks the mood of the ritual, and changes people from participants to observers.
- If you make a mistake, don't flap about and look gormless or express annoyance; pretend it did not happen, and (if necessary) move quickly and quietly to correct it. For example, if you forget to call the quarters after the water and salt, find a natural break in the ritual where it fits, and say, "Let us call the elemental powers", or something equally ritual-sounding.
- Focus on the energy first (e.g. when calling a quarter, make connection with the energy of the element, **then** say the words; don't try to do both at once. The energy is more important than the words.)
- Ritual should have a framework of set words, within which extemporisation may happen. For example, when calling the quarters, I do the extemporisation sandwich: set words to start ("Mighty ones of the [direction], powers of the [element]"), then some extemporisation appropriate to the theme or intent of the ritual, finishing with set words again ("Hail and welcome").
- Everyone needs to know what to expect in a ritual, otherwise they feel unsafe; or they need to trust the ritual leader completely.

What do all these rituals have in common?

They all involve one or more of the four elements (earth, air, fire, and water). Earth may be represented by stone, salt, crystals, or soil. Air may be represented by blades, wands, feathers, or incense. Fire may be represented by a candle flame, a bonfire, incense, or wands. Water is represented by water, chalices, and cauldrons. Each element has a sacred direction, which can vary between different traditions.

Initiation ceremonies all include a section where the candidate is asked whether they wish to be there. In naming ceremonies, where the baby cannot be asked if it wishes to take part, a simple welcome to the wider community of humanity is all that takes place.

There is an assumption that things are already sacred, because deities are immanent in the world, but sometimes we forget our connection with the divine, and need reconnecting.

They generally involve marking the transition from one phase to another – sometimes by actually crossing a threshold: stepping into the sacred space, or leaping across a fire or a broomstick.

They generally involve deities or spirits being asked for their blessing and/or protection.

The structure of a ritual

In some traditions, the coveners wait outside the ritual space until the priestess has prepared the circle.

The priestess sweeps the area of the circle. This is to purify the space for magical working.

She lays the broom at the threshold of the circle. This creates a doorway.

Next, she casts the circle with sword or athame. This is to keep power in and negative energy out.

She then lays the sword (or a wand) cross-wise over the broom. This is to protect the circle.

She consecrates the water and salt and mixes them together. These represent the elements of Water and Earth.

In some traditions, she blesses the incense. This represents the elements of air and fire.

She asperges (sprinkles) the circle with the water and salt. This is to bless and purify it.

She censes the circle with incense (wafts it around). This is to bless and purify it.

At this point, if the coveners are outside the circle, they are welcomed in. They must hold hands cross-wise with the person bringing them in, and jump over the threshold. The two then exchange a kiss.

The quarters are then called. This may be done by individual coveners, or by one person. This is to orient the circle in sacred space, seek the protection and blessing of the elemental powers, and connect the circle to the power of the universe.

The coven then dance and chant to raise power. There are many methods of doing this: the Mill of Magic, the Witches' Rune, the Cone of Power, raising power through the chakras, and the spindle of light.

Once the power is raised, it must be directed to some magical end, e.g. healing. Otherwise it will cause disturbance.

If the circle is for an esbat (Full Moon), a priest will draw down the Moon on a priestess.

If the circle is for a sabbat (one of the eight festivals), appropriate deities will be invoked.

At a sabbat, a ritual enacting a mystery relevant to the festival will be performed. This is to attune us to the cycles of the seasons.

Any small spells may be done after the main working, usually at esbats.

The coven then partake of cakes and wine. The priest adores the priestess, who sits on the altar with arms outstretched. He kneels before her and lays his arms along her thighs. He then asks her to bless the cakes, which he holds out to her on the pentacle. She blesses them with her athame.

They then bless the wine, putting wand or athame into cup or horn and willing power into it.

When the blessings are finished, the priest invites the priestess to return to the circle.

The coven then has a feast. This is very important, as eating returns you to normal consciousness. Each covener should bring a contribution of food and wine.

The quarters are closed in reverse order by the people who opened them, bidding farewell and thanking the elemental spirits.

A blessing may be recited now.

The priestess then outlines the circle widdershins. This is to unwind it.

Esbats and sabbats

An esbat is a ritual held at Full Moon, usually for the working of magic and the learning of new techniques. A sabbat is one of the eight festivals of the Wheel of the Year.

The way I organise esbats and sabbats is to start with a talking stick session where everyone takes turns talking about what has been happening for them recently; that way everyone knows everyone else's news, and it is also an opportunity to process mundane concerns and temporarily set them aside so that people can focus on the ritual. After that, we have a discussion (also using the talking stick) about a topic relevant to the ritual such as reincarnation, the nature of deities, what magic is, and so on.

There is then a comfort break, and everyone gets ready for the ritual. If it is a skyclad ritual, everyone places their clothes in a neat pile where they can find them again easily later.

The ritual begins when everyone is gathered, and people are asked to start focusing on the process as soon as the high priestess is sweeping the circle, using the outer process of sweeping to clear their minds of clutter. When the circle is cast and the quarters are called, everyone focuses on making a connection with the elemental spirits, not just the person calling the quarter. The same applies throughout the ritual. After cakes and wine at the end of the ritual, we then share a feast, usually remaining inside the circle, so as to share the merriment with the deities and spirits. Then we say farewell to the quarters and uncast the circle.

The tides of the year

Each part of the year corresponds to a different tide.

- **Resting**: during the late autumn/early winter, when everything lies still in the earth. Psychologically, this is the time when we sit by the fireside and tell tales, and go within ourselves.

- **Cleansing**: during the late winter/early spring, when the frost breaks down the earth and decayed matter. February was the month of cleansing in ancient Rome. Psychologically, this is the time for clearing old habits, spring-cleaning the house.

- **Growing**: late spring/early summer, everything is growing. Psychologically, this is the time of new projects, branching out into new ideas, being creative and extrovert.

- **Reaping**: This is the time of harvest, when the fruit and corn ripen and can be gathered in. Psychologically, this is the time of bringing things to completion and fruition.

The wheel of the year

For Pagans, the whole year is a cycle, and the movements of the Earth around the Sun, and the resulting changes in temperature and day length and vegetation (in short, the seasons) are a core part of Pagan festivals.

I think the work of spirituality is to relax, to find the inner stillness and space that is already there. All we have to do is to remember who we really are; to reconnect with the ebb and flow of the cycles of life. Everything is cyclical – the seasons, the tides, the orbits of the planets – why not human life? But it is not just a ceaseless round of the same old things, repeated ad nauseam. Everything changes; everything is always becoming something else; nothing is ever lost.

My favourite times of year are the transitional seasons of spring and autumn, when everything is changing rapidly. In spring there are new blossoms and new leaves emerging, and the days lengthen rapidly. In autumn, the leaves turn red and yellow and orange and are blown away in the wind. The smell of bonfires is in the air, symbolising the transformation of decay into the bright energy of fire.

The gathering of life experience is like the laying down of compost. The leaves of individual events fall onto the heap, fade and decay, and are transformed into memories, which feed our sense of identity, which gives rise to new experiences.

Change is constant in life; it is the one thing we can rely on. Some people find it difficult to embrace change; others enjoy it. Without change, there would be no growth, no seasons, no new life. There would also be no death, but just try to imagine what immortality would be like – a barren state of existence with no excitement.

Buddhists like to point out that there is nothing constant about our bodies. Our cells are replaced so rapidly that every cell in our bodies is replaced by the end of seven years, so you are literally not physically the same person you were seven years ago. This is possibly the origin of the phrase, "the seven year itch". Each day you acquire new experiences, new dreams, and lose old memories, so you are not the same person you were yesterday.

We constantly shape each other socially, giving approval or disapproval to certain characteristics, and each of us is a slightly different person in different social situations. We change our opinions as we hear new evidence, and this is a sign of flexibility and openness. A lack of willingness to change one's opinion gives rise to the rigidity of fundamentalism.

Willingness to change, openness and trust are essential pre-requisites for the building of spiritual community. It is why Wiccans like to do our rituals in a circle, which involves making eye contact with others, and emphasises the equality of participants.

The sociologist of religion, Emile Durkheim, said that the function of ritual is to manage changes in life, such as the transition from one state to another. Rites of passage (coming-of-age, coming out, initiation, marriage, divorce, birth, and death) are obvious examples; but in a sense all rituals are about managing change. The structure of ritual is a way of managing and enabling the change in consciousness that you experience as you make contact with the Divine by gradually relaxing into the ritual and entering into an altered state of consciousness.

The major change enabled by participating in a ritual is the building of community with others. As we share the celebration of ultimate worth, singing, praying, invoking, meditating, speaking and listening, we are focused on something other than our individual ego. We cease to worry about how we look, and focus on the experience of being together. The constant presence of the inner commentator is switched off. David Smail, a therapist who regards therapy with suspicion, writes in his book, *Taking Care*, that more therapeutic benefit is derived from participating in a communal activity than from hours of individual therapy. This is true even if it's something apparently trivial like your local bridge club.

Change involves both embracing and letting go, expansion and contraction. It is a dance of inner and outer, dark and light. It is a cycle of growth, death and rebirth. Everything is in constant flux. The plants grow, blossom, bear fruit and die. Stars and galaxies are born, expand, and then die as their energy is spent.

Sometimes change can be painful. The loss of loved ones, or the ending of relationships, are usually immensely painful, but they may also enable growth and renewal, and expand your capacity to feel.

When I reflect on the changes in my own life – the beginnings and endings of relationships, moving house, moving to a new city, meeting new friends, learning new ideas – these are always the times of greatest spiritual growth for me. Suddenly I experience a flood of creativity; poetry and prose pours onto the page in an unstoppable flood. Then there may be years of stagnation, until something comes along to shake me out of my rut and force me to move and grow. I should really try to find a way to make change constant in my life…

There could be no stories without change, because stories tell about the transition from one way of being to another – the discovery of spiritual treasure, a struggle for justice, falling in love, journeying from one place to another. The scientist Jack Cohen has suggested that we be renamed *Pan narrans*, the storytelling ape, because storytelling is a major aspect of our human nature. So let's celebrate change as being the basis of all good stories, including the unique and special story we are each currently living.

Samhain (31 October)

Samhain is a festival honouring ancestors. It is also the "harvest of meat" when cattle would be slaughtered before the winter. To the ancient Celts, however, Samhain was a festival of liberation from oppression. In East Anglia, it was known as Hollantide. Many Wiccans use Samhain rituals to honour, remember, and commune with their loved ones who have passed on.

Samhain is the Irish word for the month of November. The ancient Irish festival held at this time was about the renewal of freedom – legends associated with it tell of heroes who freed their people from bondage. So the association with the dead was probably imported to England by Christianity, as this was the feast of All Saints and All Souls. After the Reformation, of course, the importance of these festivals was downplayed, and by the early 20th century, folklorists were speculating that the origins of All Hallows were actually Pagan. The first stirrings of the Pagan revival started in the early 20th century, so the idea of Samhain being associated with the dead was imported into Paganism.

Pagans tend to focus on the preciousness of this life, not some future one beyond death. Hence all these traditions want to celebrate and remember the lives of our ancestors. Ancestors can be relatives and friends who have died, or people from the past whom we admire (we often honour both). These people have shaped who we are now – given us life, given us inspiration, guided us, comforted us, and nurtured us – and it comforts us to remember them and commune with them.

Many people believe in reincarnation, and that the consciousness resides in an in-between place between lives. In Paganism, the dead are seen as not being very far away – only a heartbeat away – and many Pagans say that "the veil between the worlds is thin" at Samhain, because the tides of life are on the ebb as winter approaches, and because the encroaching darkness of winter is seen as a time for contemplation, remembrance, and introspection.

Pagans do not see darkness and death as evil, but as part of the cycle of life, death, and rebirth. If there was no death, there would be no growth, no change, and no birth. If there was no darkness, the seeds could not gestate in the warm darkness of the earth; if there was no night, there would be no sleep, and no stars and moonlight. If there was no winter cold, there would be none of the beauty of autumn, the seeds would not germinate, and germs would not be killed by the frost. Darkness is the Yin spoken of by the Taoists – one half of the divine dance of the cosmos.

Samhain or Hallowe'en is one of eight festivals of the Pagan wheel of the year – part of the dance of the elements around the wheel of the seasons, one of the many interlocking cosmic cycles of which our lives are an intimate part.

In many cultures, especially in Mexico, All Souls is the Day of the Dead – *Dia de los Muertos* – when people go to visit family graves, and set up altars for them in the home. This is not a morbid practice, but an acknowledgement of death in the midst of life, death as part of the natural cycle.

So why should we reintegrate this festival into our spiritual practice? Because in Britain, death is swept under the carpet, ignored and feared. If we acknowledged it (at least once in the year), it would be an invitation to live more fully and mindfully. If we ignore it, it becomes part of the shadow, the part of our psyche that we reject and that contains our fears and follies, and which we project onto other people: the Other, the outsider, the transgressor.

Whereas if we recognise death as being part of the natural cycle, like the seasons of the year, then we can live more integrated lives, living in and for the moment.

Samhain is also the time when, as the nights get longer and the winter grips the land, we descend into our own depths. Summer is a time for being extrovert, creative and expansive; winter is a time for curling up by the fireside and going within oneself to find the poetic, the spiritual and the quiet side of ourselves – the forgotten aspects, perhaps even the side of ourselves that we have repressed and need to examine.

The presiding deity of winter is the Crone Goddess. She has been feared and denigrated in recent centuries – people speak of old wives' tales, haggard old witches muttering in corners, and so on. But traditionally, old women were the ones who were the keepers of stories and other traditional wisdom such as herb lore and midwifery. She is the midwife and the one who washed, anointed and laid out the dead, the one who cuts the cord of both life and death. She represents merciful release; but she also possesses the wisdom of old age. Wisdom is traditionally represented (in the *Bible* and in other traditions) as a feminine being or quality. Wisdom is the joining together of instinct and experience and knowledge. It is the wisdom of the body, the knowledge of when to act and when to refrain from acting, when to speak and when to keep silent. Wisdom comes from reflection upon experience and knowledge.

The Crone is also the Goddess of the Waning Moon, which represents a time of letting go and ebbing away, so it is traditional at Samhain to let go of aspects of your life that you do not need or want any more.

Yule (21 December)

The winter solstice is the point in the year when the day is at its shortest. The sun rises at its furthest south, and rises in roughly the same place for three days, hence the name "solstice", meaning "Sun stands still".

When I was a kid, I was told that ancient pagans used to light bonfires on top of hills at the winter solstice because they feared that the sun would not return after the longest night. I don't know if there is any truth in this idea, but I remember finding it thrilling.

The Anglo-Saxons called the festival Yule; the Old Norse word was *jól*.

The earliest references to Yule are by way of indigenous Germanic month names (*Ærra Jéola* (Before Yule) or *Jiuli* and *Æftera Jéola* (After Yule). It has been speculated that the word means "turning point", but the etymology is unclear.

At Autumn Equinox, we begin the descent into winter. At Samhain, we meet the ancestors and the beloved dead. At Yule, the furthest point in the descent of the Sun, we begin to emerge from the creative and introspective phase of winter, and start thinking about the first stirrings of Spring. The sun represents the core aspect of the personality in many esoteric symbol-systems, and so its descent into the underworld represents a journey into our own subconscious, our own depths, to bring up fertile material to feed a time of creativity. Of course we know that the Sun doesn't really descend into the underworld, but in many mythologies, that is where the sun god goes.

Yule is also a time for enjoyment; the harvest is over and done, there is little work to do in the dark time of the year, so it is time to feast, sing, dance, make merry, and kindle plenty of lights (to make up for the lack of sunshine, and to remind the sun that we would like it to start rising further north again!)

Imbolc (2 February)

Imbolc is a festival celebrating the lactation of ewes, the coming of lambs, and the first stirrings of spring. The name means either "ewes' milk" (*Oimelc*) or "in the belly" (*im bolg*).

In Ireland, Imbolc is the feast of Brigit, originally a Goddess, and now a saint. The Goddess Brigit is associated with healing, poetry, and smithcraft. The saint is associated with them too, and with the perpetual flame tended by the nuns of Kildare - which possibly goes back to pre-Christian times. There are numerous folk-customs and stories associated with Brigit.

Candlemas is the Christian festival of the Purification of the Virgin, when Mary presented Jesus at the Temple forty days after his birth, to complete her purification after childbirth in accordance with the *Torah*.

Both these festivals have traditionally focused on the increasing light and life as the days lengthen and the trees start to blossom and bud. They are also a celebration of the Divine Feminine, or the Goddess.

Spring Equinox (21 March)

Spring Equinox is a festival of balance, as day and night are equal (but after this the days get longer). It's also the time when the coming of spring is really becoming apparent. According to Bede, the ancient Germanic pagans honoured a goddess called Eostre or Ostara who was associated with hares and the Moon and eggs; however there is no reference to this goddess in any other text, so much of the modern mythology associated with her is extrapolated from Bede, and does not have any basis in older mythology. That does not mean that it is not valid as mythology, just that people should not claim ancient origins for it.

Beltane (1 May)

Beltane is a festival celebrating sacred sexuality. It is typically celebrated by jumping over fires and dancing round maypoles. Pagan rituals often include symbolic expressions of sexuality. A celebration of Beltane might include a celebration of sexuality in all its forms, and hence a social justice element. It could also include celebrations of the senses, and something to honour the coming of spring and the renewal of life.

Midsummer (21 June)

Midsummer is a festival celebrating the Sun. At this time of the year, the days are at their longest, so the Sun is said to be at the height of its power. However, after Midsummer, the days will get shorter, so the Sun is said (symbolically) to descend into the underworld. The Sun is a metaphor for our consciousness; as we descend into the depths of winter, the self goes inward and becomes more introspective.

Lammas (1 August)

Lammas commemorates the death of John Barleycorn, the dying-and-resurrecting vegetation god. The corn was believed to be inhabited by the corn-spirit, which was killed at every harvest and resurrected in the planting of the new corn. In Ireland, Lammas was celebrated with games in honour of the goddess Tailtiu, the mother of Lugh the sun god, and was called Lughnasadh. The harvest is an important symbol of cyclicity, growth, and change. The wheel turns, and what has grown must die, so that the seeds can be planted for the new cycle of growth.

Autumn Equinox (21 September)

At the Autumn Equinox, day and night are equal (but after this the nights get longer), so most Pagan rituals focus on this, and on the importance of balance. It's also the fruit harvest; for this reason, I associate it with the Roman deities Pomona and Vertumnus. A celebration of Autumn Equinox could focus on the sensual delights of food and the harvest of work and creativity, as well as the balance of light and dark.

In China, they see life as the balance of opposites – yin and yang, night and day, life and death, eternally cycling around each other in the great dance of existence, the dynamic equilibrium of nature. Equilibrium means "equal freedom" – freedom to move, to grow and to change; freedom of choice.

This dynamic balance of opposites can also be seen in the dance of the seasons – "a time to be born, and a time to die; a time to plant, and a time to pluck up that which is planted". The wheel of the year turns; falling in the autumn, rising in the spring. As it falls in the autumn, and the nights draw in, we turn inward, towards home, and hearth, and spiritual things; baking, and making jam and wine; creative projects.

In Pagan tradition, there are three harvests; the corn harvest at Lammas; the fruit harvest at Autumn Equinox; and the harvest of meat at Samhain, when some of the cattle would have been slaughtered and preserved for the winter.

Discussion and activities

- For each festival, note down ideas about what it means to you personally
- Find out the myths and traditions and festivals of your local area or

culture of origin

- How do the seasons unfold in your bioregion? What flowers come into bloom at different times of year? When do the leaves of different trees come out? What migratory birds appear around each festival?

- How do the festivals link in with other tides (life, seasons, the zodiac, etc) for you?

- Identify different rites of passage that you have experienced

- What is your preferred means of creating sacred space?

- Experiment with different ways of creating a Wiccan circle. What works best for you?

Chapter Nineteen

The shamanic ordeal in Wicca

The practice of scourging is perhaps not as widespread as it once was, except perhaps in the initiation ritual, and even there it is not done so as to hurt. There have even been suggestions that it was all invented by Gerald Gardner because he was into BDSM. However, it is clear that sexuality and spirituality have been closely associated since ancient times, and that some people have derived pleasure from pain; hence also there has been a link between BDSM and the sacred.

Pain makes you feel intensely in your body, aware of every nerve, every sinew. In a spiritual tradition where the connection between mind, body, and spirit is of paramount importance, therefore, anything which connects body and spirit more closely is a valued part of the tradition. Scourging is therefore a vital ingredient of the Craft, and BDSM is a vital ingredient of sexuality. It is a shame that the erotic enjoyment of pain has been marginalised by its association with patriarchal ideas about dominance and submission. Most people get off on the occasional fingernail digging into the flesh, or being bitten, or whatever. It is all a matter of degree.

Of course, the experience of the pain is not the only thing evoked by the practice of scourging or the practice of BDSM. In any situation where you abdicate control, power relations come into play. In BDSM, the power relations obtaining in the world are often deliberately subverted. In the Craft, all must submit to the scourge, and all must use the scourge. So there is never an imbalance of power.

The experience of scourging made me aware of a new paradigm for the experience of pain. There are various ideas to provide a mythological framework for the use of the scourge. One is that it is associated with the goddess Hecate, because it confronts the parts of the psyche hitherto considered unacceptable. Another is that it is associated with the higher self, to strip away the ego-bound consciousness (after all, you can't be very egocentric when you're bound and being scourged). In the initiation ceremony, it is a shamanic ordeal, such as is used by traditional societies. The most visually satisfying and elegant idea is that the circle is a threshing floor, the coveners are the grain, and the scourge is the flail. This fits very well with the imagery of Osiris, who carries the crook and the flail.

And of course, there is the practical aspect of heating the lower chakras to stimulate the kundalini (in which case you probably need to do it properly, so you can actually feel it). Also, there is the important aspect of safety. Scourging is not something you can just pick up a scourge and do - it needs to be thought about. It is necessary to avoid hitting the kidneys and the spine, so care must be taken not to let the ends of the thongs go over the side of the torso or above the buttocks. When the main part of the thong has been laid on, the rest travels faster, and hurts more on impact. Even someone who is deliberately doing it softly can cause the wrong sort of pain in this way. Another useful technique is to 'pull' the blow, as you do with punches in stage fighting. This is done by flicking the wrist up on impact. It hurts less, but it puts a lovely little sting in the scourging. Also, there is no need to hurry. It is a good idea to pause between the strokes so that the sensation is felt to the full. It is a bit like striking a bell - it is much lovelier if you allow the reverberation to die away before ringing it again.

Whilst we are on the subject of safety, the actual binding needs to be done with care and thought as well. The idea is to impose a certain amount of sensory deprivation by restricting the breathing and movement of the hands. Doing it too tightly, however, may pinch nerves in the wrists. It is also a good idea to use a quick-release knot. It is important that the binding does not get any tighter.

The really clever bit about the whole experience of scourging is that it is mutual (when it is done at every circle). The other person does you; then you do them. It creates an intimacy and a sense of trust. The possibility of manipulation or domination is avoided by the mutuality of it.

Within the shamanic BDSM scene, people have experienced out-of-body experiences resulting from BDSM. This is a rationale for BDSM that doesn't involve a punishment/reward view of the world. It is an experiment with pain and the boundaries of trust, which is an important aspect of bondage.

I think what Gerald Gardner had to say about scourging is extremely interesting:

> "Of the Ordeal of the Art Magical:
>
> Learn of the spirit that goeth with burdens that have not honour, for 'tis the spirit that stoopeth the shoulders and not the weight. Armour is heavy, yet it is a proud burden and a man standeth upright in it. Limiting and constraining any of the senses serves to increase the concentration of another. Shutting of the eyes aids the hearing. So the binding of the initiate's hands increases the mental vision, while the scourge increases the inner vision. So the initiate goes through it proudly, like a princess, knowing it but serves to increase her glory. But this can only be done with the aid of another intelligence and in a circle, to prevent the power thus generated being lost."

In the initiation rite, at the presentation of the working tools, the initiator says:

> "Next I present the scourge. This is a sign of power and domination. It is also used to cause purification and enlightenment, for it is written: to learn you must suffer and be purified."

In the consecration of the water, we are reminded that "as water purifies the body, so the scourge purifies the soul". The scourge is symbolic of all suffering. This of course raises the question of the purpose of suffering. There is a beautiful passage on this in *The Prophet* by Kahlil Gilbran:

> "[T]he selfsame well from which your laughter rises was oftentimes filled with your tears.... the deeper that sorrow carves into your being, the more joy you can contain. Is not the cup that holds your wine the very cup that was burned in the potter's oven? And is not the lute that soothes your spirit the very wood that was hollowed with knives?"

Scourging could also symbolise the flaying of Marsyas, who cried *"Quod me mihi detrahis?"* (Why do you tear me from myself?) Renaissance thinkers interpreted this myth as an initiatory experience, in which the dismemberment of the self resulted in a new being.

Many traditional societies use pain as a means to enlightenment. Some of these are described in the excellent book *LeatherFolk*, which is a collection of essays on BDSM. A whole section of the book is devoted to Pagan and shamanic BDSM. In the Sun Dance ritual, men would attach themselves to the central pole by hooks, and sacrifice bits of their flesh, which would be torn out as they danced ecstatically. In India, adepts learn to pass wire and knives through the flesh, thereby achieving ecstatic states.

So what is the biological basis for the ecstasy derived from pain? According to Pat Califia and Cynthia Astuto,

> "The body secretes powerful chemicals, chiefly adrenaline and endorphins, when it is under stress, and these chemicals create euphoria and change the way the brain interprets stimuli which would ordinarily be perceived as painful."

It is this euphoria which can often be so intense as to result in spiritual experiences.

However, context and meaning are very important. If a scourging is being conducted under circumstances where its meaning is not clear, and the participants do not have a clear visualisation of its purpose, they are likely to end up feeling a bit ridiculous. So a symbolic meaning and a clear magical intent for the process is very important.

The kiss is also very important. In one way it contrasts with the scourge. The binding and scourging represent Perfect Trust (in that you have to trust someone to let them immobilise you and take a scourge to you), and the kiss represents Perfect Love. However, I think the kiss has an important psychological function. The person who has been scourged has just had their outer self purified away; the kiss welcomes the inner self to the circle. Also, the prolonged experience of pain can make a different stimulus especially pleasurable, so the kiss acts as a contrast. Each is a different expression of love.

Some people may be uncomfortable with introducing this aspect of sexuality into the circle. But there is no boundary between sexuality and spirituality, everything is sacred. "All acts of love and pleasure are my rituals." It is only because the use of flagellation has unpleasant associations with punishment and patriarchy that people regard it as deviant. But the experience of pain opens up whole new realms of sensation. While it is happening, your whole body feels intensely - you inhabit your body more fully. All attention is focused on the area being stimulated. Paradoxically, this can also result in out-of-body experiences.

I once went swimming in a very cold sea. At first, the cold seems unbearable, and you think you are going to have to get out of the water. Just at this moment, you suddenly start feeling warmer, hugely euphoric, and very much alive. (This is probably the point at which hypothermia starts to set in, so be very careful.) The experience of erotic pain is very much like this - just the point at which you thought you couldn't take any more is the point at which transcendence is achieved.

The use of pain is very ancient, and was employed by people as diverse as shamans and the mystery cults. The devotees of Cybele used scourging, for example. It is one of the known paths to enlightenment, as has recently been rediscovered almost by accident in the BDSM community, with the flowering of spiritual awareness amongst some of its practitioners. The Goddesses and the Gods have many aspects; and some of them wield whips and knives.

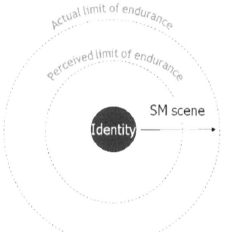

In BDSM, there is a clear understanding of consent and boundaries. The top (the one inflicting the pain) must be aware of the limits of the bottom (the one receiving the pain). Limits can be *'hard'* (non-negotiable) or *'soft'* (with the possibility of going beyond them). A personal limit is as much as you think you can take. This can vary within a scene; at the beginning of the session, you might think you can only take a certain amount of pain, but once the endorphins are triggered, you may be able to take more.

The use of pain to bring about spiritual transformation is quite ancient. In the Villa of the Mysteries in Pompeii, there is a wall-painting with a person being initiated, and part of the initiation involves being scourged (whipped). The initiate, carrying a staff and wearing a cap, is depicted returning from a night journey, and emerges from a dark place to a lighted place, as if being reborn. She is shown reaching for a covered object in a basket, the *liknon* or winnowing basket. The covered object is thought to be a phallus, or a herm. To the right is a winged deity, perhaps Aidos. She is looking to the left and is prepared to strike with a whip. In the next scene, the two themes are torture and transfiguration, the culmination of the ritual. The initiate is depicted with a lash across her back. She is consoled by another woman. To the right a nude woman is playing the cymbals and another woman is poised to give to the initiate a thyrsus, a symbol of Dionysus, god of ecstasy.[230]

---

[230] James W. Jackson (undated), Villa of the Mysteries, Pompeii, http://www.art-and-

Roman fresco, Villa of the Mysteries, Pompeii

In Sumerian legend, when Inanna descends into the Underworld, her sister Ereshkigal hangs her on a hook. Raven Kaldera, a Pagan BDSM practitioner, has written about this:[231]

> "We who are changelings of the Dark Moon, whose wiring is built for this sort of thing, we are not happy with the fruit-and-flowers sex of the upper world and its sunny gods. We are like Inanna, who walked willingly into the realm of Death, who was stripped of her name and her power, who was hung on a hook over the throne of the Queen of Death, who had to be ransomed back by those who turn gender on its head and who are willing to weep. She did it because there was no other way to touch the deep wisdom that she sought, no way but to stumble along dark paths to the katabasis point, and trust in all the wisdom of the Underworld that you may one day emerge triumphant."

archaeology.com/timelines/rome/empire/vm/villaofthemysteries.html
[231] Raven Kaldera's website: http://www.paganbdsm.org

In Hinduism, the Kavadi ritual involves the use of pain to bring about transcendence. Some have argued that the Lakota sun-dance is akin to spiritual BDSM, as it involves placing hooks in the body as an ordeal, but this is disputed. Many cultures practice body modification, scarification, and tattooing, all of which involve pain and restriction, which are related areas to BDSM, and have been enthusiastically revived by urban primitives. Some forms of monasticism also involve the use of pain and deprivation to achieve altered states. Some cultures' shamanic ordeals also involve endurance tests, pain, body modification, and sensory deprivation.

Raven Kaldera writes:

> "Throughout history, from the Hindu Kavadi ceremony to the Lakota Sun Dance, the Ordeal Path has been an honored spiritual road to the magic of the flesh, and to touching the Gods. Today many Pagans are discovering this path, by accident or by design. Simultaneously, many practitioners of secular BDSM are finding themselves having spiritual experiences in the middle of their most secular scenes."

Paganism is an embodied spirituality, honouring the flesh and the spirit intertwined. So Pagan BDSM is not about punishment, denial, or vilification of the flesh; rather it is about the joyous exploration of sensation, pain, and sensuality. Pagan BDSM is loving and consensual and celebrates the body and sensuality (and so does the BDSM community in general).

The practice of inflicting pain for sensual enjoyment was fairly widespread in the ancient world. In ancient Rome, the festival of Lupercalia was celebrated on 15 February, and involved consensual kink. Plutarch described Lupercalia thus:

> "Lupercalia, of which many write that it was anciently celebrated by shepherds, and has also some connection with the Arcadian Lycaea. At this time many of the noble youths and of the magistrates run up and down through the city naked, for sport and laughter striking those they meet with shaggy thongs. And many women of rank also purposely get in their way, and like children at school present their hands to be struck, believing that the pregnant will thus be helped in delivery, and the barren to pregnancy."

There were also a number of kinky myths. Ogmios was a Gaulish deity, whom Lucian describes as a bald old man with a bow and club leading an apparently happy band of men with chains attached to their ears from his tongue. This is thought by some scholars to be a metaphor for eloquence, possibly related to bardic practices.

Aengus went to the lake of the Dragon's Mouth and found 150 girls chained up in pairs. He found his girl, Caer Ibormeith. On 1 November, Caer and the other girls would turn into swans for one year, every second Samhain. Aengus was told he could marry Caer if he could identify her as a swan. Aengus succeeded. He turned himself into a swan and they flew away, singing beautiful music that put all its listeners asleep for three days and nights.

More recently, Donatien Alphonse François de Sade, Marquis de Sade (1740–1814) was a radical libertine, sadist, and moderate revolutionary, who wrote extensively about his fantasies, and was imprisoned. Based on his writings, the term "sadism" was coined by Krafft-Ebing in *Psychopathia Sexualis*. Various postmodern philosophers have been interested in de Sade's ideas, notably Michel Foucault.

Leopold Ritter von Sacher-Masoch (1836–1895) was a folklorist, author, journalist; socialist and humanist who favoured Jewish integration and women's emancipation. The term "masochism" was coined by Krafft-Ebing in *Psychopathia Sexualis*, based on Sacher-Masoch's novel, *Venus in Furs*, which Sacher-Masoch sought to live out with his mistress, Fanny Pistor.

Michel Foucault was a Postmodernist philosopher with an interest in Nietzsche and nihilism. He was fascinated by the exploration of power relations available in BDSM practices. He regarded it as a subversion or reversal of usual power relations; indeed, the use of power in BDSM is always subversive because it is a parody of societal power.

Foucault observed that we live in a Panopticon society, where everyone is subject to scrutiny. This was the shadow side of the Enlightenment. BDSM is a subversion of this constant control and surveillance, and the internalised imposition of social norms.

Another important writer on BDSM is Patrick Califia. He is the author of various science fiction novels and the numerous books about BDSM. Formerly a lesbian, now a trans-man, he is an advocate for BDSM, pornography and individual freedom. He was excluded by some sections of the lesbian community for his views on BDSM.

He acknowledged the inequality of power in lesbian sadomasochistic practices, but contended that exploration and open discussion of these roles would not only lead to liberation but could also be extended to other issues of inequality within the feminist movement.

Since its publication in 1991, *Leatherfolk: Radical Sex, People, Politics, and Practice* by Mark Thompson has become a classic, must-read book on human sexuality and identity. Widely acknowledged as being among the most useful books of its kind, the anthology provides historical background and analysis of queer BDSM practices. The diverse contributors look at the history of the gay and lesbian underground, how radical sex practice relates to their spirituality, and what it means to them personally.

Peter Grey is a Pagan poet who has written extensively about the use of kink in ritual, how it can be used to explore the deeper recesses of the psyche and bring about transformation. He has also explored traditional techniques of shamanic transformation using pain. He places a strong emphasis on the loving and ritual aspects of kink in his writings.

Raven Kaldera is a Pagan BDSM practitioner who has written extensively on the subject of Pagan kink. He has described a threefold ordeal path (though not everyone practices all of these at any one time).

- **Using pain applied in a ritual context** in order to bring the recipient into an altered state by triggering their endorphins, and bringing about a spiritual transformation.

- **Using ritual drama to create an ordeal** for the bottom, enabling them to travel to the dark places in themselves and come out safely, having learned useful things in the process.

- **Using dominance and submission as a spiritual path.** In this practice, the submissive effectively sees the dominant as a manifestation of the Divine, or their primary means of encountering divinity, and serves them accordingly.

He has also mapped out various BDSM correspondences for the Four Elements.

- **Fear: the Gate of Fire**
  This involves experiencing fear and going through it and beyond it

- **Shame: the Gate of Water**
  In the myth of Inanna, the Queen of Heaven who goes down to the underworld in order to find wisdom, she travels through the gates of the underworld, and is stripped of her crown (representing temporal power), her jewels (representing wealth), her rings (representing magical power), her clothing (representing protection) and finally her name. As a nameless corpse, she is hung on the wall as a decoration for her sister Ereshkigal, the Queen of the Dead. When she returns from the Underworld, she has learned the wisdom of the depths.

- **Endurance: the Gate of Earth**
  This is where the practitioner suffers and strives to gain strength, and pushes beyond perceived limits to ever greater feats of endurance. It is where you find the core of strength within.

- **Letting go: the Gate of Air**
  This is the leap of trust into the Void, into perfect trust.

- **Rebirth**
  This is the use of ritual drama as a rite of passage.

The use of pain in a ritual context can vary in its meaning and purpose. It can be used to achieve an altered state by the production of endorphins. This can be used to connect with the universe, or do magical work such as producing energy for a spell. The bottom (the recipient of the pain) is the one directing the energy, and the top's purpose is to give them the experience they need in order to do the magical work.

Pain can also be used to create energy for the top to work with. A body in pain produces energy, which is accessible to many magic-workers. In this instance, the top is the primary magician, and the bottom becomes one of their tools.

Pain can be used to bring people back in touch with their bodies; when being whipped, it is impossible to focus on anything else. This is a useful technique for people who can easily go into trance, but find it difficult to reconnect with the physical.

Pain can be used as an initiatory ordeal, to build courage and self-esteem by enduring it. It can also be used for emotional catharsis, in order to deal with negative feelings. In this case, the pain is used as a tool to reveal repressed issues that need to be brought to the surface for healing.

Obviously, the use of BDSM in ritual is not to everyone's taste, but it is good to understand it and appreciate its transformational potential.

Gerald Gardner may or may not have been kinky himself, but he did a tremendous thing by incorporating the use of scourging as one of the magical techniques available to Wiccans. The use of the scourge (and pain in general) as an initiatory and transformative tool is ancient and widespread in indigenous shamanic traditions. By releasing endorphins, magical and shamanic practitioners can experience transformation and ecstasy, and use the energy created for magical workings and spiritual renewal.

Safety considerations with BDSM

- Keep it safe, sane, and consensual
- Use safe-words:
  o Green – I need an adjustment
  o Amber – That's OK at the moment but it won't be in a minute
  o Red – stop completely
- Establish protocols
  o who can do what to whom, and how
  o Are you into B/D, D/s, S/M or some other combination?
- Script scenes and rituals beforehand
- Start low-key, establish boundaries, only push slightly beyond them
- Read a safety manual and/or how-to manual
- Be careful with hygiene around bodily fluids

BDSM glossary

- **Scene**: a session in which a BDSM interaction is staged; a good scene has a start and finish, like a ritual
- **BDSM**: Bondage/Discipline; Domination/Submission; Sadism/Masochism or any combination of these
- **Top**: the one who is in control (not necessarily active)
- **Bottom**: the one being controlled (not necessarily passive)
- **SSC**: Safe, sane, consensual
- **RACK**: "Risk-Aware Consensual Kink": RACK is intended to embrace edgeplay and play that is engaged in without safewords.
- **Edgeplay**: Play that is seen as more unusually risky than the majority of BDSM play in the scene community.
- **Safeword**: an out-of-context word that stops the scene

Chapter Twenty

Eco-spirituality and embodiment

Eco-spirituality is a new name for a set of ideas that goes back a long way. Baruch Spinoza and Giordano Bruno were two 17th century philosophers who both viewed the universe as divine. Their ideas were broadly pantheistic. In this theology, the universe is the manifestation of the Divine. The implication here is that everything is sacred, and we should take care of the Earth and other beings.

A common aspect of Western views of reality is the idea that there is an underlying essence to everything, a pure state of being, and that everything else emanates from that. This is a very pervasive idea, from Plato's concept of Ideal Forms, all the way to Cartesian dualism. Process theology was an attempt to correct this thinking; its view is that everything is always changing. It also sees the Divine as involved in the process of change, and developing as a result of the changes.

Indigenous traditions also affirm that process and becoming are natural and inevitable; many indigenous American languages do not translate well into English, because English refers to everything as a fixed state (nouns), whereas they refer to everything as a process.

Gaia theology and theory affirms the idea of the Divine as living, and therefore changing. Gaea theology was developed by Oberon Zell-Ravenheart in 1970, independently of James Lovelock's better-known Gaia Theory. Oberon Zell-Ravenheart derived his ideas in part from Pierre Teilhard de Chardin, a Catholic palaeontologist and geologist. Both Zell and Lovelock regarded the Earth as Gaia, a living organism, and named the idea after the Greek Goddess Gaia.

There is a spectrum of Gaia theories. At one end is the undeniable statement that the presence of life on Earth has radically altered the surface of the planet.

A stronger position is that the Earth's biosphere effectively acts as if it is a self-organizing system which works in such a way as to keep its systems in some kind of equilibrium that is conducive to life.

An even stronger claim is that all life-forms are part of a single planetary being, called Gaia. In this view, the atmosphere, the seas, the terrestrial crust would be the result of interventions carried out by Gaia herself.

Eco-spirituality embraces an ethic of non-violence and sustainability. Non-violence includes respect for life in all its manifestations (human, non-human, animal, vegetable and mineral); harmonious use of natural resources, with respect for the natural order and cycles of the environment, and development compatible with the ecosystem; and listening to Nature, not dictating to it. In Hinduism, non-violence is known as *ahimsa*.

Sustainability means not using up or depleting the resources available, and maintaining the diversity of ecosystems. Reducing the diversity of an ecosystem, or doing something that creates an imbalance in it, upsets the food web (what eats what in a specific ecosystem).

A key idea in eco-spirituality is deep ecology, which advocates the inherent worth of living beings regardless of their usefulness to humans. Deep ecology argues that the natural world is a subtle balance of complex inter-relationships in which the organisms depend on each other for their existence within ecosystems. This philosophy was named "deep ecology" by Arne Næss in 1973. It is becoming increasingly apparent that a deep ecological approach is needed to ensure sustainability, biodiversity and the continued existence of the human species. Vandana Shiva writes:

> "Deep ecological solutions are the only viable solutions to ensuring that every person on this planet has enough food, has enough water, has adequate shelter, has dignity and has a cultural meaning in life. If we don't follow the path of living in ways that we leave enough space for other species, that paradigm also ensures that most human beings will be denied their right to existence. A system that denies the intrinsic value of other species denies eighty percent of humanity, their right to a dignified survival and a dignified life. It only pretends that is solving the problems of poverty, it is actually at the root of poverty. And the only real solution to poverty is to embrace the right to life of all on this planet, all humans and all species."

Another important strand of eco-spirituality is eco-feminism, the idea that the exploitation of the Earth is symbolically linked to the domination of women, with talk of conquest, dominion, and so on; whereas respect for the Earth can be equated with respect for women. This is a big part of contemporary Goddess spirituality, and is obviously related to Gaia theology.

Another green precept is "Think global, act local", the idea that before acting, we should look at consequences for the whole biosphere, as well as for the local environment. This precept relates to the idea of spirit of place. The Romans honoured the *genius loci* (spirit of place) and the Greeks honoured the *daemons* (nature spirits). The spirit of place is the consciousness inhabiting wood and grove, tree and well, river and lake. Pagans have found that specific locations have a different atmosphere, a sense of presence. Christians have started to talk about 'thin places' – liminal places where the numinous can readily be encountered.

One of the things that keeps me Pagan is the importance of wildness. For me, this concept includes the erotic, the instinctive, the intuitive, a sense of connection to Nature, intimacy, freedom, and solitude. It also links in with deep ecology – the valuing of wild places and wild beings for themselves and not for their utility. An excellent book on the subject of reclaiming wildness is *Women Who Run With The Wolves* by Clarissa Pinkola Estés, a Jungian psychotherapist and traditional storyteller.

Ancient cultures regarded the landscape itself as sacred, and devised sacred geography to describe it. This includes the concept of the four cardinal directions and their associated symbolism; the idea of the World Tree at the centre; and cosmologies with the heavens above, the underworld below, and the Earth in the middle.

One thing that is often suggested as a way to connect with Nature is celebrating the seasonal festivals. I have certainly found it helpful to have the seasonal festivals in my life as markers of time, and they have made me more aware of the passing seasons, but I don't know if they have made me more connected with Nature. I also worry that we sometimes impose our own patterns on Nature, rather than listening and looking to see what's there.

Another way to connect with Nature is to get out more, and walk in the woods, by the sea, in the mountains. Meditating in Nature is excellent, and is a very old pagan practice called "sitting out". Adrian Harris writes, on his blog Bodymind Place:

> "The principle of the sit spot could hardly be simpler: Find a place outdoors and sit there everyday for at least 15 minutes. Though it's generally traced to Native American teachers, this ancient practise is cross-cultural. What modern Pagans call 'sitting out' has a more explicitly spiritual purpose, but is essentially the same thing."

The sit spot is one of thirteen core practices outlined in *Coyote's Guide to Connecting with Nature*. They are:

- Sit spot
- Story-telling
- Expanding sensory awareness
- Questioning and tracking
- Animal forms
- Wandering
- Mapping
- Exploring field guides
- Journaling
- Survival living
- Mind's eye imagining
- Listening for bird language
- Thanksgiving

These core routines were developed by the Wilderness Awareness School and Jon Young. Jon is inspired by his childhood mentor, tracker Tom Brown Jr., who was taught by Stalking Wolf, an Apache elder. Jon also draws from nature connection techniques from all over the world, and from ecopsychology. Many of these techniques are already in use in Wiccan covens under other names.

Storytelling is important because it allows us to connect with the history and mythology of place, and create our own entertainment, rather than relying on television. It cultivates the art of observation and a mythopoetic awareness.

Expanding our senses involves being aware of sights, sounds, smells, peripheral vision, taste, proprioception (bodily awareness), taste, and touch. You can use sound to judge distance, wind speed, and other environmental features. This technique needs to be practiced until it becomes a habit.

Questioning and tracking animals and birds cultivates pattern recognition and observation. Looking for subtle signs such as footprints, broken vegetation, and droppings helps you to identify animals and birds, and perhaps to use them for augury too.

Animal forms are a technique used all over the world to connect with nature and attune oneself to the flow of wyrd. Many martial arts have forms which imitate animals (such as tiger, crane, monkey, and snake). This can be done as part of a martial arts practice, or as a dance practice, inside or outside the Wiccan circle. This technique can be developed by watching the way that animals move, and imitating it.

Wandering through the landscape without a destination or an agenda, paying attention to what is in front of you, and not thinking of other things, is an excellent form of meditation. One way to do this is to go for a walk and look around you; notice something you feel drawn to or curious about, such as a leaf or a tree or a stone; really look at it, noticing its texture, colour, and scent. Then let it go and see what you feel drawn to next; follow the same level of awareness with the next thing.

Exploring field guides is a great way to learn about flora and fauna and fungi. Choose one that appeals to you, or that is reasonably portable in the field. Learn how to use the keys in these guides to identify plants and animals, grasses and fungi. Start to identify the structure and shape of plants.

Mapping is a way of attuning to the features and contours of a landscape. Draw your own maps, with the sacred directions, hills, trees, special places, places where you saw a particular bird or animal. If you have ever read *Secret Water* by Arthur Ransome, you will remember how the Swallows and Amazons explored the creeks and islands around Pin Mill in Essex, making their own maps and naming the islands and waterways. Have a look at the wonderful maps of the Burren and Connemara by Tim Robinson, and his wonderful books about the landscape and history of Connemara, and you will see how deeply it is possible to engage with a place, its natural history, geology, and history.

You could use a **journal** to write about sit spot experiences; keep a record of birds and plants seen; draw pictures and maps of the landscape, flora and fauna around you. *The Country Diary of an Edwardian Lady* by Edith Holden is a wonderful example of a nature diary.

Listening to bird language and animal cries is another way of connecting with the natural world. Birdsong is a herald of spring, and is a wonderful sound in its own right. Some birds can sing very fast, and use multiple vocal chords to produce the sounds, which is why it is very hard for humans to replicate birdsong. It may well be that the earliest music was an attempt to imitate birdsong; certainly, many composers have been inspired by it.

Survival living, or living off the land, is a great way to understand the power and complexity of the natural world. Some covens use spending a night in the wilderness as an initiatory ordeal. Indigenous American tradition includes the vision quest, a journey into the wilderness for inspiration.

Imagining things in your mind's eye also develops the powers of imagination, memory, observation, and concentration. Being able to recall the details of a landscape, bird, or plant, and find your way in the woods, is a very useful skill.

Putting food on the table is a good way to connect with the natural world – gathering wild food, or growing your own, gets your hands into the earth. It is very satisfying to cook with fruit that you have gathered from the hedgerows, or make your own wine.

Thanksgiving for all the beauty and bounty around you, and asking the spirits of place if you may enter their sacred space, and thanking them when you have finished, is very important. It is one of the key ideas of the animist worldview that humans are a part of Nature, and should be mindful that we are surrounded by other beings – trees, rocks, animals, birds, spirits of place – all of whom have a right to exist in this world.

Cultivating a sense of place is important too. The excellent book *The Art of Conversation with the Genius Loci* by Barry Patterson is one that I recommend highly, because it offers specific techniques for engaging with place, including learning about its history, geology, flora and fauna, mythology, archaeology, and what flowers, fruits and vegetables are in season at what time.

We also need to be in right relationship with Nature, so reducing your carbon footprint and your ecological footprint and auditing your lifestyle are important.

Eating food that is local and in season helps the environment, but it also makes you more aware of your surroundings. It's very hard to eat seasonally in some places, but we should at least be aware of the air miles on what we eat, and try to buy more local produce.

Another emerging aspect of eco-spirituality is embodiment. Adrian Harris writes,

> "You have a body that's always located somewhere and at some time. ... your mind and body are part of a single unified system. That means that what you think, how you feel and ultimately perhaps who you are, emerges from your fleshy embodied existence."

Recently, I have been trying to listen more to my body. There is an excellent Buddhist meditation called Vipassana, where you pay attention to every part of the body, which can help develop a deep connection between mind and body.

However, I am sure we have all had those "gut feelings" about situations and people, which we ignore at our peril. If I am in a situation where I am unhappy about something, it goes straight to my digestive system. If I meet someone dogmatic and rigid, it makes my solar plexus hurt.

Being a permeable body in a physical space with other physical bodies, rather than a mind or a spirit in a conceptual space, is very important for feeling connected to your surroundings. We take in our surroundings in the form of sensations, food, breath, and water; and we interact with our environment through touch. So our physical well-being is just as important as our emotional well-being, and the two are intimately connected.

So, rather than aspiring to be a spiritual person, I aspire to be a fully embodied person.

Attunement to the landscape

When you move to a new area, you feel uprooted. It takes a long time to put down roots and settle in the new place. That said, there are many magical techniques which can help you with this process.

When you move in, you may need to cleanse your new home of vibes from previous owners, then install your own vibes and a protective aura. To install your own vibes, simply walk around your old home before you leave with a candle, visualising burning negative vibes and storing positive vibes.

When you get to your new home, first talk to the house, get to know it and any wights that might live there. Only when you are sure you have their permission can you light incense in each room, sprinkle water and salt, and ring a bell. Then call upon the four elements to protect the house. Touch every wall in each room. Then light your candle in which you stored the vibes from your old home, and walk around the house, visualising them being spread into each room. You also need to assert ownership of your new house - one very effective way of doing this is putting up at least one picture as soon as you arrive. You may also find there are house brownies or other elementals sharing the house with you. Be careful not to disturb them with the cleansing of the house. They like airing cupboards and other warm places. If yours does not yet have a name, ask it if it would like one.

However, magical attunement to the new home is not just about the immediate hearth and home, but also the local landscape. All landscape is sacred, so attuning yourself to a new landscape is not just about visiting the obvious sacred sites, but also making your own connections with the mythology of the landscape. You must connect with the landscape, learn its pattern, contact its guardian deities, let your personal mythology and favourite deities fit in with the landscape about you. Link the mindscape to the landscape. It is very important, however, to show respect to the spirits of place - do not impose your will on the land, let it talk to you.

Walk around your new landscape at different times of the day. Walk north, east, south and west. Look for landscape features which appeal to you - trees, rocks, hills, streams, ponds, etc. Do they correspond to a particular deity or element? Can they be incorporated into your rituals? Do they want to be incorporated into your rituals? What are the sounds, sights, smells, tastes, sensations there? What emotions do they evoke in you? Talk to the spirits of place. Do a circular walk, noting landscape features on the route. Anglo-Saxon land charters were written by this means - describing the features around the edge of a domain. Many parishes re-establish their boundaries in this way each year in the ceremony of "beating the bounds".

Look for a feature in the North which corresponds to Earth, a feature in the

East for Air, in the South for Fire, in the West for Water, and in the centre for Spirit. Again, seek inspiration from the land-wights. Now draw a magical map of your landscape which shows these features. It need not bear much resemblance to physical reality. The central point should be at or near your covenstead or place of working. You could use any hills or other landscape features of your choice.

Always ask the spirits of place before working anywhere - show respect to the land and the land-wights. Don't leave litter (psychic or physical), candles, tea-lights, incense, scorch-marks, unclosed circles, crystals, graffiti, or conspicuous libations. Take time to feel the energies of the space.

This process of personal attunement to the landscape is the quickest way that I know of becoming rooted in a new place. The only problem is, if you decide to move on, it's very difficult to uproot yourself again!

Presumably it would be even more powerful if it was the collective vision of a group, as is the case with tribal mythologisation of the landscape. The landscape dreams its own dreams - attune yourself to these and your connection will be even deeper.

- Leave nothing but footprints, take nothing but memories

- Draw or photograph local features (landscape features and buildings).

- Before taking photographs, walk around the site without a camera, taking in the atmosphere.

- Write poetry or prose about the places you have visited.

- Take time to meditate at the places you visit.

- Keep a note of features which may have folkloric or mythological significance and look them up when you get home.

- Read local history, folklore and mythology. Find out about local historical characters, local deities, spirits of place, etc.

Nature religion in the city

Many writers suggest that Paganism is a nature religion, or that Wicca is a fertility religion. But do these statements actually hold any water? Classical paganism existed in both cities and countryside. Ronald Hutton points out in *Triumph of the Moon: A history of modern Pagan witchcraft* that there were many goddesses who were patrons of cities. In addition, he points out, these city goddesses (also patrons of smithcraft, surveying, architecture, learning, and so on) would make excellent role-models for feminists, unlike the 'Great Mother Goddess' (invented by Jacquetta Hawkes, a conservative, and later enthusiastically adopted by feminists).

In fact, every pagan culture has had cities and/or towns, from Çatalhöyük in Neolithic Turkey to the Iron Age Celts. And research into ritual suggests that with the widespread movement of people into cities, more ritual is practised, perhaps because the need to escape from the self becomes more pressing in a *'civilised'* context.[232]

The reason that Paganism was revived was because people felt they had lost their connection with Nature after the Industrial Revolution; and certainly ancient paganisms (or perhaps polytheism would be a better word in this context) involved propitiation of the gods of nature; but they also involved the Fates, Justice, and other personifications of concepts.

So connection with (or propitiation of) Nature is certainly an important part of Pagan practices; but it is not the whole story. And Nature does not stop at the edge of the city; there are trees, animals and birds in the city. Actually foxes prefer the city to the countryside because in urban contexts they are not pursued by the unspeakable who do not realise that they are uneatable. The countryside is full of conservative people (in both the political and the social sense). Try being a Pagan in the countryside for five minutes and see how long you would last. I know a few people who have tried this and been rewarded by local suspicion and distrust; even if your chosen label does not include the word 'witch', country people will still assume that any practising Pagan is likely to put spells on them or their cattle. If you want to be in a religious minority, opt for safety in numbers and a nice tolerant environment to do your thing in.

Rather than giving up on the cities, we should be trying to make them more beautiful, more sustainable, more elegant, and more civilised. Cities have always been the places where innovation and change happen. Cities were the birthplace of democracy, the middle classes, artisans, radical politics, libraries, and beautiful architecture. It is possible that the first towns in some societies were created by the coming together of artisans to share ideas; and it is true that some radical political groups went to the countryside to try to realise their ideals, but towns have not always been polluted disaster zones, and they could be sustainable and beautiful.

I am very happy that there is countryside within walking distance of my house. But it's also very useful to have a 24-hour supermarket nearby, and very pleasant to be able to pop into town to go to the arts cinema or theatre. Okay, so I am actually a suburban Pagan... But the suburbs are very close to the ideal expressed by William Morris, in his utopian novel *News from Nowhere*, that every house should have a little plot of land to cultivate, and the towns should be full of trees and happy artisans plying their trade or craft. When I had time, I used to cultivate an allotment, growing organic vegetables.

As a polytheist, I honour spirits of place (also known as land wights and *genii loci*) and every kind of being up to and including gods and goddesses. I'm also an animist, so I honour rocks and trees, too. But artefacts can have soul, too. Maybe even machines. In *Skinny Legs and All*, a novel by Tom Robbins, five of the characters are inanimate objects (a spoon, a sock, a can of beans, a conch shell and a painted stick - the last two survived from ancient times and were originally objects of veneration in a Pagan temple).

Much of the modern yearning for Nature is due to our alienation from the industrialised urban world, and from machines. But Pagans have taken to the web

---

[232] Durkheim (1912), *The Elementary Forms of Religious Life*, p220

with alacrity, so we are clearly not averse to computers. So it's not technology in itself that is the problem, it's our use of it (as with any tool or weapon – the sword can be a symbol of higher consciousness, truth and justice, or it can be a deadly weapon).

The problem with the modern world is our failure to connect. We no longer see the connection between our desire to eat fresh fruit and vegetables all year round (whether they are in season or not) and the problems this might cause elsewhere in the world, for example, in terms of the pollution created by the aircraft that bring us the fruit and vegetables.

So we need to practice eco-spirituality, and audit our ethical and ecological choices, to ensure that we are living sustainably.

Chapter Twenty-One

Running a coven

"Really, there's plenty of room for growth and improvement of all that we do. I think we also need to be very strong about resisting the threat of commercialism, which corrupts everything it touches. I think it's also essential that we celebrate and cherish -- and maintain -- our traditional structures: covens and lineages. It's a bad mistake to think that eroding this will promote individual freedom. Structureless mass movements turn individuals into interchangeable parts. In small affinity groups, like covens, each person matters. Externally, defending our own right to exist is necessary but not sufficient. Besides a right to exist, we need a reason to exist. What I think this means is that we need to develop an effective advocacy for the sacred value of Mother Earth. In terms of our interactions with the larger society, I think we should model ourselves on the Quakers. They have been a minority for 300 years, but a respected minority because of their consistent and honorable lifeways and their clear advocacy for social justice. We could offer a similar clear and steady voice speaking for ecological sanity."

~ Judy Harrow, from a 2001 interview[233]

Counter-culture, sub-cultures, and mainstream culture

The Pagan movement started in the late nineteenth century as a counter-current to the effects of the industrial revolution: corporate capitalism, consumerism, and regarding people as cogs in the machine, measuring their

---

[233] I am indebted to Jason Pitzl-Waters for this quote, which he posted on Facebook not long after the Pagan community received the sad news of Judy Harrow's death. Judy Harrow (3 March, 1945 – 20 March, 2014) was a third-degree Gardnerian initiate, founder of the Protean tradition, a counsellor, and the Chair-emerita of the Pastoral Counseling Department at Cherry Hill Seminary. She founded the Pagan Pastoral Counseling Network in 1982, and served as the first editor of that Network's publication. She also wrote several books.

contribution to society by how much they could afford to consume. The early advocates of a return to Nature and to Pagan values were people like Edward Carpenter – a gay Pagan vegetarian socialist, and one of the first people to live openly with another man, and get away with it. His friend Goldsworthy Lowes Dickinson was not only an advocate for a return to Nature and the values of ancient Greek paganism, including the right to love another man, but also the man who came up with the idea for the League of Nations, which eventually became the United Nations.

So Paganism has never been part of the mainstream culture. The people who embraced it were usually Bohemians, hippies, and other radicals. The values of the Pagan revival are profoundly opposed to the mainstream culture, when that is materialist, consumerist, and regards people (both human and animal) and land as units to be exploited. The Pagan movement values individual creativity, and is egalitarian, feminist (where feminism is defined as the belief that women are equal to men), and LGBT-inclusive. There are right-wing Pagans, to be sure, but they are generally of the libertarian persuasion.

However, the Pagan movement, the mainstream culture, and other subcultures, are not hermetically-sealed bubbles floating around in a vacuum. They influence each other; over the years, polyamory has become less common in the Pagan movement, but also less controversial generally. The idea of Nature being sacred and the Divine including both male and female has become more widespread. Other religious traditions read books by and about Pagans, in an effort to understand the cultural phenomenon of the Pagan revival. Pagans read mainstream books, and interact with other religious liberals (though perhaps not as often as we should).

The dynamics of how religious movements become less radical over time have been noted by sociologists; basically, the first generation is a small group of radicals with fire in their bellies and a vision of what needs to change; the second generation is either the offspring of the first generation, in which case they receive the ideas of the religion second-hand from their parents; or they are newcomers with a different set of cultural expectations, having grown up in a new generation, which may already have taken on board some of the counter-cultural ideas of the first wave. In the early days of Christianity, Christians lived in communes and shared everything they had; this was quickly and quietly dropped (probably as richer people started joining, for whom the idea of sharing everything in common was less attractive). The generation of Pagans who started out in the 1960s were much more into free love than the current generation, because it was part of the zeitgeist.

So, how can Wiccans maintain our countercultural stance in the face of assimilation by the mainstream culture? Initiation and small groups like covens are an excellent way of maintaining our values, because the coven is small, close-knit, and bound together by the initiatory oath and the shared experience of working powerful rituals.

It is my view that Pagan values of egalitarianism, feminism, deep ecology, LGBT-inclusiveness, co-operation, valuing the individual, and regarding everything as sacred, are what will save the world from the rapacious and destructive machine of corporate capitalism, which places profits and shareholders above every other consideration.

I realise that not all Pagans share all these values, but enough of us share a significant number of them to make it worthwhile to co-operate on the basis of what we do share.

As Pagans are not very numerous, we also need to forge alliances with other liberal religions, such as the Unitarian Universalists, the Unitarians, the Religious Society of Friends (Quakers), and the Liberal Jews. We need to help defend other minority groups (whether they are Muslims, LGBT people, or atheists) from the fascists who would attack them. And we need to forge alliances with non-faith groups with similar values, such as secular humanists, environmentalists, feminists, and LGBT activists.

So we need to find a way to preserve and develop what is unique about the Pagan movement, and not merge with the mainstream. As Judy Harrow remarked, "we need to develop an effective advocacy for the sacred value of Mother Earth", and I agree with her that the coven, where every member is valued, is a very good way of achieving that aim.

Structuring coven meetings

When a group meets, all sorts of considerations need to be taken into account: group dynamics; individual personality types (introvert, extrovert, and so on); the building of magical energy, group mind, and rapport between participants; physical needs (toilet breaks, food, allergies, disabilities); social needs (telling others about recent events in your life, catching up with their lives); transport needs (if someone needs to leave at a particular time to get the last bus home, or if they need to stay overnight and get a bus in the morning).

With all this in mind, over time my group and I developed the following structure for coven meetings.

7:15 to 7:30 Coveners arrive, settle in, use the toilet, put food in the kitchen or the temple, put tools on the altar, etc.

7:30 to 7:45 Talking stick circle where coveners share recent events in their lives. This saves having to tell people more than once, means that everyone gets an opportunity to speak, starts the energy moving in a circle, helps to build the group mind because everyone knows how the others are feeling, helps people by offloading their troubles or sharing their triumphs, and prepares coveners for ritual by letting go of whatever is on their mind.

7:45 to 8:15 Talking stick discussion.

The chosen topic of the evening is discussed using a framework of two or three questions (see Appendix 2 for examples). For example, a discussion on reincarnation might be framed around the questions: do you believe in reincarnation, and why? How do you think it works? Do you have any past-life memories?

The way a talking stick discussion works is quite different from a debate.

Rather than trying to eliminate differing points of view, participants share their ideas, and the group arrives at a multiple perspective on the topic, a synthesis of participants' views. There is no summary or plenary; all the perspectives stand together and participants can choose to adopt or ignore others' ideas.

It also works better for shy people, and people who take longer to formulate their thoughts, as then they don't have to worry about getting a word in edgeways; and for people like me who always get told that we talk too much, as then we do not have to worry that the less talkative can't get a word in edgeways!

The stick is passed clockwise (*deosil*) around the circle, and whoever is holding it is the only person who can speak. They may choose to say nothing, in which case they hold the stick for a moment and then pass it on. If there are three discussion questions, the stick is usually passed round three times, once for each question. Generally people do not respond to others' contributions, but stick to expounding their own ideas. Once you have the protocols fairly firmly in place, it is possible to bend or break these guidelines. Our group had an additional rule that you could ask to interrupt another person's turn by touching the stick (but you could not interrupt until they gave you leave to do so).

8:15 to 8:30 Toilet break, followed by **assigning ritual roles** (who will call the quarters, consecrate the elements, and act out other parts in the ritual). Whoever has written the ritual explains anything about it that they feel needs explaining.

8:30 to 9:00. Start ritual.

9:30 to 10:00. Finish ritual. If anyone needs to leave early, close the circle before starting the feast.

10:00 onwards. Feast, sit around chatting.

Obviously there is plenty of room in this structure for discussions taking longer, ritual set-up taking longer, the ritual itself taking longer, people being a bit late, and general faffing about. However, we did have a rule that social talking stick started no later than 7:45, even if someone was late arriving. We generally finished by about 11:00 pm.

Group dynamics

The dynamics of the group can be affected by a number of things. The person who is the most volatile or quickest to get angry often has a disproportionate amount of power as a result. If someone doesn't want to do something, this can prevent the rest of the group doing it while they are around.

One way to get around this problem is to have one person in charge of everything. This is usually the high priestess of the coven. However, she should not arbitrate disputes according to personal whim, but have a clear set of guidelines.

My personal preference is to have a set of guidelines for acceptable behaviour and expectations of the group that has been collectively produced by the group in a brainstorming session. Whilst the high priestess is the final arbiter of disputes (and she is high priestess because she is the most experienced person in the group, and/or the founding member of the group), the guidelines are the collective will of the group, and the high priestess is also bound by them. This prevents complaints that she is merely acting on a whim. The guidelines should be reviewed by the group at the annual general meeting.

It is also a good idea to make it clear to all members which things are core activities of the group, such as working skyclad. Not all groups work skyclad, but for me, it's not Wicca without it, so it is non-negotiable in my coven. If you don't want to work skyclad, don't join my coven. Another area that is non-negotiable for me is that I would not initiate anyone who was homophobic.

Another aspect of group dynamics is the ingroup and the outgroup. It is alright for a coven to be a cohesive group and regard the rest of the world as the outgroup, but it must also be capable of welcoming new members, and not scapegoating those who do not conform to coven norms. For example, if you expect all your members to read a large number of books as part of the training, or expect them to copy out your *Book of Shadows* by hand, you may be excluding people with dyslexia. If they are then made to feel less a part of the group because of this, you have then relegated them to the outgroup. I have also seen situations where people changed considerably on joining a coven, suddenly adopting the interests and clothing styles of the coven they had joined, which varied considerably from their original interests and clothing style. That does not strike me as a healthy group dynamic.

If left unchecked, an outgroup situation can develop into scapegoating (blaming one person for everything that goes wrong). I have not seen this happen in a coven, only in workplaces, but it is very unpleasant when it happens, and should be nipped in the bud with dialogue about any issues that arise. It is also a good idea to have a rule that if a coven member has a problem with another coven member, they raise it with that person in the first instance, and if it cannot be resolved that way, then bring it to a group meeting or ask the high priestess to mediate, whichever is more appropriate.

It is also a good idea to have a session with your group about Myers-Briggs types, as these can affect group dynamics. If everyone knows their own type and that of others, it can help them to understand each other's communication style. You can do the Myers-Briggs test for free on the internet, and there are lots of resources explaining the different personality types.

There are four aspects of personality according to the Myers-Briggs model:

- **Introvert / Extrovert:** An introvert will gain energy from spending time alone, and may feel depleted after spending time with others. An extrovert will gain energy from spending time with others, and may feel depleted after spending time alone.

- **Intuitive / Sensing:** An intuitive person gains insight through inner feelings and ideas; a sensing person gains insight from external perceptual data.

- **Thinking / Feeling:** A thinking person prefers to base their decisions on logic; a feeling person prefers to base their decisions on their emotions.

- **Perceiving / Judging:** A perceiving person tends to see things as being on a spectrum of possibilities; a judging person tends to see things as either this or that, with nothing in between.

Developing group cohesion

Theorists of group dynamics have described the way that groups work towards group cohesion as going through four phases known as *"forming, storming, norming, and performing"*. This theory was developed in 1965 by Bruce Tuckman.

The **forming** stage is when the group comes together, and individual goals are secondary to the needs of the group, as people seek what they have in common with each other, and look for consensus.

This is followed by the **storming** stage, when people realise that their individual goals may be in conflict with the group goals, or their ideas about what the group's goals should be are different from those of other members. The tension and conflict that is part of the storming stage can be very uncomfortable for people who don't like conflict, or who have an under-developed sense of self.

The next stage is **norming**, when consensus about the group's goals, and the roles of the members within the group, is achieved. Some people may have to compromise on what they want to ensure cohesion; the danger of this stage is that people may avoid sharing creative ideas because they seem controversial, or outside the expected norms of the group. For example, one person may dislike singing, so it becomes difficult to include singing in the activities of the group; or someone may dislike spell-work, so that gets sidelined.

The last stage is **performing**, when all the conflicts and problems with not being able to raise controversial ideas are ironed out, and people are able to participate in the group's activities, feel safe and valued, and offer suggestions, and the group functions well in achieving its goals.

A final stage, added by Tuckman and Mary Ann Jensen in 1977, is **adjourning**, where the group dissolves, having completed its task. If a coven decides to go its separate ways, there are ways of ensuring this happens harmoniously; one way is to do a closing-down ritual, where any differences are symbolically reconciled, and everyone takes away a symbol to represent their happy memories of being in the group.

It is also possible that whenever a new person joins the group, these stages happen again, only less intensively, as the group seeks to integrate the new person.

It is a good idea to agree consensually what the goals of your coven are, and to review them regularly. Are you primarily about celebrating the seasons, honouring the deities, personal and collective spiritual development, eco-activism, transforming consciousness, a combination of these, or some other aim entirely?

Group dynamics and systems theory[234]

Group dynamics can be looked at from different perspectives: anthropological, sociological, and theological.

The sociological perspective includes systems and organisation theory. Systems have an input and an output, and if one part of a system is changed or

---

[234] For the information in this section, I am indebted to a talk given by Rev Sarah Tinker, minister of Richmond Unitarians, at FUSE 2014.

removed, the system as a whole changes. Systems theory is a view of the world as dynamic and changing (much like the Wiccan worldview).

Systems theory says don't look at the broken part, look at the whole system. If one person seems to be causing mayhem, look at the whole system, not just them. Take several steps back. Look at your and their environment and culture. Systems theory is often applied in situations of family breakdown and mental illness. The member of the family who is ill may be the 'canary in the goldmine' indicating that the family dynamic is unhealthy. If you focus on another part of the system, the broken part will change too. The same applies to covens and other groups.

Everybody has a role in a group, whether it is conscious or unconscious. People tend to fall into patterns of behaviour, form structures, settle into homeostasis, and become predictable. We need these patterns to organise our lives, but we don't want them to become too rigid.

In looking at the group dynamic of your coven, consider energy and how it flows in a system. How does the group interact with the wider community, both Pagan and non-Pagan? Tension can be healthy and creative, open to change and innovation. A healthy system is not stagnant; there is dynamic balance, not stasis. The leadership should be responsive, not reactive; in other words, listening to suggestions and concerns, not just reacting to crises and conflict.

A coven is not a family. In a group that resembles a family, it becomes difficult for new people to join (even with initiation to help you over the threshold), and members project family roles onto leaders (this might seem fine until you remember that not everyone has a healthy and happy relationship with their family, and may be projecting all their parents' or siblings' flaws onto you, not just their good qualities). Groups are complex emotional systems, and there is potential for hurt. Sometimes people need to withdraw for a while as a means of managing anxiety. A group that is too close can marginalise those with different beliefs or values.

As a leader, your responses to situations are crucial - take a step back, consider your own role, consider the system. Change your perspective; look at it from another point of view.

Differentiation

Differentiation is the ability to be an individual within the group. Healthy leaders let other people have a go, empower them. My goal as the high priestess of a coven is to empower others to become priestesses and priests in their own right. I encourage coveners to write their own rituals, and give talks on subjects they know about. They build up to this gradually by calling a quarter, then calling all four quarters; or consecrating water and salt, or casting the circle. I keep a checklist of activities they have done, so I know that everyone has had a go at every aspect of ritual. This avoids the problem of hero-worshipping the leader, and people taking a back seat and just coasting along.

A person who is less differentiated from the group may be a social chameleon, adapting their views, values, and behaviour to the group. The chameleon is vulnerable to bullies, who will try to impose their values on the group as a norm. A strong set of guidelines and an ethos of fairness will help to prevent this sort of dynamic developing.

According to Bowen Theory,[235]

> "A person with a well-differentiated "self" recognizes his realistic dependence on others, but he can stay calm and clear headed enough in the face of conflict, criticism, and rejection to distinguish thinking rooted in a careful assessment of the facts from thinking clouded by emotionality. Thoughtfully acquired principles help guide decision-making about important family and social issues, making him less at the mercy of the feelings of the moment. What he decides and what he says matches what he does. He can act selflessly, but his acting in the best interests of the group is a thoughtful choice, not a response to relationship pressures. Confident in his thinking, he can either support another's view without being a disciple or reject another view without polarizing the differences."

Triangulation

Triangulation can be positive or negative. The term refers to the tendency of two parts of a system to do something with a third, e.g. two people gossiping about a third party. It can relieve tension, but it can also become too fixed and develop into always saying negative things about the same person. One particularly unhealthy form of it to watch out for is the "Persecutor – Victim – Rescuer" triangle, also known as the Karpman Triangle,[236] named after Stephen Karpman, who first described it in the 1970s. In this situation, someone who is occupying the role of persecutor wants to reposition themselves as the victim, and be rescued by a third party, or the persecutor wants to reposition themselves as the rescuer (as in "I'm doing this for your own good"). Sometimes people occupy the positions of victim and rescuer for a long time, so that eventually the other party comes to seem like the persecutor, because they are too controlling, or too passive.

A triangle can also produce the feeling in one of its members of being the 'odd one out'. Consider the example of a couple with a newborn baby. Previously the couple were the dyad; now the mother and baby also form a strong pair-bond, which can make the father feel left out.

Triangulation can also be positive, e.g. facilitation, mediation, used to defuse and resolve conflict. It can then introduce a much-needed alternative perspective into a situation.

Over-functioning and under-functioning

An **optimally-functioning** person[237] is someone who is managing their life

---

[235] http://www.thebowencenter.org/pages/conceptds.html
[236] http://www.psychologytoday.com/blog/fixing-families/201106/the-relationship-triangle
[237] http://willmeekphd.com/item/over-functioning--under-functioning

well, has good relationships, and fulfils their roles and responsibilities. An **under-functioning** person is someone who is coasting along, allowing others to make key decisions, and may feel inadequate or disempowered. An **over-functioning** person is one who takes more than their share of responsibility in the group, and thereby actually disempowers others. They are enabled to over-function by the presence of under-functioning people, which is why this is also known as "somebody's got to do it" syndrome.

The more leaders over-function, the more others under-function because they think they will never do it as well as the leader and there are no intermediate steps between doing it all and not doing any of it. The leader needs to manage their own anxiety about things not being done properly. That is why I encourage coveners to do various aspects of the ritual one at a time, to enable them to build up to leading a whole ritual. Luckily, Wiccan ritual is easy to break down into smaller sections.

Over-functioning can lead to burn-out, so it is important for your own well-being to create the conditions where others share the responsibilities of writing and leading rituals.

Where does the power go in groups?

In any decision-making process, there are a number of dynamics at work. There is a discussion phase, which may result in a convergence of opinion, or a divergence. When trying to achieve consensus, there are good ways and bad ways to arrive at it. There is **apparent consensus** (the absence of vocal disagreement); **imposed consensus** (where the facilitator of the discussion moves on without acknowledging the dissenting voices); **hasty consensus** (where only those with a massive objection to the decision are allowed to voice their objections); and **considerate consensus** (where all the dissenting voices are given time and space to speak, and the outcome of the discussion may be modified to take them into account).[238]

Starhawk, drawing on the work of Randy Schutt, identifies a number of processes that can be used to ensure that genuine, considerate consensus is achieved. These include active listening, and working together in smaller groups to tease out the issues before returning to the larger group to air concerns and possible solutions to the problem being decided on. The outcome may not end up being the preference of any one individual, but it will usually be the best outcome for the group.[239]

Starhawk identifies several roles for the consensus process: facilitator (who usually remains neutral), note taker, name taker (a person who keeps a note of who wants to address the meeting), vibes watcher (someone who keeps the mood of the meeting on track and prevents participants verbally attacking each other), and

---

[238] Christoph Haug (2012), *Assembly publics and the problem of hegemony in consensus decision-making*, http://www.opendemocracy.net/christoph-haug/assembly-publics-and-problem-of-hegemony-in-consensus-decision-making

[239] Starhawk (undated), *Consensus is Not Unanimity: Making Decisions Co-operatively*, http://www.starhawk.org/activism/trainer-resources/consensus-nu.html

time-keeper (ensuring that the meeting does not overrun and that everyone gets time to speak). It is a good idea to rotate these roles, so that different people carry them out on different occasions.

Consensus decision making is a good way to work out how to act as a group, provided that there is not an unbridgeable divide between the participants. If there is an assumed, imposed, or hasty consensus, however, then it will cause problems for the group, and the power will default to the dominant personalities in the group.

If the power is not vested in any particular individual or role, then it is hidden, and the shadow side of power (dominance and control) comes to the fore. If this happens frequently, resentment can build up, and this can result in backbiting and grumbling. This is why it is a good idea to have a person (in Wiccan covens, this is usually the High Priestess, or the High Priestess and High Priest together) who can arbitrate disputes and facilitate discussions. However, the leadership model that I would recommend is the "servant leader" model, where the High Priestess knows that her role is to act in the best interests of everyone in the group, not to impose her will on them.

In large groups with a committee, the committee can often end up acting as a block to initiative and creativity. One solution to this problem is to have an enabling policy, where if someone wants to try a new initiative, they are empowered to do so, whether or not the larger group thinks it will work. Fortunately, covens (and most other Pagan groups) are small enough not to need a committee.

In groups where there is no formal leadership role, the power often devolves to the person with the strongest opinion, or the person who has been a member the longest, unless care is taken to achieve consensus.

One issue with consensus decision-making is that it may mean that no-one is satisfied with the outcome. If this is the case, it may be an idea to take it in turns to do things in the way that particular coven members prefer. For example, coven members may take it in turns to write and facilitate rituals. If different coven members have come from different initiatory lineages, they may have inherited different ways of doing ritual from their initiators, and people (including me) get very attached to the traditions they receive, because a particular way of creating ritual space becomes a powerful tool for transforming consciousness, and has a way of getting embedded in one's practice. So there are two possible solutions to this: create a new synthesis of the two different ways of working, or if they are incompatible, take it in turns to create the ritual space according to the two different techniques.

I have also found that it is a good idea to agree the group rules together, and then if a dispute arises, it can be resolved by referring to the group rules, which everyone in the group has assented to, rather than by the leader(s) of the group. The leader(s) may act as interpreters of the rules, and mediators in the dispute, but they are not imposing an arbitrary decision.

Relationships in groups

Problems can arise in groups with relationships. A coven is – almost inevitably – an emotionally intense environment, and whether it is a friendship or a sexual relationship that develops between coven members, things can get out of hand. Obviously it is good if coven members are friends, but sexual relationships are more difficult. What happens if the couple break up and fall out with each other whilst both are still members of the group?

There are several different solutions to this problem. One is to ban sexual relationships between coven members. This seems impractical for a number of reasons, and potentially unethical too. It is appropriate to make a rule that coven leaders may not have a sexual relationship with coveners, because of the difference in power between them. I would also strongly discourage sexual relationships between coveners if one or both of the parties was in a monogamous relationship with another person outside the coven. Obviously if they are in a polyamorous relationship, that would not be a problem, but even then, they should keep the other partner(s) informed and follow the rules of the polyamorous group of which they are a member.

Another solution is that if the couple break up and cannot stand to be in a room together, let alone in a circle together, they take it in turns to attend Sabbats and esbats. It is probably best if the rest of the coven do not take sides, unless one of the couple has done something that justifies taking sides.

If an existing couple want to join your coven together, it is always a good idea to check that they are both equally committed to Wicca, and interview them separately. It may be that one of them wants to join your coven to keep an eye on the other one. It may also be helpful to initiate them separately.

On the face of it, friendships seem less problematic, but intense friendships can develop in covens, and the shadow side of this can be that others are excluded, or even scapegoated, because they are outside the friendship bond. The best cure for this is to schedule regular coven socials where people can get to know each other outside the intense atmosphere of the circle.

Because we work a lot with the archetypes and the psyche in Wiccan ritual, it can happen that projections and identifications and transference can occur. It is a good idea to make your coven aware of Jungian archetypes and how people project them on each other. When invoking deities, it is a good idea not to invoke the same deity, or the same type of deity, on the same person. For example, if someone feels very attracted to the Morrigan, and wants to aspect her a lot, they should also balance this with a different goddess such as Rhiannon or Blodeuwedd. If they always want to call the same quarter or avoid a particular quarter, ask them to call all the quarters, or a different one.

It is always best to nip any problems in the bud before they develop into anything really serious. If a dispute arises, encourage the parties to seek mediation, either with the coven leaders, or with another trusted third party outside the coven. Many disputes arise out of misunderstandings rather than any genuine malice or negligence.

Spiritual burnout and how to avoid it

Spiritual burn-out is a real risk for coven leaders. I have suffered from this myself in the past, and have found that if I was getting nurtured by others, and receiving energy from the universe, it didn't happen, whereas if you fail to do these things, you will get burn-out, and the symptoms can be quite nasty.

The symptoms of spiritual burnout or psychic burnout can include exhaustion, depression, dread before or after working, feelings of unbearable responsibility, feeling overwhelmed, crying for no reason, crying often, being overtired, insomnia, difficulty getting out of bed, restlessness, procrastination, avoidance, constant illness, problems with the heart, difficulty breathing, anxiety and panic attacks, extreme weight loss or weight gain, hair loss, irritability, and a desire to avoid people.

How to avoid spiritual burnout can be summed up in six key points:

- **Have a rest** – have regular scheduled time for your own rest, healing, and renewal; times when you are nurtured by someone or something else. This is necessary to avoid burnout. If you do experience burnout, take a complete break from coven leadership.

- **Make sure your needs are met** - physically, emotionally, mentally and spiritually. Make an inventory of the areas of your life, and check regularly that you are fulfilled in all of them. This includes time spent alone, time with friends and family, time with your partner, time at work, and time sleeping.

- **Draw your energy from the universe** - don't use up all your personal energy; make sure to be replenished from the source. This is particularly important when practising psychic healing, or any magical practice involving energy.

- **Make sure you benefit from rituals that you lead** - there always has to be an exchange of energy. Whilst Wiccan covens do not charge participants for training or rituals, coveners should contribute by helping to set up the temple space, bringing food and drink to share, and helping with the washing up after the ritual.

- **Maintain strong boundaries** - visualise yourself surrounded by white light; set aside a special room for magical work. Do not create dependencies on you among the coven by over-functioning.

- **Only do magical work when you are on top form** - don't deplete yourself by working when you are ill, distracted, or upset. I have often said that the mark of a true priestess or priest is a person who can switch to ritual mode even when they are feeling under the weather, disgruntled, or otherwise upset. This is true, but don't do it all the time, or it will lead to burnout.

If you think you are suffering spiritual burn-out, get help - don't leave it until you are absolutely exhausted.

Ritual nudity

Seeing the body as natural and not shameful is a pre-requisite to regarding it as a source of power and a sacred place. I have had a number of inquiries recently from prospective trainees who had no idea that Gardnerian Wicca involves ritual nudity. Really? Don't the Wicca 101 books mention it?

I regard ritual nudity as a core element of Gardnerian Wicca; a ritual without it feels completely different. I also think that robes are not a Pagan garment. Having special clothes for ritual is a great idea; having special clothes that are designed to deny the physicality and shape of the human body, not such a good idea. The erotic aspects of Wiccan ritual are very important; the idea that the God and the Goddess of the Craft make love is a core part of the ritual (usually represented symbolically).

Ritual nudity does not lead to orgies in the circle (contrary to what some people with prurient attitudes to nudity might think); it does lead to being at ease with one's own body and the bodies of others, regardless of shape or size. The human body (especially when lit by candlelight or firelight) is a beautiful thing, no matter the shape or size.

Obviously, partly due to the presence of ritual nudity, and partly because of the psychological impact of the rituals, there is a rule that no-one under the age of eighteen should be initiated into a Gardnerian coven, or take part in a skyclad (nude) ritual.

Role of initiation and secrecy: social cohesion

Initiation, being a transformational experience, allows a person to cross a threshold and become part of the group. The more intense the initiatory experience, the more one feels part of the group. Some religions have a very minimalist joining ritual, and so people feel less certain about whether they are really part of the group.

I have written about both secrecy and initiation in two separate chapters; in this section, I want to focus in their role in group dynamics.

The reason that many aspects of Wiccan ritual are secret is because they would be dangerous for unskilled and uninitiated practitioners, which is why Gardnerian and Alexandrian Wiccan groups are so keen on ensuring valid initiations and lineages. That is why this book is not a 'how-to' manual of Wiccan ritual, so people can set up their own groups; if you feel drawn to Wicca after reading this book, you should seek out a genuine coven to join. There is nothing wrong with solitary practice, if that is your choice, but it is less intense than working in an initiatory coven and lineage.

However, secrecy has another function beyond keeping secret practices which could cause damage if performed without the necessary safeguards. This function is less acknowledged in the Craft. Secrecy binds a group together around the shared secret – even if it happens to be relatively trivial.

Confidentiality – keeping secret and confidential any personal information which has been divulged by other members of the coven – is a vitally important aspect of group cohesion. However, if someone divulges that they have sexually molested a child, or murdered someone, then that should be reported to the police (apart from the moral considerations, you would be an accessory to the crime if you did not report it). As a coven leader, if one of your coveners has a problem which requires professional help, you are entitled to discuss it with another coven leader (preferably anonymising the covener), or with a professional such as a therapist. That is why I advise my coveners that what they are offered is extended confidentiality – that disclosures of their confidential information will normally be with their consent, and in order to further the aims for which it was disclosed, except in cases where there is an urgent need to prevent them harming themselves or others, or where the law requires disclosure.

There are negative aspects of secrecy, and the disadvantages may well outweigh the advantages, as Wiccans could exchange more ideas with other initiatory traditions if we were less obsessed with secrecy; and in that sense, we may be holding ourselves back by insisting upon it.

I personally feel that one should be able to make one's own judgment about who is a magical adept (of any path) and discuss with them the dynamics of invocation, or other magical practices. I had a very fruitful discussion with an esoteric Buddhist about invocation, which formed some of the ideas in the chapter on invocation. If I had not had that conversation, I would not have learnt about the difference between possession and transcendence which is outlined in that chapter.

Training others

When training other people in Wicca, there is a delicate balance to be achieved between spoon-feeding them and chucking them in the deep end to sink or swim. Most training requires the trainees to make an effort and do the background reading and practice required. I set homework for my trainees, but I don't check up on whether they have done it (apart from anything else, it is obvious who is making the effort and who is not, from how much they are able to participate in the next session, which usually follows on from the homework). I also recognise that different people have different amounts of other commitments in their lives (child-care, jobs, etc). However, I do expect that the Craft will be very important in coveners' lives, which means showing up to rituals and putting in the effort, and not turning up late on a regular basis, or regarding other activities as more important than the Craft most of the time. Sorry if that is unreasonable, but it's just how I roll.

It is important to note that different people have different learning styles, and adjust one's expectations accordingly. Some people are visual learners, and learn best by seeing things done; others are auditory learners, who retain what they hear; and others are kinaesthetic learners, which means they learn by doing: moving through the ritual actions and the ritual space. So your training should offer opportunities for all three learning styles. Fortunately, Wiccan rituals are a combination of visual, auditory, and kinaesthetic elements, so that should not be too difficult to manage.

Learning words is difficult for most people; some learn best by writing out the words and reading them over and over; others learn best by recording the words onto a tape or CD and playing them back; others learn best by doing the ritual and associating the words with the actions. However, the most important thing is being able to connect with the magical and spiritual energies in the circle. I always recommend that people make a connection with the energies first, and then worry about the words. I have known people who are very wordy and who said they couldn't feel energies do a very good invocation, simply because they were very eloquent, but because the invoker couldn't feel the energies and didn't know when to stop, the invokee was invoked about halfway through the invocation, and had to wait until the invocation had finished before they could start channelling the deity.

Another thing that some people just cannot do is visualisation, because they don't see images in their mind's eye – this is rare, but I have come across several people like this. You can help these people by building emotional and spatial and auditory ideas into the visualisation.

I personally disagree with making people write out their *Book of Shadows* by hand. Of course, if some people find it valuable, I wouldn't stop them from doing it. But I would not make it a requirement.

The advantages of doing it are that some people learn well by copying things out; some people find it a meditative exercise, where they really engage with the text; others find it to be a way of ensuring that every member of the coven really values the text, because they have had to make a big effort to copy it out.

The disadvantages of doing it are that it is very difficult for people with dyslexia. Some people learn through auditory means and not through reading. When I need to learn a ritual off by heart, I learn by listening to a recording of it. Some people have arthritis, which makes it hard for them to write at length; some people have poor handwriting, so what they have copied out is illegible (though this is an excellent argument for learning calligraphy).

Being a pragmatic sort of person, if I am going to engage in any activity, I like to have a reason for doing it. If the reason is because someone else says so, that is insufficient reason for me. Of course if I trust them (as one does trust one's elders and peers in the Craft) and they said, there's a good reason for this but I can't put it into words; you'll know what I mean when you've done it, then that would be different.

As it happens I have copied out a lot of rituals by hand, and generally I tend to wish they were in electronic form so as to be easier to reproduce and store (not to be disseminated widely, but to share with my initiates).

If you happen to have elegant calligraphic handwriting and enjoy illuminating your manuscripts, that's great, of course. If you're one of those people who memorises things by writing them out, that's great too. But for people with dyslexia, copying the *Book of Shadows* is just a form of torture. For people with dyslexia, the problem with copying texts is that they can only hold a small amount of stuff in working memory, so they have to refer to the text much more frequently, and are much more likely than other people to make mistakes copying, especially when it involves unfamiliar words (which occur frequently in magical texts).

Furthermore, we are not a religion of the book, and elevating the *Book of Shadows* to a quasi-authority and keeping it always the same text creates a danger of turning Wicca into a form of fundamentalism and the *Book of Shadows* into its scripture.

My *Book of Shadows* is a growing document that includes the material that was handed down to me, but also includes rituals written by our coven members over the years. Perhaps it would be a good idea for people to copy the initiation rituals out by hand, and the eight sabbat rituals, and other core material, but not the whole corpus of material available.

There are other activities in learning the Craft that I consider to be more important than hand-copying a *Book of Shadows* – like learning to visualise, learning the theory of magic, learning divination, learning to construct and lead a good ritual.

Your Book of Shadows

Each individual witch, coven, and lineage should have different material in their *Book of Shadows*. It has been said that originally, a *Book of Shadows* was the written version of rituals and spells that had been performed, and was called the *Book of Shadows* because the written versions are mere shadows of the actual ritual that was enacted. As any experienced witch will tell you, a ritual is much more than the words that were spoken; it is the experience of being in circle, and encountering deities and spirits. It is the sight of candlelight and firelight playing on naked bodies; the experience of jumping over the Beltane fire, or being in a space that is between the worlds.

Each coven will develop particular and special rituals and traditions that it performs (and other covens have been kind enough to share some of their special rituals with me). Each lineage will have variations, large or small, on the 'core' material that most Gardnerian and Alexandrian Wiccans share. Gerald Gardner gave different version of his *Book of Shadows* to Madge Worthington, Monique Wilson, and Patricia Crowther – all of whom went on to found their own lineages and create their own rituals which were handed down in those lineages; and other covens continue this practice of handing on material. According to Fred Lamond, in his book *Fifty Years of Wicca*, Gerald Gardner also told his initiates that they could adapt, add, and remove things from the *Book of Shadows*. I (and many other Wiccans) would also add that if you don't like a particular ritual, you should hand it on to your initiates anyway, because someone else might like it in the future.

The development of different Books of Shadows is not something to be deplored, but something to be celebrated. A *Book of Shadows* is a unique record of the rituals of a coven and the lineage of which it is part. Because of that, I always put the date and the author of the ritual at the top of the document, and encourage my coven members to do the same.

I also feel that it would be a good idea to make a record of any channelled utterances of invoked deities, outcomes of magical work, how people responded to visualisations, and so on. These might be written in a separate book that is always kept in the temple (if you have a dedicated temple space). Some covens do this, and it is a great idea.

Creating ground-rules for your group

Through trial and error, I have worked out that the best way to create meaningful coven etiquette is not to write it yourself and attempt to impose it, but to have a brainstorming session where you invite the members to suggest ground rules for interaction within the group. If the brainstorming session omits a guideline that you feel to be important, you can always suggest it yourself.

The advantage of inviting the group to create their own set of rules is that when someone breaks one of them, the rules are owned by the whole group, including the person who has broken a rule, so they are not seen as rules imposed by the coven leaders.

There is a general consensus on how people should behave in small groups, which has been arrived at in many different traditions, both spiritual and secular. It is likely that the coven will arrive at a set of rules that looks similar.

Here's an example set of rules:

- Don't interrupt others when they are talking
- Everyone should have an equal chance to participate
- When offering criticism, do so with compassion
- Don't criticise others behind their backs
- State how something makes you feel, rather than blaming the other person for making you feel that way
- Allow participants to decline to take part in any activity (but people should also try to 'push the envelope' of their comfort zone)
- Arrive on time for coven activities

I also hold an Annual General Meeting of the coven, so that people could renegotiate the ground-rules and the collective goals of the coven, suggest new ones, and discuss any issues that had arisen which they had not got around to mentioning when they first cropped up. Of course, people can raise issues at any time and discuss them during the feast after the circle, but having an Annual General Meeting ensures that issues that arise do not get ignored or sidelined.

The rules could also be based around the Eight Wiccan Virtues: honour and humility, mirth and reverence, strength and beauty, power and compassion.

Ritual safety

Ritual safety has two aspects, physical and psychological. The Wiccan circle needs to be a safe place for participants to explore their spirituality, work magic, and grow and develop as witches. However, individual witches can also protect themselves.

Protecting yourself

Learn what the warning signs are of a manipulative group, and withdraw from any situation where those warning signs appear. See the section "some danger signals to watch for" in the excellent article by Phil Hine, *Approaching Groups*. Find out about group dynamics and how they work. Be aware of what triggers you into a state of passivity or compliance, and seek to avoid situations where that may occur.

I once attended a ritual where the temple (a basement room) had a polystyrene ceiling, and there was a cauldron of burning methylated spirit, which we danced round. I was very scared when I thought about it afterwards – but I didn't leave the ritual. Not because I felt coerced into being there, or anything like that, but because I was "away with the fairies", and because it would have felt rude to leave. Another time, I left a ritual without making sure that I was properly grounded, and parked my car in a stupid place where it got broken into. If you are in an altered state, it is very difficult to make rational judgements. It is not a matter of being gullible or stupid – it is how group dynamics work, as any social psychologist will tell you. As soon as people become part of a group identity, they start aligning their views and values to those of the group, and/or the most powerful person in it (not necessarily the named leader; this can be someone with a dominant personality). This happens even in small ad hoc groups such as pub conversations; it happens in healthy groups as well as unhealthy ones (but it is alright if the values of the group are healthy values; not okay if they are unhealthy). If you are planning to join a group, speak to all the members as well as the leader before joining. If there are warning signs, don't ignore them. Does the leader seek to impose their values or lifestyle on members with different values or lifestyles?

Creating safe rituals

We need to examine our own ethics and safety procedures, both physical safety and psychological safety.

Psychological safety: Do our practices and rituals empower people? Are we helping to develop people into competent ritual practitioners and functional human beings? Can people leave our rituals if they feel uncomfortable? Do we have an option for them to vent their feelings constructively if they are unhappy about something? Do people feel psychologically safe and nurtured in our rituals? If we are pushing at boundaries, do we have their informed consent to do so? Make sure your group has sensible guidelines about personal interaction between members. Write the guidelines as a group exercise, so that everyone feels that they own them, and that they are not imposed from above. Hold regular meetings where people can air any problems that arise (an annual meeting is probably enough, but any member of the group should be able to call a meeting whenever a sufficiently serious issue arises). Make sure ritual participants are properly grounded after the ritual, especially if they are driving home. Have a feast (eating is grounding) and some "mundane time" after the circle.

Physical health and safety: If you have a lot of incense, make sure the room is well-ventilated. If you have asthmatics in your group, make sure they have access to their inhaler whilst in circle. If people are allergic to cats or dogs, have they taken anti-histamine tablets? If someone feels ill in your circle, stop everything and make sure they are OK before carrying on with the ritual. Their well-being is more important. If you are planning to include dancing in your ritual, are there trip hazards such as loose carpet? Are there fire hazards in the room (naked flame, incense burners)?

Authoritative versus authoritarian leadership

As a high priestess, I don't expect automatic acceptance of everything I say as being true or valid; but I do expect respect for my knowledge and experience in the Craft. I also expect courtesy among the members of my coven, both towards me and towards each other.

For example, whilst people are at first degree level, there is a custom that they should ask their high priestess's permission before guesting with another coven or tradition. This is because there is a magical tradition that you learn one set of magical practices in its entirety before learning another one and mixing and matching ideas from them. My approach to this is that they should inform me that they are intending to do so and ask my advice about it; I would normally give the go-ahead, but I reserve the right to request that they refrain from visiting another group if I disapprove of that group's practices, or think that the person is not ready for certain aspects of that group's practice, however valid it may be.

Starhawk and others have described various different types of power: power-over (an authoritarian approach where the leader expects never to be questioned); power-from-within (a more egalitarian approach where everyone cultivates their own power. There is also power-among, a consensus approach to decision-making.

As suggested earlier, the Pagan movement came together out of many different strands – American Transcendentalism, the occult orders of the nineteenth century, a rebellion against consumerism and capitalism, egalitarianism and socialism, feminism, a desire for greater sexual freedom, and a sense that we have lost our connection with Nature.

I first realised that I am a Pagan when I read *Puck of Pook's Hill* by Rudyard Kipling, but the thing that got me really interested in witchcraft was reading Starhawk's books about it. So I tend to be very egalitarian in my approach to coven working, rotating the role of ritual leader, and listening to suggestions and comments. My aim in taking on trainees is not to have perpetually dependent acolytes, but to empower and develop them into priestesses and priests in their own right – developing their own power-from-within.

However, because this approach is different to that of the mainstream culture, and people will not automatically understand it or respect it, I have found that it is still necessary to make it clear that the high priestess is the leader. She is neither a complete pushover nor a tyrant; she is a servant leader. The art of leadership requires cunning, tact, and subtlety. If you think of leaders whom you admire, they generally make it look effortless – this is because they have set clear boundaries and expectations (probably by the consensus of the group) and are respected for their knowledge and authority, not feared for their autocratic manner and unpredictable temper.

Power-from-within is utterly different from power-over. Starhawk writes:

"My spirituality has always been linked to my feminism. Feminism is about challenging unequal power structures. So, it also means challenging inequalities in race, class, sexual preference. What we need to be doing is not just changing who holds power, but changing the way we conceive of power. There is the power we're all familiar with — power over. But there is another kind of power — power from within. For a woman, it is the power to be fertile either in terms of having babies or writing books or dancing or baking bread or being a great organizer. It is the kind of power that doesn't depend on depriving someone else."

Coven leaders should be an embodiment of power-from-within. They should be authoritative but not authoritarian; they should know what they are talking about, and walk their talk. They should encourage others' creativity, and empower others to do things. As W.B. Yeats once said, "Education should be the lighting of a fire, not the filling of a pail". Coven training should be like that too – people's enthusiasm should be kindled, not stifled, and they don't need to be spoon-fed, but rather encouraged to seek out knowledge for themselves.

Discussion and activities

- Discuss the role of the coven leader and other members of the coven
- Try rotating the role of ritual facilitator
- Identify any manifestations of the shadow side of power that occur in your group. How can you work through them and prevent negative consequences?
- Practice active listening and other techniques for working towards consensus
- Do a ritual exploring the different aspects of power
- Create a mind-map of the different aspects of power
- Invite the whole coven to do the Myers-Briggs personality inventory and discuss how the results might enhance how you work together as a group
- Discuss the rights and responsibilities of coven members

Practical

- Identify all the fire risks in your temple and do something to fix them
- Work through the section in this chapter on creating safe rituals. Make a list of the physical and psychological hazards, and how you can create safe space for participants.
- Hold an annual general meeting of your coven where members can raise issues for discussion and resolution

- Keep a checklist of roles and activities in ritual (calling the quarters, facilitating a discussion, writing and leading a ritual, casting the circle, consecrating the circle, invoking, being invoked on, etc) and make sure that every coven member has had an opportunity to do them.

Chapter Twenty-Two

Wiccan values

"Let my worship be within the heart that rejoiceth, for behold: all acts of love and pleasure are my rituals. And therefore let there be beauty and strength, power and compassion, honour and humility, mirth and reverence within you."

~ Doreen Valiente, *The Charge of the Goddess*[240]

I believe that the basis of Pagan ethics is the idea that the divine is immanent in everything. All beings partake of the Divine nature, so everything is sacred. Wiccan values reflect this belief.

The basic Wiccan ethic, known as the Wiccan Rede,[241] is "An it harm none, do what ye will". Simply expressed, this means, if it harms no-one, follow your true will. ("An" is an archaic word for "if"). Many critics of Wicca have derided this, because it is impossible to harm no-one; every action can have harmful consequences for someone. However, my friend Dee Weardale suggested that what the Rede is actually saying is that as it is impossible to harm no-one, you can't actually do anything that you want. Therefore the consequences of each possible course of action should be weighed carefully before proceeding.

But there is more to Wiccan ethics than the Rede. Ancient pagan cultures cultivated the virtues. Epicurus advocated the cultivation of virtue as leading to a happy life (and was criticised by his contemporaries for his purely utilitarian view of virtue).[242] The Stoics, on the other hand, identified happiness with virtue, and Aristotle identified happiness with virtuous activity.

Epicurus wrote that all the virtues spring from wisdom, which:

---

[240] Doreen Valiente, *The Charge of the Goddess*, http://www.doreenvaliente.com/Doreen-Valiente-Poetry-11.php

[241] *The Wiccan Rede* is also the title of a long poem written in America in the 1970s which expands on this basic idea, but originally, the phrase 'the Wiccan Rede' referred only to the ethic "An it harm none, do what ye will."

[242] *Epicurus, Internet Encyclopaedia of Philosophy*, ww.iep.utm.edu/epicur/

"is a more precious thing even than philosophy; from it spring all the other virtues, for it teaches that we cannot live pleasantly without living wisely, honourably, and justly; nor live wisely, honourably, and justly without living pleasantly. For the virtues have grown into one with a pleasant life, and a pleasant life is inseparable from them."[243]

Eight Wiccan virtues

In *The Charge of the Goddess* by Doreen Valiente, eight virtues are mentioned: honour and humility, mirth and reverence, strength and beauty, power and compassion. Each of these pairs is carefully balanced.

Too much honour can mean excessive touchiness on every potential ethical dilemma, perhaps even pomposity. Too much humility could make you a doormat, or a Uriah Heep figure. Taken together and balanced, honour and humility make for dignity and integrity. The word humility derives from *humus*, earth, and so implies closeness to the earth. This is not false humility or self-deprecation, but rather an accurate assessment of one's powers. This is especially important in magic, where it can be disastrous to overreach one's capabilities. Also, leaders in Wicca are usually servant leaders, who are aware of the needs of their coveners. We do not lord it over the initiate, but receive them with humility, aware of the talents and insights they bring to circle. Behaving honourably is also important – keeping one's word and behaving with a high standard of integrity.

Too much mirth can lead to cynicism, and too much reverence can lead to boredom – but balanced, these two virtues can lead to good companionship. Mirth is a wonderful thing, especially for pricking the pomposity of the powerful, but we have all met people who can never take anything seriously, and after a while, one wishes that they would take off the mask of comedy and show their real face. But those who always insist on reverence are rather puritanical, and one wishes that they would lighten up. Hence a balance between mirth and reverence is vital.

Beauty and strength also need to be

Pillar of Grace / Pillar of Severity / Pillar of Mercy — Crown, Understanding, Wisdom, Gnosis, Strength, Mercy, Beauty, Splendour, Victory, Foundation, Kingdom

[243] Epicurus, Letter to Menoeceus, http://wwv

balanced – a graceful person is often also a strong person, because they are in control of their body and their mind. Beauty alone can be weak, and strength along can be brutal; but together, they create balance.

Too much power can lead to cruelty, and so can too much compassion. The Buddhists call compassion without wisdom "silly compassion" – the compassion that gives without insight into the situation of the recipient can actually do more harm than good. Too much power can be corrupting, especially if it is not tempered with compassion. When we wield the power of magic, we had better be sure we do so wisely and compassionately.

The balance of these opposites recalls the twin pillars of the Kabbalistic Tree of Life, which are reconciled in the central pillar. Together, Wisdom and Understanding create Gnosis or Knowledge; Strength combined with Mercy creates Beauty; and Power and Glory create the Kingdom. All the Sephiroth (Spheres) of the Tree of Life proceed from the Divine Source. Some of the names of the Sephiroth are also similar to the virtues listed by Doreen Valiente.

Balancing different qualities seems to be important in many esoteric world-views: yin and yang in Taoism, the pillars of mercy and severity in Kabbalah, and what are frequently referred to as "masculine" and "feminine" qualities in Wicca. This terminology is confusing, however, as it does not mean literally that you need a man and a woman to create harmony. What it means is that expansive, hot, active energy is needed to balance contracting, cool, receptive or passive states. These qualities do not necessarily map directly onto men and women; there are cool and receptive men, and women who are expansive and active.

We need a more nuanced and complex understanding of gender to ensure that we do not automatically equate women with "feminine" qualities and men with "masculine" qualities, and expect them to embody those qualities.

Most Wiccans that I know are very relaxed about variations of gender expression, but as soon as it is suggested that these should carry over into ritual, some people start to fall back on gender stereotypes, talk of "fertility religion", and "tradition". But Wicca at its best is an experimental, creative, and evolving tradition that is open to change and growth.

Another important aspect of Wicca is the emphasis on 'perfect love and perfect trust'. Whilst the coven is not a family, the bonds of friendship that develop among coveners are often deep and lifelong. Love among coveners might be seen as *agape*, the experience of fellowship, but it is less impersonal than *agape* often is.

Because coven-based rituals are intense and involve a lot of personal transformation and work with archetypes, it is necessary for coven members to trust each other, and to have a deep concern for each other's wellbeing (more commonly referred to as love). Trust and love is required because we make ourselves vulnerable to each other, revealing our inmost thoughts and feelings, and this would be impossible if we did not trust each other and care deeply about each other.

Cyclicity

Most Pagans regard cyclicity as an important part of the Pagan understanding of the cosmos. We view life as cyclical rather than linear (an example of this is the belief in reincarnation and the emphasis on seasonal festivals). That is, rather than being a progression from non-existence to birth to death to an afterlife, Pagans view existence as a progression from life to life (birth, death and rebirth). This view is often based on the cycles of Nature and the seasons, and the progression of morning, afternoon, evening, and night.

Balance and harmony

In Wicca, darkness does not symbolise evil. The darkness is necessary for rest, growth, and regeneration. Death is not evil, but a necessary adjunct to life. If there was no death and dissolution, there could be no change or growth. The cycle of birth, life, death, and rebirth is part of the interaction of the polarities. Suffering is also part of the process of growth; just as a tree is shaped by the wind, we are shaped by our experiences. It is only by experiencing suffering that we acquire sufficient depth to know the fullness of joy. It is then that the full light of consciousness dawns in us, and we achieve mystical communion with the divine.

But what if we never emerged into the light? What if we were always suffering? This would only be the case if time were linear and not cyclical. In the Wiccan worldview, we go through cycles of birth, death, and rebirth, but not in an endlessly repeating, always-the-same kind of way, rather there is change and growth. The pattern is an ascending spiral, not a treadmill. We pass through light (spring and summer) and descend into darkness (autumn and winter). But just as the seasons are not the same each time, nor are the greater cycles.

Good, in my scheme of things, means balance, and evil means imbalance. Otherwise you get into a terrible mess with people claiming to have a hotline to God, and to represent the forces of good fighting the forces of evil.

Any quality balanced by an opposite quality is not cancelled out but creates a third quality. Balance is often assumed to mean cancelling out, but if you think about two equal weights in a scale, they do not cancel out each other's weight, they only cancel out each other's impact on the scales. In a complex system, such as climate, high pressure in one area will result in comparatively low pressure in another area, so the flow will be from the high pressure area to the low pressure area. But as it is not a closed system, this will create another flow due to another difference in pressure, so you might say that the system was in dynamical balance (like the concept of Equilibrium in Ursula le Guin's *Wizard of Earthsea* trilogy). Equilibrium means 'equal degrees of freedom'.

Reciprocity

Although the ethic of reciprocity is not strongly emphasised in Wicca, it is present in our ethical values. One example of this is the very strong prohibition against charging for training in Wicca. This is based on a 'pay-it-forward' model: the idea that you received your training for free, and so you pass on the knowledge and skills that you received without charging for them. The relationship among coveners is regarded as sacred, and the exchange of money would destroy the relationship by ending the mutual web of obligation.

In ancient times, hospitality was regarded as sacred. In English, the words 'guest' and 'host' are very closely related. In German, the words are *'Gast'* (guest) and *'Gastgeber'* (host, or literally, guest-giver). There were rituals of giving and accepting hospitality, and it was regarded as a sacred exchange. A guest under your roof was to be protected. That is why stories where the relationship of hospitality is betrayed are so powerful and shocking. In Germany and in Pakistan, it is still the custom for a guest to bring a gift for the host on their first visit to a house (even if they are not staying the night). This is the custom in other countries too. Hospitality was regarded as a sacred obligation in ancient Greece; it is mentioned several times in Homer's *Odyssey*. When Odysseus is shipwrecked, it is because of the obligations of the host towards the stranger that Nausica comes to his aid; and when he returns home to Ithaca disguised as a beggar, the shepherd Eumaios welcomes him as a guest. In India, the guest is regarded as a manifestation of the Divine, and hospitality is based on the principle *Atithi Devo Bhava*, meaning "the guest is God."

The exchange of gifts is a way of establishing relationship. In gift economies, gifts are given without any formal agreement as to when the favour will be returned; however, the ethic of reciprocity is so strong that the gift creates an obligation to return the gift or favour, and in this way, an ongoing relationship is created. We can see this ethic at work in the giving of gifts for Yule and birthdays. If a friend gives me a gift, I feel an obligation to get them a gift in return. If someone looks after your cat while you are on holiday, you get them a gift while you are away.

Sadly, the giving of gifts has become bound up with monetary considerations, as we feel the need to buy something of equal value to the gift we were given. However, the point of a gift is the amount of effort that went into it. Perhaps your friend went to a lot of effort to find something that they knew you would like; perhaps they went to a lot of effort to make something beautiful. Either way, it is the effort that counts, not the money. It is the idea that the friend cares enough about you to spend time making something for you, or finding a gift that expresses something about who you are. The gift then becomes an outward and visible symbol of your relationship with the giver. This is why I disagree with the idea that we should give up on all material things and get rid of stuff; quite often the stuff that you have around your home represents friendships and relationships.

The giving of money in exchange for something does not create relationship, it ends it. If I pay in full for a service or a commodity, my obligation is discharged, and that ends the relationship. If I pay for a massage, a Tarot reading, or a workshop, that is because the masseur, Tarot reader, or workshop leader is not going to receive from me (at some unspecified future date) a massage, a Tarot reading, or a workshop. The relationship is ended by the payment. This is, I think, why Wiccans believe strongly that we should not charge trainees for training. Members of a coven are in a relationship, and payment for training would end that relationship. What you gain in return for teaching is an opportunity to formulate, clarify, and refine your own views in the process of transmitting them to others. You can also learn from your trainees. And in due course, you will have a coven to work with who can write rituals for you to take part in. All members of a coven are expected to contribute food for the feast and candles and incense for rituals, and help with the washing-up, however.

A similar situation exists in the development of friendships. A friend is someone you can open up to, who will not judge you for your actions; they may offer constructive criticism, but they do not reject you for your oddities and quirks. However, the process of opening up to each other is gradual and reciprocal. One person will reveal something about themselves, and the other will reciprocate. Revealing your innermost thoughts and feelings is to make yourself vulnerable, to give the gift of yourself. If the other person does not reciprocate with a revelation of similar import, it feels as if there is a major imbalance in the relationship; you have made yourself vulnerable, giving the other person power over you; so you need them to reciprocate. The gradual peeling away of layers of the onion applies both to thoughts and feelings, and to social space. First you meet a new friend outside the home, in a pub or other neutral space; only later do you invite them to your house. At first you talk about current affairs and other relatively impersonal topics; only later do you reveal your more inward feelings and experiences.

This ethic of reciprocity appears in many cultures, but is grounded in the idea of creating relationships. We are social animals and like to form bonds and associations – friendship groups, clans, tribes, and families. These groups gradually form their own traditions, rituals, and symbols, but they are grounded in the mutual relationships of the members, who help each other, forgive each other, and form bonds of obligation through the exchange of gifts and hospitality.

It can be a good thing that the money economy has developed; sometimes we do not want to enter into relationship with a person who has done something for us, because they are not part of our social group. But it is important not to confuse the practice of gift exchange with the money economy. The two "systems" work differently, and have different rules.

Traditional Pagan and other cultures had a strong ethic of reciprocity, hospitality and gift exchange, and it is worth investigating these ideas. They can help us to understand the dynamics of gift-giving (always fraught with social minefields, especially at Yuletide), and to learn to value what is of real worth (the emotional associations of a thing, rather than its monetary value), and not feel guilty about having stuff. They can also make us more aware of the underlying currents of social intercourse – always a valuable insight for a magical practitioner who aims to be effective in all the realms (physical, spiritual, astral, social, and mental).

Reciprocity also exists in nature, in the form of balance. Birth is balanced by death; growth is balanced by decay; darkness is balanced by light. This natural reciprocity is found in ancient myths too. In order to gain wisdom from Mimir's Well, Oðinn had to sacrifice an eye. He gave up part of his physical sight in order to gain inner sight or wisdom. In order to gain the knowledge of the runes, Oðinn hung nine days and nights on the World Tree. The gain of one thing entails the loss of another; that is how equilibrium is maintained.

Caring for the environment

Because we believe in balance and cyclicity, it makes sense to work with the environment and Nature, rather than against it. We honour the immanence of the divine in the world, and we regard the physical world as the primary locus of spiritual experience. There may be other worlds, but we cannot usually experience them directly and unambiguously, so we should act as if our beautiful and precious world is the only one there is.

Many Wiccans are animists, that is, we believe that the world is a community of living persons, only some of whom are human. Animists attempt to relate respectfully with the persons (human, rock, plant, animal, bird, ancestral, etc.) who are also members of the wider community of life.

Most Wiccans believe that the Divine is immanent in the physical world, and can be experienced through nature and the celebration of the cycle of the seasons. Many of us therefore engage in environmental activism and try to reduce our carbon and ecological footprints.

Ethical and ecological audit

Household

Area	Issues	Solutions
Cleaning products	• Many cleaning products contain chemicals which are harmful to the environment and to animals, birds, and fish • Washing your car swills harmful chemicals into rivers	• Use environmentally-friendly products • Use waterless car-wash
Furniture and textiles	• Was the producer of the furniture fairly paid for their work? (is it Fair Trade?) • Was it made from a renewable resource? • If the fabric is made from plant fibre, was the plant grown organically?	• Check wooden items to see if they are certified by the Forest Stewardship Council • Buy things made from recycled materials
Disposals	• Anything you throw away will end up in a landfill site, emitting methane into the atmosphere • Many materials are from non-renewable resources (e.g. metal & plastic)	• Think before you throw it away. • Can it be recycled? • Could you give it to a charity shop / thrift store / goodwill store?

Area	Issues	Solutions
Energy use	• Is your electricity coming from a sustainable source? • Have you considered solar panels? • What about wind power?	• Switch to a green energy supplier • Don't leave electrical items on standby • When boiling the kettle, only put in as much water as you need (this makes the tea taste better too!) • You can get grants to switch to solar panels
Heating	• Gas is extracted from the Earth and is a non-renewable resource. • Electricity is frequently generated from nuclear energy (and 25% of the power is lost in transmission through the National Grid) or from coal-fired power-stations, another non-renewable resource.	• Consider using a wood-burning stove (it's carbon-neutral) • If you have central heating, turn your thermostat down a few degrees and put a jumper on instead
Insulation	• No point having green energy if it escapes out of the roof. • Is your loft insulated? • Is the insulation material non-polluting and from a sustainable source? • Do you have double-glazing?	• Use recycled or natural materials such as thermal fleece, "denim wool" or shredded newspapers for insulation

Area	Issues	Solutions
Recycling	• Glass, plastic, clothing and textiles, paper and metal can all be recycled	• Sort your waste • Don't buy items with packaging which cannot be recycled
Lighting	• Uses electricity • External lighting can cause light pollution and disturb animals	• Use energy-saving light-bulbs • Don't leave lights on • If you have an external security light, make sure it is only triggered by a sensor, not left on all the time

Personal

Area	Issues	Solutions
Clothing & shoes	• Was the producer of the clothing fairly paid for their work? (is it Fair Trade?) • Was it made from a renewable resource? • If made of leather, was the animal humanely treated?	• Buy fair trade and organic clothes • Make your own clothes • or buy from a charity shop / thrift store / goodwill store • Buy vegan / vegetarian shoes
Jewellery	• Was the producer of the jewellery fairly paid for their work? (is it Fair Trade?) • If it contains gemstones, were they strip-mined?	• Look for the fair-trade label • Check that the gemstones were not strip-mined
Personal hygiene products	• Was it tested on animals? • Will it pollute the environment?	• Buy only from ethical suppliers • Look for the mark "Not tested on animals" or "Against animal testing"
Gifts	• Is it fair trade / organic / sustainable?	• Make your own gifts and cards • Send e-cards • Buy someone membership of an organisation, or shares in a

		forest project
		• Buy gifts from charitable organisations
All products	• Was the producer of the product paid at all for their work?	• Check your slavery footprint (how much of the product was produced using slaves or indentured labour?)
		• Write to the companies from which you buy things to make sure there is no slavery in their supply lines

Food and drink

Area	Issues	Solution
Meat, eggs and dairy	• Factory farming • Antibiotics in the animal's diet can kill the flora and fauna in your gut which you need to digest your food properly	• Buy from your local farmer's market • Buy organic and free-range
Vegetables and fruit	• Air miles - how far was the item transported? (causing pollution and carbon emissions)	• Only buy local produce when it's in season • Get your fruit and veg delivered in a box
Bottled drinks	• Plastic and glass bottles accumulating in landfill sites • Plastic is made from oil (a non-renewable resource) • How far has the water or other drink been transported? • Is it drawn from underground aquifers, which can cause land collapses	• Buy water that supports water projects in the Third World • Filter your tap water • Reuse and recycle plastic and glass bottles
Fish	• Sustainability - the fish species may be endangered	• Check one of the various sustainability websites that lists fish species and sustainably sourced fish suppliers

Genetically modified foods	• Allowing one company to own genetic material • Decreasing biodiversity • Cross-breeding of GM crops with wild plants • Lack of consumer choice • Once farmers have bought GM seeds, they are stuck with them • Unpredictable effects on the environment	• Campaign against GM crops • Look at online GM foods checklists to avoid buying food with GM ingredients
Pesticides in food	• About half of all UK fruit and vegetables contain pesticide residues • Some of these can bio-accumulate in our bodies or harm our hormone systems. They also pollute drinking water; removing pesticides costs the UK £120m a year	• Buy organic vegetables & fruit (from a farmers' market or a box scheme)
Disposal	• Putting it in the bin means that it ends up in a landfill site	• Compost it!

Transport

Area	Issues	Solution
Driving to work	Pollution & carbon emissions	Seek alternative forms of transport, such as walking, cycling, bus or train
Flying	Pollution & carbon emissions	Do something to offset the carbon emissions - e.g. tree planting Go by train (if possible)
Going by ship	Pollution & carbon emissions Noise of propellers prevents long-distance communication by whales	Sail

Chapter Twenty-Three

Witchcraft and Activism

"No sane person with a life really wants to be a political activist. When activism is exciting, it tends to involve the risk of bodily harm or incarceration, and when it's safe, it is often tedious, dry, and boring. Activism tends to put one into contact with extremely unpleasant people, whether they are media interviewers, riot cops, or at times, your fellow activists. Not only that, it generates enormous feelings of frustration and rage, makes your throat sore from shouting, and hurts your feet.

Nonetheless, at this moment in history, we are called to act as if we truly believe that the Earth is a living, conscious being that we're part of, that human beings are interconnected and precious, and that liberty and justice for all is a desirable thing."

- Starhawk (2003), "Towards an activist spirituality". In: *Reclaiming Quarterly* (Fall 2003)

Many witches and Wiccans are activists for one cause or another: campaigning for the environment, against racism, for reproductive rights, LGBT rights, freedom of religion, ethical treatment of animals, and more. Some of us supplement our campaigning with magical activities; others prefer to keep politics out of their spiritual lives.

For myself, I have always thought that changing the world and changing yourself go hand in hand. The aim of my magical practice is to be as fully developed as possible in every sphere: mental, physical, spiritual, and astral.

There is, however, a major conflict at the heart of the Pagan movement, between individuality and community, and between environmentalism and consumerism.

Being a post-Enlightenment phenomenon, the Pagan revival is strongly wedded to the idea of individual freedom. In many ways this is a good thing, but it comes at a cost – the loss of a sense of communal obligations and communal culture.

The other problem is that in order to express our individuality, we require artifacts to remind us of our identity. As soon as an idea becomes popular, consumer culture appropriates it and turns it into a commodity – consider the commodification of the Pagan lifestyle in the form of jewellery, art work, clothing, crystals, wands, and other paraphernalia. A counter-current to this consists of the "fluffy bunny" label[244] – the more commercially-produced paraphernalia you own, the more likely you are to be considered a "fluffy bunny".

Both the lack of a sense of community, and the assimilation of new forms of cultural expression into the dominant cultural discourse, make activism difficult. It is often easier to give up hope of real change and accept the status quo. However, this is the counsel of despair. Do we really want to accept the despoliation of the earth, the disenchantment of reality, the commodification of everything? Even landscape has been assigned a monetary value by some neo-conservatives.

Rhyd Wildermuth writes[245] that if we regarded belief, not as an interior state of mind, only to be expressed in private, but instead as a call to act out our belief in public space, we would be more active in making our vision of the world a reality. By comparison with cultures where it is the norm to be able to make offerings to deities, to worship deities in public, and to celebrate them in public space, Paganisms in the west look peculiarly private and circumscribed. Our lack of action in support of our beliefs (that the Earth is sacred, for example) begins to look like a lack of imagination, or a lack of will. If we really believed that magic worked and the deities exist and are our allies, we would behave consistently with that belief. In ancient times, belief did not mean merely an opinion – it meant to love and trust. If we love and trust each other, then we can build a way of life that is both sustainable and sacred.

In magic, there is a fourfold practice: to know, to will, to dare, to keep silent. Activists need all four of these to bring our visions to fruition. We need to know the conditions in which we are working, and what needs to change. We need to have the will to bring about change. We need to dare to speak out for our beliefs, and to act upon them – whether that is in demonstrating, letter-writing, signing petitions, making magic, and acting in ways consistent with our vision. We also need to know when to keep silent, in order to bring about the magical change that we require.

Peter Grey argues[246] that we are sleepwalking into an apocalypse; that environmental collapse is now inevitable and irreversible, and therefore we must radically reorient our witchcraft and our activism to deal with this. We certainly cannot continue to drive cars and unthinkingly collaborate with global capitalism as if we were not on the brink of environmental disaster. Grey proposes a radical reorientation of witchcraft:

[244] A Coco & I Woodward (2007), Discourses of Authenticity Within a Pagan Community: The Emergence of the "Fluffy Bunny" Sanction, *Journal of Contemporary Ethnography* October 2007 vol. 36 no. 5 479-504 (doi: 10.1177/0891241606293160)
[245] Rhyd Wildermuth, Manifesting An Other World, *The Wild Hunt* blog, 5 July 2014, http://wildhunt.org/2014/07/manifesting-an-other-world.html
[246] Peter Grey, Rewilding Witchcraft, *Scarlet Imprint*, 13 June 2014, http://scarletimprint.com/2014/06/rewilding-witchcraft/

"I will argue that Witchcraft is quintessentially wild, ambivalent, ambiguous, queer. It is not something that can be socialised, standing as it does in that liminal space between the seen and unseen worlds. Spatially the realm of witchcraft is the hedge, the crossroads, the dreaming point where the world of men and of spirits parlay through the penetrated body of someone who is outside of the normal rules of culture. What makes this all the more vital is the way in which the landscape of witchcraft is changing. Ours is a practice grounded in the land, in the web of spirit relationships, in plant and insect and animal and bird. This is where we must orientate our actions, this is where our loyalty lies."

I certainly agree that witchcraft is inherently queer and that we must resist assimilation into mainstream culture, which seeks to turn us all into consumers, to stifle our creativity, our connection to the land, and our sense of community with the whole biosphere and its inhabitants. I do not know whether the collapse of civilization is imminent, as Grey opines, but it is an eventuality we need to prepare for. We need to get angry about the destruction of the wilderness, and to become active in its defence, and for the reintroduction, conservation, and proliferation of wild species which can reinvigorate ecosystems. We need to educate ourselves about the environment and what we can do to save it. We do not need to become "acceptable" and spend hours arguing about what consists of "proper" witchcraft and Wicca.

Recently I read an article by George Monbiot about the reintroduction of the beaver[247] in a number of European river systems; after its reintroduction, fish stocks increased because of the pools created by the beavers, and there were many benefits to the environment. The reintroduction of wild species, including the wolf and the queer activist witch, can help to save the environment.

The Pagan movement is at its best when it runs counter to mainstream consumerist values. This is not always the case in every manifestation of apparently counter-cultural Paganism, as those who have dropped out of the system can sometimes be just as consumerist as those who are part of the system.

We need to develop strong Pagan values and a strong sense of community that also celebrates diversity, so that we can resist assimilation by the mainstream culture. This is difficult when we are faced with the need to survive in the existing system, but we can start by getting involved in activism, daring to dream, and daring to translate our dreams and visions into action.

I recently read the *Emberverse* series of novels by S.M. Stirling, in which electronics, guns, the internal combustion engine, and gunpowder all stop working overnight. The laws of physics have been tampered with by some unknown power. The books explore the consequences of this strange event, known as the Change. Part of the story follows a small group of Georgian Wiccans who take to the hills;

---

[247] George Monbiot, Stop the control freaks who want to capture England's wild beavers, *The Guardian*, 4 July 2014.
http://www.theguardian.com/environment/georgemonbiot/2014/jul/04/stop-control-freaks-capture-englands-wild-beavers

another part deals with a man who decides to set up a feudal Norman-style state. The people who do best are those with some skills in farming, making things, but also, the ones who are rich in stories that help make sense of the world, which help them to build just and cohesive societies.

I think that the Change is shorthand, or a metaphor, for what happens when the oil runs out. It won't happen overnight, and if we are lucky, it will be managed sensibly. But all the current indications are that it will *not* be managed sensibly. Instead of reducing our dependency on fossil fuels, companies are inventing ever more destructive ways of wresting them from the ground, the worst of these being fracking. We are also not investing in sustainable power sources, or taxing carbon consumption, or anywhere near enough of the things we should be doing. The warning signs of climate change are being ignored, and more species are becoming extinct.

I also recently attended a ritual in my local area that was part of a global magical working to protect the waters of the world from fracking, which is about the most irresponsible and damaging thing anyone could possibly do to the environment. It was a very moving and beautiful ritual, and it brought together eco-activists, Pagans, shamans, and others.

So what can Pagans and other ecologically-minded people do to prepare for the eventual crash, or shift?

We can reduce our own dependence on fossil fuels; campaign for investment in sustainable energy sources; campaign for environmental and social justice. But in addition to these, we can do magic (the art of changing consciousness in accordance with Will) to heal and protect the Earth and other living beings, and we can learn skills such as building roundhouses and coracles and boats, raising livestock, weaving, growing our own food, and so on. We can get involved with the transition towns movement and other sustainability initiatives, support organic farming, and check our own ecological footprint. We can build strong communities – not only of Pagans, but including others of good will. And we can engage with stories that show how to build just, cohesive, and inclusive societies. We are already doing all this to a certain extent – we just need to do it more.

If we cannot be involved in direct action ourselves, then we can support and empower those who are involved. We can make magic – always a tool of resistance for the oppressed. We can dare to dream that a different world is possible; we can educate ourselves and the young about sustainability, community, deep ecology, and a culture of inclusiveness and consent; we can try to heal and support those who are broken by the consumerist system; we can choose to live sustainably, and empower others to do so.

> "Another world is not only possible, she's on the way and, on a quiet day, if you listen very carefully you can hear her breathe." – Arundhati Roy[248]

---

248   From a speech entitled *Confronting Empire* given at the World Social Forum in Porto Allegre, 28 January 2003

Appendices

Appendix 1

Visualisations

Walpurgisnacht

Sitting in a cottage by the fire. Stone walls, simple furniture. Feel yourself getting lighter and more insubstantial. Fly up the chimney. Riding on a broomstick over a moonlit landscape. The moon shines silver on everything. The land seems blue and silver in the moonlight. There is mist in the hollows. You become aware of the roads glowing silver in the moonlight, only they are not roads, but spirit tracks. Fly above them, following them. You see people moving along them. Then you realise that all the tracks converge on a very high round hill. Other witches are coming from all directions, heading for the great round hill. It is a Sabbat, and there is dancing and feasting. Magpies and hares and cats weave in and out among the dancers. Towards dawn, retrace the route to the cottage.

The island in the lake in the island in the lake

You travel among hills and find a lake. A small boat is tied to a jetty by the shore. You row across to an island in the centre of the lake. Within that island is another lake. Within the inner lake is another island. You swim across and discover what is on that island.

The plain of horses

Follow a stream and then cross it, and enter a cave. The cave is dimly lit by the daylight coming in at the entrance. There is a vertical wall in the cave, painted with horses and handprints and the outlines of hands. You place your hand in one of these and the wall becomes insubstantial, and you pass through into the realm of spirit. You pass into another cave which is the mirror image of the one you have just left, and opens out into a landscape of rolling steppe, in which the yellow grass moves softly in the wind. There is a herd of horses just beyond the cave, and you run to catch up with them. They are white dappled, grey, brown, and piebald. Eventually you catch up with them and mount your chosen horse, then ride it across the steppe. When finished, thank the horse, and retrace the route through the cave, using a handprint as the key back to the first cave.

(This visualisation is good with a drum, and can be used as a job spell – the horse represents a job.)

The sea shell

Start from a high tower in an upper room. Descend ten steps. Walk down the hill on which the tower stands, along a track down to a round cove, where rocky outcrops enclose a calm stretch of water and a smooth slope of sand, and a stream runs down the beach to the sea. Walk to the edge of the sea (you can paddle or dive in, whatever you like) and find something which is meant for you under the water (could be a shell or a pebble, or whatever). When you are ready, return to the shore.

Now it is time to return back up the slope, through the fields to the door by which you entered. Retrace your steps up to the door, open it and close it behind you. You can lock it if you want. Then climb back up the steps, and return to the space in which you are sitting.

(This visualisation is good for preceding a story-in-the-round exercise, as it helps people to access the subconscious.)

The house with nine rooms

You are in a square white house with nine rooms. Wander from room to room. Note how you feel in each room. Is there another floor – above or below? What objects are in each room? How do the rooms relate to each other? The centre room may be a small courtyard with a pool and a tree.

(This visualisation could form the basis of a memory house.)

The place of orientation

You are on a flat circular plain surrounded by mountains. The sun is rising in the east and the moon is setting in the west. You lie with your head towards the north and your feet towards the south. Connect outwards to the four directions and inwards to the centre.

Archetypes visualisation

It is twilight. You are standing in a sacred grove, trees all around you. Look at the trees and touch their bark. Feel the earth beneath your feet, the cool grasses brushing against you. Smell the breeze and listen to the wind rustling the leaves of the trees in your grove.

Now look beyond the grove to the landscape beyond. Ahead of you is a small hill. As you walk towards it, you see an opening in the side of the hill, with a low stone doorway – two uprights and a huge lintel. A small ochre-coloured stone stands outside, with three bands of red around it, and moss around its base. You may pour a libation here if you wish.

You stoop down to enter the doorway, and find yourself in a tunnel which goes upwards into the hill. It is not too dark, as there seems to be a light source up ahead.

Eventually you emerge into a big open space, and as you stand blinking, your eyes adjusting to the light, you see that there are two people in the cave: an old person and a child. They are sitting by a fire, which reflects its warmth and light onto their faces.

Look at the old person: how are they dressed? Take their hand: how does it feel? Look into their eyes, listen to them, talk to them, give them a gift. Perhaps they will give you a gift.

Now the child: how is it dressed? What will it tell you? Talk with the child, look into its eyes. Maybe you exchange gifts.

And now, look into the fire, and notice how its dancing flames form shadows on the walls of the cave: hairy arms, hands, tongues, and beast shapes rise up and flicker on the walls of the cave. They are scary but you have the reassuring presence of the old person and the child.

And now you look again into the flames and see a person forming in the fire, beautiful and golden. The person rises out of the fire, the embodiment of your inner self. The person smiles at you. Gaze into their eyes, let your gaze caress them, but do not touch.

In turn, the firelight illuminates a deep pool at the back of the cave. Its dark waters are smooth and peaceful, rippling gently towards the shore, as the pool is fed by a spring.

You see that the moon has risen and is shining through a small opening in the roof of the cave, and is reflected in the dark water. You can stoop down and drink the water. Feel the silver moonlight filling you.

Now it is time to go, and when you turn around, you see that the flames have died down to embers, the fire being has disappeared, and the old person and the child are two stalactites in the cave.

You turn and walk back down the passage, stoop low to go out of the entrance, and are back on the green slope of the hill. Ahead of you is your grove. Walk back to the grove, greet the trees, and sit down once more on the earth. As you sit, close your eyes, and feel yourself gradually returning to this place and this time and this room.

The sea cave

You are descending a slippery, dark, winding stair. Down into the earth and the darkness, down and down and down. The only sound is the far-off dripping of water, the only light is the faint glimmer of phosphorescence. Down and down you go into the earth, down into the cold and dark. At last you come to a great cavern, filled with dark water. Above you, you can hear waves booming on the cliffs, and you know that this deep cave must be connected to the sea. The dark water stretches away in front of you, very cold and very deep. It is entirely still, like a mirror, but every now and then a drop of water falls from the roof far above, and a circular ripple shines softly and dimly in the darkness, illuminated by some unknown light source. The water is dark as ink, and you feel afraid. Dive into the water.

[Long pause – can stop talking here if required and let people free-visualise before bringing them back out of the water and up the winding stair.]

You find that the water is cold but refreshing. As you become accustomed to it, you open your eyes and see that all is bright beneath the surface of the water – blue and silver and turquoise and green, and in some places all the colours of the rainbow woven together – the ocean of the streams of story – a many-coloured land beneath the wave. You swim on and on, and out of the winding tunnel that connects the cave to the ocean, and then play and tumble in the great rolling waves, riding the surf, letting the salt sea enfold you and caress you.

(Can meet sea deity here, e.g. Yemaya, Manannan.)

You become one with the sea, you are the water. As you are swept up on the crest of a wave, you are carried up into a cloud, then fall as rain in the mountains, run down into caves, then rise up into the world as a bubbling spring, and run gurgling and chuckling over the rocky stream bed and down to the sea again. Rejoin your body at this point. Return to the room and fully conscious awareness.

(Do not do the above until you are ready to dive into the subconscious)

The city of alchemy

You sit in a warm book-lined room by a fire, with French windows and a balcony, overlooking the roofs of a middle-European city. Domes and cupolas and tiled roofs are spread out below you. You rise from your chair and cross the room to the window, and push open the window and step out onto the balcony.

Below you is a square, tiled with a mystic symbol. It is sunset, and the doves are settling to roost on the rooftops and gutters. Just as you are about to turn back into the room, you hear beautiful singing, deep and melodious. Into the square comes a procession of robed figures carrying torches. They stop beneath your window, and you know that you have to join them. You walk out of your room, down a spiral staircase, out into the hall, which has black and white tiles on the floor, and open the great oak front door. Then you walk down the front steps of the house.

The leader of the procession gives you a cloak, a rose and a flaming torch, and then silently the procession continues up some gracious stone steps and onto a bridge lined with statues of gods and goddesses, heroes and heroines out of some dimly-remembered legend of the far past.

As you process over the bridge, the flaming torches are reflected in the river. By now it is twilight, and as you reach the other side of the bridge and look up at the tower at the end of it, you see the first star twinkling among the pinnacles atop the tower.

The procession wends its way among the tall gabled houses with their ornate and brightly-coloured façades, finally coming to a magnificent town house, painted with designs depicting the nine Muses.

As the procession approaches the house, the double entrance doors open silently and each person extinguishes their torch in a large vat of water either side of the entrance.

The procession forms a circle in the great baroque courtyard. The doors to the street are shut, and two great iron doors that open into the inner recesses of the house are opened. In the centre of the courtyard is an enormous bronze dish. Each person produces a rose from beneath their cloak and lays it reverently in front of them, the flower facing the centre of the circle.

Now a man and a woman enter the circle, through the great iron doors, from within the house. They are carrying flaming torches, and light the coals and driftwood within the bronze dish in the centre.

As the flames spring up, the flames illuminate the faces around the circle, and you recognise the features of people from all around the world.

Now the man produces a curiously shaped box from beneath his robes, and the woman produces a cup. The man walks slowly and solemnly around the circle, showing the contents of the box to all present. As each person sees the contents of the box, they join in the high sad thin keening that has arisen. As the box is shown to you, you see that it appears to contain a dead raven.

At last all present have seen the melancholy contents of the box. Now the man takes the raven gently out of the box and places him on the red-hot coals of the great bronze dish. Then the woman pours half the contents of the cup onto the coals. At once the fire turns white and golden, and the flames rise higher. As they take shape, you see that a phoenix has risen from the flames. It rises up, spreads its wings – almost too bright to look upon – and flies up and around the courtyard, over the heads of all present, so that a spark from its tail lands on every head, without burning it, and illuminates the brow chakra of each person, so that it seems that a star has settled on their brows.

Then, with a final flourish, the phoenix flies up and away, singing its beautiful song, spreading magic and beauty once more over the earth. And now each member of the circle bows to the man and the woman, and each is given to drink from the cup that she poured on the flames.

And silently the procession departs once more from the great courtyard, returns over the bridge – where now you see stars reflected in the river, and the moon climbing over the hill beyond. Then you walk back down the steps into your square, and back into you house – up the steps and through the oak front door, back up the spiral stairs into your warm book-lined room. There you latch the window and close the curtains and settle back into your chair, musing on all that you have seen.

Introduction to Wicca course

There is a tradition in Wicca of waiting until you have known someone for a year and a day before initiating them. Many covens choose to use this time to provide a series of introductory sessions on witchcraft, Paganism, and magical techniques. Here is a suggested structure for an introductory course. I have run this course (with slight variations) three times now, and it seems to be a good preparation for initiation. Sessions can be every two weeks or every three weeks, depending on your preference.

Undergoing training does not automatically lead to initiation – initiation is a privilege, not a right. It is an induction into the priesthood, and not everyone can be a priestess or priest.

Session	Discussion	Practical / ritual	Homework
1	**What is the sacred?** What kind of quality is sacredness? What makes a thing, concept, person, place or time sacred? How do you make something sacred? (consecration)	Grounding and centring; casting the circle	Do an energy cleansing at home – use bells, sweeping, incense, water (whatever seems appropriate)
2	**What is ritual?** What is ritual for? How does it differ from theatre? What types of ritual are there?	Meditation	Meditation

	Do we need a circle for our rituals? What is the significance of performing ritual in a circle?		
3	**Archetypes and symbols** What are archetypes and symbols? How are they different from each other? How do we relate to them? Are they helpful?	Visualisation of archetypes (see Appendix 1)	List symbols which have resonance for you personally, and reflect on why they are meaningful for you
4	**The four elements** Why are they assigned to the four directions? How do they correspond to aspects of the personality and the life cycle? Why do we call on them to create sacred space?	Casting a circle and sweeping; four elements meditation (see appendix 1)	Make your own altar at home – add your own special symbols, deities, magical tools, pictures of ancestors, etc.
5	**Deities and spirits** What are deities and spirits? Are they "real"? Why do we honour them? What different types of deities and spirits are there? (Land-wights, spirits of place, personified concepts, forces of nature…)	Calling the quarters	
6	**Reincarnation, karma, wyrd** What is the nature of reincarnation? What is the goal of reincarnation?	Chakras	Practice opening the chakras

	What is wyrd? What is karma? How are they different from each other?		
7	**What is magic, how does it work?** What is magic? What is magic for? How does it work?	Raising energy	
8	**Ethics of magic** How can you ensure that your 'results magic' is ethical? When is it ethical to work magic for another person?	Protection techniques	Protect your house
9	**The tides of the year and the eight festivals** Have you experienced similar cycles – within the year? Within a project or process? What other cycles are there? How do they interact with each other?	The use of sound in ritual	Draw a year-wheel; find out some folk customs to go with the festivals
10	**Moon meanings and symbols** Why is the Moon so important in Wicca? In what ways do you feel connected to the Moon (or not)?	Some spells	Do a solo ritual
11	**Magical tools** Why use tools instead of just visualising or pointing? What is the symbolism of the tools?	Healing techniques	Make a wand or other magical tool
12	**The nature of space-time** Is fate fixed; is our destiny written in the stars? Or is fate fluid? Can we	Various divination techniques	Do a divination

	change our destiny? Do we determine our own destiny by our choices? **What is divination for?** For discovering the future? For investigating the choices available to us in the present moment? For finding out the consequences of various courses of action? For discovering the roots of our current situation in the past?		
13	**Folklore and folktales** Which folktales are particularly meaningful for you? Which folktales are especially relevant to Wicca?	Folklore ritual	Read a folktale
14	**Local deities** Why honour local deities? How are they connected with the landscape? How are they connected with the wider divine realm?	Local deity ritual	Research local deities Find out a ritual or custom honouring a local deity Find a poem or picture of them; add it to your home altar or shrine area Visit one of their sacred sites Find out when their festival is and keep it as a holy day Find out about their myth or legend

15	**Pagan cosmology** How is a magical diagram of the cosmos useful? How can it be used in ritual? What does it say about our place in the cosmos?	Cosmology ritual	Draw a World Tree
16	**Magic and science** Are the magical and scientific worldviews compatible? Will science one day explain how magic works? What insights from science can we incorporate into our Craft?	Science ritual	Read about the Hero Journey
17	**The Hero Journey** How useful is the Hero Journey as a model of the spiritual journey? Does it resonate with your experience?	Labyrinth/The Hero Journey	Write a visualisation
18	**Spirituality and sexuality** How does spirituality connect with sexuality? Is there an overlap? Where does LGBT sexuality fit in? What does fertility mean? Is Wicca a "fertility religion"?	Sacred Play (Mirth and Reverence)	Play!
19	**Secrecy/confidentiality** Why is secrecy necessary? Why is confidentiality necessary? How are they different? What things would you prefer to keep private to your coven?	Silent ritual	Watch sunrise or sunset

20	**Rites of passage** What is a rite of passage? What significant events should have a rite of passage devoted to them? Do you feel you have missed out on any rites of passage?	Aura-cleansing ritual	Prepare ritual for next time
21	**Preparing for initiation** What is the purpose of initiation? What do you think makes someone ready to be initiated?	Ritual written by a trainee	
22	**Wiccan priest(ess)hood** What is a priestess or priest? How does a Wiccan priest or priestess relate to themselves, their group, wider society?	Ritual written by a trainee	

Extra sessions can be added for trainees to give a talk as well as running a ritual.

Progressive Wicca, talk given in 1988 by Tam Campbell

The Progressive Movement is a group of Wiccans which have a commitment to personal growth, experimentation and free thinking within a supportable structure, moving away from the idea of an orthodox dogma towards a new and fresh approach. They emphasise the need for linking and networking and a desire to share and incorporate experiences. We value people from different traditions who may use differing and alternative methods of magickal expression.

To become a Progressive Wiccan, it is not necessary to be re initiated into a tradition. Progressive Wicca is a movement rather than a tradition in the sense of Alexandrians' or Gardenerianism, or of any other tradition, indeed we have groups within the movement who are of these and other traditions. Instead we are more of a brother and sisterhood linked with a supportive network structure to each other and within which the individual and the groups can grow and learn from each other. It is also important that our convictions should carry over into our everyday lives; therefore we try to espouse a greener and more humanitarian lifestyle. We have people active within both the civil rights and green movements and who are taking direct and concerted action to make life better for all those living on the earth, both human and animal and have a concern to preserve and conserve the earth itself.

Many groups are now taking this approach, we do not claim to be exclusive in this, and however we make it an aim within the movement. The Progressive Movement offers itself as a framework to support the growth of this kind of group and to aid them in the enhancement of their personal, religious and magickal development and furtherance of their knowledge by cross linking and mutual exchange of experiences, techniques and training. It is therefore descriptive of a broad approach to the path of Wicca rather than a conventional tradition and we wish to network with more groups for mutual support, friendship and sharing.

We also wish to come into closer contact with Pagans of other paths for our mutual benefit and to co-work, with them also in whatever ways seem mutually satisfactory within the constraints of our respective traditions and working practices and as the opportunity presents itself.

The Movement does not wish to be seen as a rival to the traditions within Wicca, indeed we have much to learn from them also and they have much of value to contribute to the Wiccan and Pagan word in general. Rather we see ourselves as an alternative means of development. The individual Witch within the Progressive Movement, being encouraged to take as full role, as their experience and training will allow them, take as active a part in the coven life as they can and in the responsibilities and decision making of the group as they are able, will we believe lead to an increasing involvement and responsibility to the group of the members and a growth of personal confidence in their own abilities within the group. Each individual will therefore take responsibility for their own development within the framework of a supportive environment. We know that this approach does no suit those who would be spoon fed or told what to do nor those who are of a consumerist frame of mind. The covens therefore have a democratic structure and seek to, develop power from within rather than the power over/ powerlessness relationship found more commonly within our society. Less assertive members are encouraged to find their voice and we try to create an atmosphere within which they feel confidant to claim their own power, participate in the decision making process within the group rather than being told what to do by an autocratic leader or personality and thus neither change nor grow, nor to develop their own experience of self confidence and responsibility. It is in the interests of both the individual and the group that we have a self reliant group of people who can take their own responsibility rather than do nothing without the caveat of the High Priest/ess. The role of the High Priestess and High Priest is therefore not one of autocratic leaders but along with the experienced members, is more that of facilitators and catalysts who encourage the group members to find and use their powers and develop themselves and enrich the group as a whole, and through this the Movement. In the more experienced groups the role of High Priestess and High Priest within individual group workings are taken by different people at different meetings and rituals and when appropriate different members will take training sessions. The High Priestess within my own group the "Company of Witches" acts as the central facilitator and focus of the group identity.

The Progressive Movement also believes in the importance of comprehensive training in all techniques of Magick, lore and group and individual ritual, both at the level of the beginner and more advanced continuing development up to and including the most experienced members, on to inter group skills enhancement. Members from all the groups may take time off to meet and work together, even go to week long inter group retreats where they work and learn from each other and run courses for mutual development. This could be called continuing professional development. At the beginner level it is usually a condition of acceptance and initiation within to the group for the applicant to undergo a course of training meetings, focusing on personal development, basic ritual and magickal techniques. This is seen as part of the assessment of the applicant by the whole group and is an opportunity for the applicant to get to know the group as a whole. We also enhance the individual members experience by fostering members to other groups in the area, therefore giving the member not just the chance of seeing different techniques and experiencing the atmosphere of different groups but of making new contacts and friends within the groups therefore enhancing the bonds between the groups. We encourage the individual to do their own research and learning and to visit and work with as wide a range of groups as the can.

The groups usually work at different levels; we run open, semi open, outer and inner group rituals. The first type open to anyone of a Pagan persuasion, the second by invite, to pagans, the third to probationers and all group members and the last for power workings and experimental and advanced techniques in a closed environment open only to members of sufficient experience and who know each other well and have worked together for a reasonable time. We prefer to work outdoors and in places of significant sacred atmosphere and power as near to unspoiled nature as it is possible to get, in mountains and woods, by river and sea. We also have and work within, Men's and Women's mystery groups associated with an individual coven or a number of covens within an area, These groups work and explore orders of spirituality other than the basic Dialectic of male/ female found in the Wiccan tradition, specific to the development of the personality and magickal experience of the individual witch thus complementarily to the magick of the main coven.

Initiations and degrees are seen as markers and symbolic signs of a significant advance in the progress of the individual's magical development. Degrees within the Progressive Movement distinguish between different levels of commitment and experience and not as a hierarchical badge of rank. They are taken when the coven and the individual agree that there is a readiness for greater commitment and responsibilities to the coven and the craft. In the words of the Roman Catholic sacraments, they are "an outward sign of inward grace". Wicca views itself as a Priesthood of the Goddess and God, not by any means the only one, however. There are many other Pagan paths which may take this attitude also. There is a pre initiation degree within the Progressive movement when the individual takes upon themselves the intent to become an initiate but who have yet to fully prepare themselves for the commitment of full priesthood. They have publicly declared intent to become full coven and Wiccan brothers and sisters It is , within Wicca, the acceptance into the family of the brotherhood and sisterhood of Wicca and the coven. The beginning of a new view of one's self as no longer simply a Pagan, but an especially chosen devotee and priest of the Goddess and God. A new and significant phase in one's magickal life and development. It is in many ways the most significant signpost of the development of the individual within the path of Wicca and marks the beginning of a new awareness of themselves as Pagans. They are now ready to partake of and enter into the more esoteric workings of the coven and are accepted into the family of the Coven, formally into the brotherhood and sisterhood of the Craft as a whole. It is part of the change to being fully committed to the responsibilities of priesthood, to fully develop one's self upon the path of Wicca and to even deeper levels of commitment and understanding which lie beyond the point of initiation. It therefore needs to be a real and significant experience to the new initiate. This is of course also true of the many other pagan paths and not exclusive to Wicca. It marks a rite of passage and the death of the old personality and the birth of the new priest. Rituals of initiation within the Wicca reflect this. Within the Progressive Wiccan movement we make the First degree elevation and perhaps the Probationary degree, to a lesser extent, take place in a site of deep spiritual and macickal importance and sacredness. In caves, waterfalls, cliffs seashores, woods and hilltops with traditions of being sites of sacredness and power to pagans for millennia. We also tend to precede the initiations with tasks and quests, pilgrimages and the gathering of significant symbols, to further impress upon the pre initiate the impact of the initiation and so make them more ready for the impact of initiation. It gives concrete form to the idea of what initiation is and therefore a deeper understanding of the responsibilities and commitments implicit within the initiation rituals.

As I have already said, degrees within the progressive movement, are not to be viewed as hierarchical or competitive ranks but as markers and acknowledgments of changes within the individuals development and personal progress and as declarations of deeper commitments taken on. They are rites of passage in other words to more intense commitments and responsibilities. The degree system is as follows.

Non-initiated Pagans, People who have a feel for paganism but do not wish to be actively involved on an ongoing basis or with a specific group or path within Wicca. It may be that they either do not wish to or for some reason cannot commit themselves to a group at present but wish to come to open events occasionally.

The Probationers' Oaths and Declarations.

For those who have decided to make a commitment to join a group, and the Craft. It is a point where the decision has been made, the intention has been formally recognised and acknowledged and a deeper commitment to the group and the craft is now expected. As a sign of this commitment, the individual is usually set a task and basic vows are made in front of the coven members. There follows a time of study and preparation. The basics of magick, meditation and personal insight are studied. There is formal training group sessions set up, though there should be some very basic trainings started when the person has decided to go for probationary initiation, into the workings of basic paganism, Sabbats and festivals, and cycles of nature. The probationer is getting to know the coven members more deeply and fitting in to the group at this time. In our coven we usually require a certain frequency of attendance at the formal training sessions also as a sign of competence and commitment to the next step.

Initiation into the First Degree and into Wicca.

A major turning point in the development of the person, they are accepted into the family of Wicca as a witch and priest in a ritual which involves symbolic death and rebirth. A new name is taken and the new Witch takes his or her place within the Coven. They continue and intensify their training in this degree and begin to learn the more esoteric elements of Magick and Wicca. They begin to contribute more to the group energy and bring their own contribution into the group, thinking more about what they can offer in terms of sharing knowledge and the teaching of others. They also begin to think about specialising in specific areas of craft work, Astrology, Tarot, herbalism, runes, therapy, voice work, ritual and crafting objects. They will study and research on their own and bring their specialist knowledge into the group and be writing and designing rituals, take the group for the first time, after practice in ritual and circle casting and work etc. Bringing their own contribution back to the group. The initiation takes place when the person feels themselves ready to fully enter and commit themselves to the group and Wicca in general and both they and the group feel that they are ready to enter into the group. If the person does not feel right within a particular group, they may be referred to another group, or be given Initiation and work as a solitary witch.

Elevation to the Second Degree.

This marks a time when they are really coming into their own power. The will in our coven produce and run a Masterpiece ritual with the group and offer this for judgement of their competence to the group. Also within our group, they will have had experience with at least one other group in a fostering situation and possibly more than one, therefore broadening their contacts and relationships within the Progressive Movement. The ritual is part written by the witch themselves but retains all the main elements of the second degree ritual, and involves a willing of power into the individual empowerment by magickal method and a facing of death that we may learn from it. This has a different emphasis from the death and rebirth of the first degree. The witch should be working with channelling of the God/ Goddess, polarities such as light and dark, anima/ animus/ yin yang et cetera, and be ready to understand and face their shadow sides. It is a mark of the growing maturity and competence of the witch both individually and within the group/ movement.

Third Degree elevation.

The individual should have a thorough understanding of Wicca, be able to channel the Goddess/ God effectively and see their partner as the Goddess/God in ritual. They are becoming aware of the Gods within themselves and the divinity of themselves and all within Nature and upon the earth. They should be seeing the divine inherent in others and love and accept themselves with understanding. They should be training others and running workshops and events for all pagans to attend as well as running and organising covens. This is not an ego trip for self love does not mean that you do not recognise your faults, rather the acceptance of yourself with your faults, coming to terms with these faults and improving yourself at every step. Being in contact with your emotions and to channel them in the most positive way. There will be other changes to mark beyond this, and there may be rituals to mark these changes, development and evolution is continuous.

There are certain standards agreed within the Progressive Movement, these above all else are what links the Progressive covens. These are some of those standards. Working closely with Nature, both on a practical level and in everyday life and to a greener lifestyle, protecting the earth and our environment and to humane action to our fellow humans and animals.

A commitment to personal development through meditation, ritual, therapy, path-workings, self exploration and importantly a willingness to change and grow through our learning and experiences, letting go of prejudices, outmoded ideas, attitudes, beliefs and behaviour patterns. A commitment to networking, sharing of skills ideas and information with other groups. It may include Fostering of members to other groups and the ready acceptance of foster members from other groups.

Rejection of autocracy and power over others, to seek to cultivate inner power with the more experienced members taking a facilitating role. Encouraging less demonstrative members to come into their own power and participate in making decisions. Willingness to experiment and grow through experience as a group, to try new things and keep an open mind. Confront and challenge problems without blame, hostility or aggression, especially in ourselves.

Deeper understanding of the dialectic of Male/ Female energy, and of different energy types and exploring these energies. For this we also work in Men's and Women's groups so that these energies may be fully explored to be brought together more powerfully. Introduction of fun into rituals, chanting, drumming, laughter and games. The enjoyment of ritual experience and the celebration of life and nature. The recognition that each individual brings something new and unique into the craft and group, that we can learn from each other and that even the most inexperienced member has a lot to contribute.

The development of close working groups with the understanding of group energy. Being a supportive environment for the growing and learning magickal personality. Covens are like nuclear families within a network of an extended family. Member covens care and look after each other and the interests of the other coven's members as well as their own.

The Progressive movement is a part of the evolving and growing process within a living religious belief system. As such it takes its place within the varieties and diversities inherent within and non dogmatic religion. It has much to contribute and a spirit of intersection and experimentation which I believe is valuable to all Paganism, in parallel with the other vibrant traditions of that system. In the words of an old Chinese proverb:

"Let a hundred thousand flowers bloom".

Bibliography & further reading

Introduction

Blain, J. (2002) *Nine Worlds of Seid-Magic: Ecstasy and Neo-Shamanism in North European Paganism.* London and New York: Routledge.

Bourne, L. (2006 [1998]) *Dancing with Witches.* London: Robert Hale. ISBN 0-7090-8074-3.

Bourne, L. (1979) *A Witch Amongst Us.* London: Satellite.

Conner, R.P., Sparks, D.H., and Sparks, M. (1997) *Cassell's Encyclopedia of Queer Myth, Symbol and Spirit.* London and New York: Cassell.

Foltz, T.G. (2000). 'Sober Witches and Goddess Practitioners: Women's Spirituality and Sobriety.' *Diskus*, 6 (1). [online] available from: http://web.uni-marburg.de/religionswissenschaft/journal/diskus/foltz.html

Gardner, G. (1954) *Witchcraft Today.* London: Rider.

Goss, R.E. (1999) 'Queer Theologies as Transgressive Metaphors: New Paradigms for Hybrid Sexual Theologies.' *Theology and Sexuality*, 10: pp 43-53. [online] available from Ebscohost: Academic Search Elite.

Hawley-Gorsline, R. (2003) 'James Baldwin and Audre Lorde as Theological Resources for the Celebration of Darkness.' *Theology and Sexuality* 10(1) pp 58-72 [online] available from: Ebscohost.

Heselton, P (2003), *Gerald Gardner and the Cauldron of Inspiration: An Investigation into the Sources of Gardnerian Witchcraft,* Capall Bann Publishing (ISBN: 1861631642)

Hine, P (1998), Approaching groups, http://www.philhine.org.uk/writings/gp_appgrps.html

Hutton, R. (1999) *The Triumph of the Moon: a history of modern Pagan witchcraft.* Oxford: Oxford University Press.

Landstreet, L. (1999 [1993]) *Alternate Currents: Revisioning Polarity Or, what's a nice dyke like you doing in a polarity-based tradition like this?* [online] available from http://www.wildideas.net/temple/library/altcurrents.html

Owen, A. (2004) *The Place of Enchantment: British Occultism and the Culture of the Modern.* Chicago: The University of Chicago Press.

Chapter 1, What is sacred?

Starhawk, M. Macha NightMare, and the Reclaiming Collective (1997), *The Pagan Book of Living and Dying: Practical Rituals, Prayers, Blessings, and Meditations on Crossing Over*, Harper One

Chapter 3, Gender and sexuality

Jenny Blain (2001), *Nine Worlds of Seid-Magic: Ecstasy and Neo-Shamanism in North European Paganism*, Routledge.

Lou Hart (2005), *Magic is a many-gendered thing*, http://www.philhine.org.uk/writings/flsh_gendered.html

Philip Heselton (2003), *Gerald Gardner and the Cauldron of Inspiration: An Investigation into the Sources of Gardnerian Witchcraft*, Capall Bann Publishing

Ronald Hutton (1999), *The Triumph of the Moon: A History of Modern Pagan Witchcraft*, Oxford: Oxford University Press

Alex Owen (2004), *The Place of Enchantment: British Occultism and the Culture of the Modern*, Chicago: University of Chicago Press

Ceisiwr Serith (2003), *The Sources of the Charge of the Goddess*, http://www.ceisiwrserith.com/wicca/charge.htm

Chapter 4, Polarity

Blain, J. (2002) *Nine Worlds of Seid-Magic: Ecstasy and Neo-Shamanism in North European Paganism.* London and New York: Routledge.

Bourne, L. (2006 [1998]) *Dancing with Witches.* London: Robert Hale. ISBN 0-7090-8074-3.

Bourne, L. (1979) *A Witch Amongst Us.* London: Satellite.

Hawley-Gorsline, R. (2003) 'James Baldwin and Audre Lorde as Theological Resources for the Celebration of Darkness.' *Theology and Sexuality* 10(1) pp 58-72 [online] available from Ebscohost.

Landstreet, L. (1999 [1993]) *Alternate Currents: Revisioning Polarity Or, what's a nice dyke like you doing in a polarity-based tradition like this?* [online] available from http://www.wildideas.net/temple/library/altcurrents.html

Chapter 6, Progressive Wicca

'Terminus' (undated), *What is Progressive Witchcraft?* http://www.sacred-texts.com/bos/msg0015.htm

Chapter 8, Queer Paganism

Ali, S., Campbell, K., Branley, D. and James, R. (2006) 'Politics, identities and research.' *In:* Seale, C, ed. (2006), *Researching Society and Culture.* London: Sage, pp. 21-32

Althaus-Reid, M. (2003), *The Queer God.* London: Routledge.

Becker-Huberti, M. (undated) *Aussehen wie die Heilige Kümmernis: über eine erfundene Heilige".* [online] available from: http://www.religioeses-brauchtum.de/sommer/heilige_kuemmernis.html

Blackwood, E. and Wieringa S.E. (2001) 'Sapphic Shadows: Challenging the Silence in the Study of Sexuality.' *In:* Juschka, D.M. *ed.* (2001) *Feminism in the Study of Religion: a Reader.* London and New York: Continuum, pp. 452-473

Blain, J. (2002) *Nine Worlds of Seid-Magic: Ecstasy and Neo-Shamanism in North European Paganism.* London and New York: Routledge.

Boisvert, D (1999). 'Queering the Sacred: Discourses of Gay Male Spiritual Writing.' *Theology and Sexuality* 10, pp 54-70.

Bourne, L. (1979) *A Witch Amongst Us.* London: Satellite.

Cherry, K. (2006) *Jesus in Love.* Berkeley: AndroGyne Press.

Cherry, K. (2007) *Art That Dares: Gay Jesus, Woman Christ, and More.* Berkeley: AndroGyne Press.

Conner, R.P., Sparks, D.H., and Sparks, M. (1997) *Cassell's Encyclopedia of Queer Myth, Symbol and Spirit.* London and New York: Cassell.

Dewr, C. (1998) *Why Pagan Pride?* [online] available from: http://www.paganpride.org/what/why.html

Foltz, TG (2000). 'Sober Witches and Goddess Practitioners: Women's Spirituality and Sobriety.' *Diskus*, 6 (1). [online] available from: http://web.uni-marburg.de/religionswissenschaft/journal/diskus/foltz.html

Ford, T.M. (2005) *The Path of the Green Man: Gay Men, Wicca and Living a Magical Life.* New York: Citadel Press.

Foster, N. (undated) *A Prayer in the Dark.* Lesbian and Gay Christian Movement. [online] available from: http://www.lgcm.org.uk/archive/archive4a.html

Foucault, M. (1978) *The History of Sexuality Volume 1: An Introduction.* Trans. Hurlet, R. Harmondsworth: Penguin Books.

Francis-Dehqani, G.E. (2004) 'The Gendering of Missionary Imperialism: The Search for an Integrated Methodology.' *In:* King, U. and Beattie, T. (2004), *Gender, Religion and Diversity: Cross-Cultural Perspectives.* London and New York: Continuum.

Gill, S. (2004) 'Why difference matters: Lesbian and gay perspectives on religion and gender.' *In:* King, U. and Beattie, T. (2004), *Gender, Religion and Diversity: Cross-Cultural Perspectives.* London and New York: Continuum.

Goss, R.E. (1999) 'Queer Theologies as Transgressive Metaphors: New Paradigms for Hybrid Sexual Theologies.' *Theology and Sexuality*, 10: pp 43-53. [online] available from Ebscohost: Academic Search Elite.

Gross, R.M. (2004) 'Where have we been? Where do we need to go?: Women's studies and gender in religion and feminist theology.' *In:* King, U. and Beattie, T. (2004), *Gender, Religion and Diversity: Cross-Cultural Perspectives.* London and New York: Continuum.

Hart, L. (2005) *Magic is a many-gendered thing.* [online] available from: http://www.philhine.org.uk/writings/flsh_gendered.html

Hawley-Gorsline, R. (1996) 'Facing the Body on the Cross: A Gay Man's

Reflections on Passion and Crucifixion.' *In:* Krondorfer, B., *ed.* (1996) *Men's Bodies, Men's Gods: Male Identities in a (Post-) Christian Culture.* New York and London: New York University Press.

Hawley-Gorsline, R. (2003) 'James Baldwin and Audre Lorde as Theological Resources for the Celebration of Darkness.' *Theology and Sexuality* 10(1) pp 58-72 [online] available from: Ebscohost.

Haxton, N. (2003) *Adelaide hosts first ever Queer Spirituality Festival.* Australian Broadcasting Corporation [online] available from: http://www.abc.net.au/am/content/2003/s995098.htm

Hine, P. (1989) *Some musings on polarity.* [online] available from: http://www.philhine.org.uk/writings/flsh_polarity.html

Hoff, B.H. (1993) *Gays: Guardians of the Gates. An interview with Malidoma Somé.* [online] available from http://www.menweb.org/somegay.htm

Hutton, R. (1999) *The Triumph of the Moon: a history of modern Pagan witchcraft.* Oxford: Oxford University Press.

Juschka, D.M., *ed.* (2001) *Feminism in the Study of Religion: a Reader.* London and New York: Continuum.

Juschka, D.M. (2005) 'Gender.' *In:* Hinnells, JR, ed. (2005) *The Routledge Companion to the Study of Religion.* London and New York: Routledge.

Lamond, F. (1997) *Religion without Beliefs: Essays in Pantheist Theology, Comparative Religion and Ethics.* London: Janus Publishing Company.

Landstreet, L. (1999 [1993]) *Alternate Currents: Revisioning Polarity Or, what's a nice dyke like you doing in a polarity-based tradition like this?* [online] available from: http://www.witchvox.com/va/dt_va.html?a=usxx&c=gay&id=2458

MacThearlaich, S. (2000) 'Let's Undermine Polarities'. *Queer Spirit*, 1:2.

Marcadé, B., and Cameron, D. (1997) *Pierre et Gilles: The Complete Works, 1976-1996.* Paris: Taschen.

Matthieu, N.-C. (1996) 'Sexual, Sexed and Sex-Class Identities: Three Ways of Conceptualising the Relationship between Sex and Gender.' *In:* Leonard, D & Adkins, L, *eds.* (1996) *Sex in Question: French Materialist Feminism.* London: Taylor and Francis.

Moon, T (2005). *Spirit Matters IV: Ten Queer Spiritual Roles.* San Francisco Bay Times. [online] Available from: http://www.sfbaytimes.com/index.php?sec=article&article_id=3772

Moore, S.D. (2001) *God's Beauty Parlor and other queer spaces in and around the Bible.* Stanford: Stanford University Press.

Odih, P. (2006) 'Using the Internet.' *In:* Seale, C, ed. (2006), *Researching Society and Culture.* London: Sage.

Owen, A. (2004) *The Place of Enchantment: British Occultism and the Culture of the Modern.* Chicago: The University of Chicago Press.

Prosser, J. (1998) *Second Skins: The Body Narratives of Transsexuality.* New York, Columbia University Press.

Reid-Bowen, P. (2007) *Goddess as Nature: Towards a Philosophical Thealogy.* London: Ashgate Publishing.

Rodgers, B. (1995) 'The Radical Faerie Movement: A Queer Spirit Pathway.' *Social Alternatives*, 14 (4) pp 34-37. [online] available from Ebscohost, Academic Search Elite

"Mama Rose" (undated). *Why go Dianic?* [online] available from: http://www.iit.edu/~phillips/personal/philos/dianic.html

Saadaya (undated) *Coming Out as a Rite of Passage.* [online] available from: http://www.angelfire.com/journal/saadaya/ComingOut.html

Sawyer, D. (2004) 'Biblical Gender Strategies: The Case of Abraham's Masculinity.' *In:* King, U. and Beattie, T. (2004), *Gender, Religion and Diversity: Cross-Cultural Perspectives.* London and New York: Continuum.

Schüssler Fiorenza, E. (1992 [1983]) *In Memory of Her: A Feminist Theological Reconstruction of Christian Origins.* New York: Crossroads.

Seale, C. (2006) 'History of Qualitative Methods.' *In:* Seale, C, ed. (2006), *Researching Society and Culture.* London: Sage.

Seneviratne, T. and Currie, J. (2001) 'Religion and Feminism: A Consideration of Cultural Restraints on Sri Lankan Women.' *In:* Juschka, Darlene M., *ed.* (2001), *Feminism in the Study of Religion: a Reader.* London and New York: Continuum.

Simplicity, Sr M.T. (2004), Meet the Sisters. [online] available from: The Sisters of Perpetual Indulgence, http://thesisters.org/bios/mts.html

Sisters of Perpetual Indulgence (2007), Meet The Sisters. [online] available from: The Sisters of Perpetual Indulgence, http://thesisters.org/meet.html

Standing, E. (2004) 'Homophobia and the Postmodern Condition.' *Theology and Sexuality* 10 (2), pp 65-72 [online] available from: Ebscohost, Academic Search Elite

Starhawk, Nightmare, M.M., and the Reclaiming Collective (1997) *The Pagan Book of Living and Dying: Practical Rituals, Prayers, Blessings and Meditations on Crossing Over.* San Francisco: HarperSanFrancisco.

Stemmeler, M.L. (1996), 'Empowerment: the Construction of Gay Religious Identities.' *In:* Krondorfer, B, ed. (1996). *Men's Bodies, Men's Gods: Male Identities in a (Post-) Christian Culture.* New York and London: New York University Press.

Summerskill, B. *ed.* (2006) *The Way we are now: Gay and Lesbian Lives in the 21st Century.* London and New York: Continuum.

Tatchell, P. (2001) *Equality is Not Enough.* [online] available from: http://www.petertatchell.net/Equality%20-%20Limits%20and%20Deficiencies/equality%20is%20not%20enough2.htm

Taylor, P. (1998) *Edward Carpenter Biographical Note.* The Edward Carpenter Archive. [online] available from: http://www.edwardcarpenter.net/ecbiog.htm

Wallis, R.J. (2003) *Shamans / Neo-shamans: Ecstasy, alternative archaeologies and contemporary Pagans.* London and New York: Routledge.

Wilde, O. (1996 [1905]) *De Profundis.* New York: Dover Publications, Inc.

Horrocks, R. (1997), *An Introduction to the Study of Sexuality.* Basingstoke and London: Macmillan Press.

Pemberton, C. (2004), 'Whose Face in the Mirror? Personal and Post-colonial Obstacles in Researching Africa's Contemporary Women's Theological Voices.' In:

King, U. (ed) Gender, Religion and Diversity: Cross-Cultural Perspectives. London and New York: Continuum.

Vallet, Odon (2006) *Les Corps Divins - Pierre et Gilles*. Editions du Chêne

Wahba, Rachel (1989). "Hiding is Unhealthy for the Soul." In: *Twice Blessed: On Being Lesbian or Gay and Jewish*, ed Christie Balka and Andy Rose. Boston: Beacon Press.

Chapter 9, Deities and spirits

G. W. Bowersock (1990). *Hellenism in Late Antiquity, Thomas Spencer Jerome Lectures.* Ann Arbor: The University of Michigan Press.

RM Ogilvie (1969), *The Romans and their gods*.

Lou Hart (2005), *Magic is a many gendered thing*,

http://www.philhine.org.uk/writings/flsh_gendered.html

Ronald Hutton (2001), *The Triumph of the Moon: a history of Modern Pagan Witchcraft*. Oxford Paperbacks.

Yvonne Aburrow (1993), *The Sacred Grove: Mysteries of the forest*, Chieveley: Capall Bann

Bob Trubshaw (2002), *Explore Folklore*, Explore Books, an imprint of Heart of Albion Press.

Yvonne Aburrow (2000), *Between Mirrors*, Queer Spirit, issue 13.

Douglas A Marshall (2002), <u>Behavior, Belonging and Belief: A theory of ritual practice</u> in *Sociological Theory* 20:3, 3 November 2002, pp 360-380

Frederic Lamond (2004), *Fifty Years of Wicca*, Green Magic

Alex Owen (2004), *The Place of Enchantment: British Occultism and the Culture of the Modern*, University of Chicago Press.

Janet Farrar and Gavin Bone (2004*), Progressive Witchcraft: Spirituality, Mysteries & Training in Modern Wicca*, New Page Books.

Barry Patterson (2005), *The Art of Conversation with the Genius Loci.* Capall Bann Publishing.

Pagan Religious Worldviews - http://web.ics.purdue.edu/~rauhn/ancrelig.htm

Eliezer Segal (1995), *The Ten Sefirot of the Kabbalah*
http://www.ucalgary.ca/~elsegal/Sefirot/Sefirot.html

Colin Low, *Memory Theatre: The Tree of Life considered as a Memory Theatre.*
http://www.digital-brilliance.com/kab/theatre/theatre.htm

H. J. Carol Thompson (2004), *Yggdrasil, World Ash Tree,*
http://www.earth-dancing.com/yggdrasil.htm

Hesiod's *Theogony* - http://www.sacred-texts.com/cla/hesiod/theogony.htm

Hesiod's *Works and Days* - http://www.sacred-texts.com/cla/hesiod/works.htm

The Four Worlds, http://www.byzant.com/kabbalah/worlds.asp

Chapter 10, What is truth?

Frank Pajares (2004) 'The Structure of Scientific Revolutions' by Thomas S. Kuhn, A Synopsis from the original, Philosopher's Web Magazine, http://www.emory.edu/EDUCATION/mfp/kuhnsyn.html

The Lady of the Lake, http://www.sacred-texts.com/neu/celt/wfb/wfb03.htm

Ursula K Le Guin (1985), *Always Coming Home*, Grafton Books, London. ISBN: 0586073833

George Lakoff and Johnson, *Metaphors We Live By*,

Joseph Campbell, *The Inner Reaches of Outer Space: Myth as Metaphor and as Religion*,

George Lakoff (18 March 2003), Metaphor and War, Again, AlterNet, http://www.alternet.org/story.html?StoryID=15414

C G Jung, *Psychology and Religion*, Collected Works, Vol. 11.

Victoria Lynn Schmidt (2001), *45 Master Characters*, Writer's Digest Books

Pamela L. Travers (1993), *What the Bee Knows: Reflections on Myth, Symbol and Story*, London: Penguin Arkana. ISBN 0140194665

John Halstead (2014) *"A mighty host respond": Pagan unity through diversity*, http://www.patheos.com/blogs/allergicpagan/2014/03/10/a-mighty-host-respond-pagan-unity-through-diversity/

Chapter 11, Wicca and science

Adler, M. (1986) *Drawing Down the Moon: Witches, Druids, Goddess-Worshippers, and Other Pagans in America Today*. Boston: Beacon Press.

Alspector-Kelly, M. (2001) 'Should the Empiricist Be a Constructive Empiricist?' *Philosophy of Science*, 68 (4), pp. 413-431 [online] Available from: http://www.jstor.org/stable/3081045

Attwood, R. (2008) 'High IQ turns academics into atheists.' *Times Higher Education*, 12 June 2008. [online] Available from: http://www.timeshighereducation.co.uk/story.asp?sectioncode=26&storycode=402381

BBC (2006) 'Atheism.' Religion and Ethics. *BBC*. [online] Available from: http://www.bbc.co.uk/religion/religions/atheism/types/rationalism.shtml

Beliefnet (2000), *Belief-O-Matic, Religion Beliefs, What Religion Am I Quiz*. [online]

Berman, M. (1981) *The Re-enchantment of the world*. New York: Cornell University Press.

Bienkowski, P. (2006) 'Persons, things and archaeology: contrasting world-views of minds, bodies and death', *Respect for Ancient British Human Remains: Philosophy and Practice*. [online] Available from: Manchester Museum, http://www.museum.manchester.ac.uk/medialibrary/documents/respect/persons_things_and_archaeology.pdf

Blain, Jenny and Wallis, Robert (2006), 'A Live Issue: Ancestors, Archaeologists and the "Reburial Issue" in Britain.' *Association of Polytheist Traditions* [online] available from: http://www.manygods.org.uk/articles/essays/reburial.html

Blain, Jenny and Wallis, Robert (2007) *Sacred Sites – Contested Rites/Rights: Pagan Engagements with Archaeological Monuments*. Eastbourne: Sussex Academic Press.

Bloch, A. (2004) 'Doing social surveys.' In: Seale, C., ed. *Researching Society and Culture*. London: SAGE Publications.

Bowman, M. (2000) 'Nature, the natural and Pagan identity.' *Diskus* (6) [online] Available from: http://www.uni-marburg.de/religionswissenschaft/journal/diskus

Bregman, L. (2006) 'Spirituality: a glowing and useful term in search of a meaning.' *Omega*, 53(1-2), pp. 5-26. [online] Available from Ebscohost: Academic Search Premier, AN 21808441.

British Humanist Association (undated), '*About the BHA*'. [online] Available from:
http://www.humanism.org.uk/site/cms/contentChapterView.asp?chapter=333

Brock_tn (2008), *'Thoughts on Pagan community.' Half a Kilogramme of Well-Crottled Greeps...* [online] Available from: http://brock-tn.livejournal.com/16019.html

Byrne, B. (2004) 'Qualitative Interviewing'. In: Seale, C., ed. *Researching Society and Culture*. London: SAGE Publications.

Chaves, M. (1994) 'Secularization as Declining Religious Authority.' *Social Forces*, 72(3), pp. 749-774. [online] Available from JStor

Clifton, C. (1998) 'Nature Religion for Real.' *Gnosis*, 48. [online] Available from: http://www.chasclifton.com/papers/forreal.html

Clifton, C. (2006). *Her Hidden Children: The Rise of Wicca and Paganism in America*. New York: Altamira Press.

Coco, A., and Woodward, I. (2007) 'Discourses of Authenticity Within a Pagan Community: The Emergence of the "Fluffy Bunny" Sanction.' *Journal of Contemporary Ethnography*, Vol. 36(5), pp. 479-504 [online] Available from: SAGE Publications

Collins, G.P. (2008) 'Remembering Sir Arthur C. Clarke, 1917-2008. Graham Collins reflects on meeting the famous author in New York City'. *Scientific American*. http://www.sciam.com/article.cfm?id=remembering-sir-arthur-c

Connelly, P. (1994) *'Towards a Postmodern Paganism.'* [online] Available from: http://www.darc.org/connelly/pagan1.html

Cooper, Q. (2008) 'Material World: Hay-on-Wye Special'. *Radio 4*. 29.05.2008 [online] Available from:
http://downloads.bbc.co.uk/podcasts/radio4/material/material_20080529-1800.mp3

Covenant of the Goddess (2006) *The 2005-06 Wiccan/Pagan Poll Results*. [online] Available from: http://www.cog.org/05poll/poll_results.html

Dawkins, R. (2006) *The God Delusion*. London: Bantam Press.

Demeritt, D. (1996) 'Social Theory and the Reconstruction of Science and Geography', *Transactions of the Institute of British Geographers*, New Series, 21 (3), pp. 484-503 [online] Available from: http://www.jstor.org/stable/622593

Diaz-Bone, R. (2006), 'Kritische Diskursanalyse: zur Ausarbeitung einer problembezogenen Diskursanalyse im Anschluss an Foucault.' *Forum Qualitative Sozialforschung*, 7 (3), p. 1 [online] available from: Ebscohost/SocINDEX (AN

21734748)

Dobbelaere, K. (1998) 'Secularization.' In: Swatos, W.H., ed. (1998) *Encyclopedia of Religion and Society*. Lanham: Altamira Press. [online] available from: http://hirr.hartsem.edu/ency/Secularization.htm

Fish, S. (2008) 'French Theory in America.' *New York Times*, April 6, 2008. [online] available from: http://fish.blogs.nytimes.com/2008/04/06/french-theory-in-america/

Folse, H.J. (1986) 'Niels Bohr, Complementarity, and Realism'. *Proceedings of the Biennial Meeting of the Philosophy of Science Association*, 1, pp. 96-104 [online] Available from: http://www.jstor.org/stable/193111

Friedman, M (2002) 'Kant, Kuhn, and the Rationality of Science.' *Philosophy of Science*, 69(2), pp. 171-190 [online] Available from: http://www.jstor.org/stable/3080974

Frisk, T. (1997) 'Paganism, Magic, and the Control of Nature.' *Trumpeter: Journal of Ecosophy*, 14 (4). [online] Available from: http://trumpeter.athabascau.ca/index.php/trumpet/article/viewFile/169/206

Gallagher, E.V. (1994) 'A Religion without Converts? Becoming a Neo-Pagan'. *Journal of the American Academy of Religion*, 62(3), pp. 851-867. [online] Available from JStor

'Genexs' (2006) *'Witches and Scientists.'* (blog) [online] Available from: http://witchesandscientists.blogspot.com

Godfrey-Smith, P. (2002) 'Dewey on Naturalism, Realism and Science.' *Philosophy of Science*, 69 (3), Supplement: Proceedings of the 2000 Biennial Meeting of the Philosophy of Science Association. Part II: Symposia Papers, pp. S25 -S35 [online] Available from: http://www.jstor.org/stable/3081079

Griffin, D. R. (1988) *The Re-enchantment of Science: Postmodern Proposals*. Albany: SUNY Press

Haila, Y., and Dyke, C. (2006) *How Nature Speaks: The Dynamics of the Human Ecological Condition*. Durham, NC: Duke University Press. [online] Available from: http://books.google.co.uk/books?id=MgUGA5T2ADQC

Haraway, D. (1988) 'Situated Knowledges: The Science Question in Feminism and the Privilege of Partial Perspective.' *Feminist Studies*, 14(3), pp. 575-599 [online] Available from: http://www.jstor.org/stable/3178066

Harris, G. (2005) 'Pagan Involvement in the Interfaith Movement, Exclusions, Dualities, and Contributions'. *Crosscurrents*. [online] Available from Ebscohost: Academic Search Premier, AN 16501005.

Harrison, P. (1999) *The Elements of Pantheism: understanding the divinity in nature and the universe*. Shaftesbury: Element Books.

Harvey, G. (1997) *Contemporary Paganism: Listening People, Speaking Earth*. New York: New York University Press.

Heelas, P. and Woodhead, L. (2005) *The Spiritual Revolution: Why Religion is Giving Way to Spirituality*. Oxford: Blackwell.

Hutton, R.E. (1999) *The Triumph of the Moon: A history of modern Pagan witchcraft*. Oxford: Oxford University Press.

Keating, C. (2008) 'The Wiccan What?' *The Wiccan Scientist* (blog) [online] Available from: http://thewiccanscientist.blogspot.com/2008/02/wiccan-what.html

King, R. (1999) 'Orientalism and the Modern Myth of "Hinduism".' *Numen*, 46(2), pp. 146-185 [online]

Kosmin, B. A., Mayer, E., and Keysar, A. (2001), *'American Religious Identification Survey.'* The Graduate Center of the City University of New York. [online] Available from: http://www.gc.cuny.edu/faculty/research_briefs/aris.pdf

Kraemer, C., and Lewis, A.D. (2007) *'Re: [Pagan Studies] Re: Religion & Comics CFP.'* [online] Available from: http://groups.yahoo.com/group/paganstudies/message/2199

Landstreet, L. (1993) 'Alternate Currents: Revisioning Polarity, Or, what's a nice dyke like you doing in a polarity-based tradition like this?' *Wild Ideas, an online exploration of the wild.* [online] Available from http://www.wildideas.net/temple/library/altcurrents.html

Landstreet, L. (1996) 'The Soul of Nature: The Meaning of Ecological Spirituality.' *Wild Ideas, an online exploration of the wild.* [online] Available from http://www.wildideas.net/forest/library/ecospirit10.html

Lazar, D. (2004) 'Selected issues in the philosophy of social science.' In: Seale, C., ed. *Researching Society and Culture.* London: SAGE Publications._

Lee, R. L. M. (2003) 'The Re-enchantment of the Self: Western Spirituality, Asian Materialism'. *Journal of Contemporary Religion*, 18(3), pp. 351–367 [online] Available from Ebscohost: Academic Search Premier, AN 11234629.

Lemke, J. J. (1998) 'Analysing Verbal Data: Principles, Methods and Problems' In: K Tobin & B Fraser, eds, *International Handbook of Science Education.* Boston: Kluwer. [online] available from: http://academic.brooklyn.cuny.edu/education/jlemke/papers/handbook.htm

Letcher, A. (2003) '"Gaia told me to do it" - Resistance and the Idea of Nature within contemporary British Eco-Paganism.' *Ecotheology*, 8(1), pp. 61-84. [online] Available from Ebscohost: Academic Search Premier, AN 12446132.

Letcher, A. (2006) *Shroom: A cultural history of the magic mushroom.* New York and London: Harper Perennial.

Levitt, N. (2007) 'What a Friend We Have in Dawkins.' *Skeptic*, 13(2), pp. 48-51. [online] Available from Ebscohost: Academic Search Premier, AN 25486037.

Livingstone, D. N. (2002) 'Ecology and the Evironment.' In: Ferngren, G. B., *Science & Religion: a historical introduction.* Baltimore and London: Johns Hopkins University Press.

Luhrmann, T. (1989) *Persuasions of the Witch's Craft: Ritual Magic in Contemporary England.* Cambridge, MA: Harvard University Press.

McGrath, A. E. (1999) *Science and Religion: An Introduction.* Oxford: Blackwell Publishing.

McGrath, A. E. (2007) *The Dawkins Delusion?* London: SPCK.

Muller, A. and Livingston, P. (1995) 'Realism/Anti-Realism: A Debate'. *Cultural Critique*, No. 30, The Politics of Systems and Environments, Part I, pp. 15-32 [online] Available from: http://www.jstor.org/stable/1354431

National Statistics Office (2004), 'Religious Populations: Christianity is main religion in Britain.' *National Census Online* [online] Available from http://www.statistics.gov.uk/cci/nugget.asp?id=954

Naturalism.org (2001) 'Spirituality Without Faith.' *The Centre for Naturalism.* [online] Available from http://www.naturalism.org/spiritual.htm

Naturalism.org (2006) 'Deny God, Then What?' *The Centre for Naturalism.* [online] Available from http://www.naturalism.org/new_atheism.htm

Nuyen, A.T. (2001) 'Realism, Anti-Realism, and Emmanuel Levinas.' *The Journal of Religion*, 81, (3), pp. 394-409 [online] Available from: http://www.jstor.org/stable/1206402

O'Gaea, A. (2002) *Raising Witches: Teaching the Wiccan faith to children.* Franklin Lakes, NJ: New Page Books.

PaganSpace.net (2007) 'Who are we?' *Pagans and science.* [online] Available from http://www.paganspace.net/group/paganscience/forum/topic/show?id=1342861%3ATopic%3A90790

Partridge, C. (2004) *The Re-enchantment of the West, Volume 1: Alternative Spiritualities, Sacralization, Popular Culture and Occulture.* London and New York: T & T Clark

Paulson, S. (2007) *'The atheist delusion: Theologian John Haught explains why science and God are not at odds, why Mike Huckabee worries him, and why Richard Dawkins and other "new atheists" are ignorant about religion.'* Salon.com [online] Available from: http://www.salon.com/books/feature/2007/12/18/john_haught/

Pickstone, J. V. (2000) *Ways of knowing: A new history of science, technology and medicine.* Manchester: Manchester University Press.

Porter, R. (2001) *Enlightenment: Britain and the Creation of the Modern World.* Harmondsworth: Penguin.

Rayner, A. D. M. (2003) *'Inclusional Science - From Artefact to Natural Creativity'* [online] Available from http://people.bath.ac.uk/bssadmr/inclusionality/inclusionalscience.htm

Ringel, F. (1994) 'New England Neo-Pagans: Medievalism, Fantasy, Religion.' *Journal of American Culture*, 17(3) pp. 65-68. [online] Available from Ebscohost: Academic Search Elite, AN 9501170957.

Rountree, K. (2003) 'How Magic Works: New Zealand Feminist Witches' Theories of Ritual Action.' *Anthropology of Consciousness*, 13(1), pp. 42-60.

Sagan, C. (1994) *Pale Blue Dot: A Vision of the Human Future in Space.* Ballantine Books.

Segal, R. A. (1999) *Theorizing about myth.* Amherst: University of Massachusetts Press.

Starhawk (2007) 'Pagans embrace science.' [online] Available from: *On Faith,* http://newsweek.washingtonpost.com/onfaith/starhawk/2007/10/pagans_embrace_science.html

Star Stuffs (2003), *'Physics and Consciousness: Our Quantum Interconnectedness'* [online] Available from: http://www.starstuffs.com/physcon2/index.html

Stubbs, Michael (1983), *Discourse Analysis: The Sociolinguistic Analysis of Natural Language*, Oxford: Blackwell.

Thomas, K. (1971) *Religion and the Decline of Magic: Studies in popular beliefs in sixteenth and seventeenth century England*. Harmondsworth: Penguin.

Toulmin, S. (1982) 'The Construal of Reality: Criticism in Modern and Postmodern Science'. *Critical Inquiry*, 9 (1), The Politics of Interpretation, pp. 93-111 [online] Available from: http://www.jstor.org/stable/1343275

Turner, W. (1908). 'Giordano Bruno.' In: *The Catholic Encyclopedia*. New York: Robert Appleton Company. [online] Available from New Advent: http://www.newadvent.org/cathen/03016a.htm

Whitehead, C. (1998) 'The Re-enchantment of Science'. *Anthropology Today*, 14(5), pp 20-21. [online] Available from JStor.

Chapter 12, What is magic

Nigel Pennick (1995), *Practical Magic in the Northern Tradition* (2nd edition, Thoth Publications)

Aleister Crowley (1994), *Magick in Theory and Practice*, Weiser Books

Brian Bates (1983), *The Way of Wyrd*, Arrow Books

Freya Aswynn, *The Leaves of Yggdrasil*, Llewellyn Publications

Naomi Ozaniec (1995), *Dowsing for beginners*, Trafalgar Square Publishing

Juliet Sharman-Burke, *The Complete Book of Tarot*, Pan Books

Chapter 14, The hidden children of the Goddess

Moon, T (2005). Spirit Matters IV: Ten Queer Spiritual Roles. *San Francisco Bay Times*. [online] Available from:
http://www.sfbaytimes.com/index.php?sec=article&article_id=3772

Chapter 18, Mythology for Wiccans

Yvonne Aburrow (2013), *What is cultural appropriation?*
www.patheos.com/blogs/sermonsfromthemound/2013/03/cultural-appropriation/

Catherine Beyer, *Plastic Shamans: Commercialization of Native American Practices*
http://altreligion.about.com/od/controversymisconception/a/Plastic-Shamans.htm

On reverse cultural appropriation
http://mycultureisnotatrend.tumblr.com/post/781005138/on-reverse-cultural-appropriation

Cultural (Mis)Appropriation
http://www.uua.org/multiculturalism/introduction/misappropriation/index.shtml

Reactions to Ray Verdict from Native Voices, Victim's Families, and Pagan Community (*Wild Hunt blog*) http://wildhunt.org/2011/06/reactions-to-ray-verdict-from-native-voices-victims-families-and-pagan-community.html

Hinduism, Indo-Paganism, and Cultural Appropriation (*Wild Hunt blog*)
http://wildhunt.org/2010/06/hinduism-indo-paganism-and-cultural-appropriation.html

The Elephants in the Room (*Wild Hunt blog*)
http://wildhunt.org/2009/03/the-elephants-in-the-room.html

"Talking About the Elephant: An Anthology of Neopagan Perspectives on Cultural Appropriation" (edited by Lupa)

Chapter 19, Wiccan rituals

Ronald L Grimes (1982), *Beginnings in Ritual Studies*, Lanham & London: United Press of America

Starhawk, M. Macha NightMare, and the Reclaiming Collective (1997), *The Pagan Book of Living and Dying: Practical Rituals, Prayers, Blessings, and Meditations on Crossing Over*, Harper One

Chapter 20, The shamanic ordeal in Wicca

Mark Thomson (1991), *Leatherfolk: Radical Sex, People, Politics and Practice*
Patrick Califia (1989), *Macho Sluts*
Patrick Califia (2012), *Speaking Sex to Power: The Politics of Queer Sex*
http://www.ravenkaldera.org/
http://www.paganbdsm.org/
http://pagantheologies.pbworks.com /Sexuality

Chapter 21, Eco-spirituality and embodiment

https://roehampton.academia.edu/AdrianHarris
https://independent.academia.edu/AndyLetcher
http://phranqueigh.blogspot.co.uk/2005/12/meditation.html
http://www.wikihow.com/Practice-Body-Mindfulness-Meditation
http://www.adrianharris.org/blog/2011/03/the-sit-spot/
http://wildernessawareness.org/coyotes-guide/cg-faq/
http://www.wildernessskillsinstitute.com/mentorResourcesNatureConnetion.html
http://www.wildernessawareness.org/
http://www.adrianharris.org/blog/2011/04/nature-connection-core-routines/
http://connectedbynature.com/2010/01/happy-2010-where-you-at-a-bioregional-quiz/
Landstreet, L. (1996) 'The Soul of Nature: The Meaning of Ecological Spirituality.' *Wild Ideas, an online exploration of the wild.* [online] Available from http://www.wildideas.net/forest/library/ecospirit10.html
Richard Mabey (1993), *Food for Free*, Collins Gem
Barry Patterson (2007), *The Art of Conversation with the Genius Loci*, Holmes

Emile Durkheim (1912), *The Elementary Forms of Religious Life*

Chapter 22, Running a coven

Bowen Theory, http://www.thebowencenter.org/pages/conceptds.html

http://www.psychologytoday.com/blog/fixing-families/201106/the-relationship-triangle

http://willmeekphd.com/item/over-functioning--under-functioning

Christoph Haug (2012), *Assembly publics and the problem of hegemony in consensus decision-making*, http://www.opendemocracy.net/christoph-haug/assembly-publics-and-problem-of-hegemony-in-consensus-decision-making

Starhawk (undated), *Consensus is Not Unanimity: Making Decisions Co-operatively*, http://www.starhawk.org/activism/trainer-resources/consensus-nu.html

Ronald Hutton (2003), 'A modest look at ritual nudity' in *Witches, Druids, and King Arthur*. Hambledon Continuum.

Index

Also published by Avalonia:

Circle of Fire by *Sorita d'Este & David Rankine*
The symbolism and practices of Wicca (Introduction to the practices)

Cunning Man's Handbook *by Jim Baker*
The Practice of English Folk Magic 1550 - 1900

Dionysos: Exciter to Frenzy *by Vikki Bramshaw*
A study of the god Dionysos: History Myth and Lore

HATHOR *by Lesley Jackson*
A reintroduction to an Ancient Egyptian Goddess: The Cow Goddess Hathor

THOTH *by Lesley Jackson*
The history of the Ancient Egyptian God of Wisdom

Thracian Magic: Past & Present *by Georgi Mishev*
A treasure trove of folklore & magical practices from the Balkan Peninsula

Wicca Magickal Beginnings *by Sorita d'Este & David Rankine*
A exploration of the historical origins of the practices found in modern Pagan Witchcraft.

*For more information on these, and the many
other titles published by Avalonia, go to:*

www.avaloniabooks.co.uk

Lightning Source UK Ltd.
Milton Keynes UK
UKHW050048281221
396187UK00006BA/376